Adam Smith

D1605926

DATE DUE

GAYLORD			PRINTED IN U.S.A.

SUNY SERIES, RHETORIC IN THE MODERN ERA

Arthur E. Walzer and Edward Schiappa, Editors

The goal of this series "Rhetoric in the Modern Era" is to prompt and sponsor book-length treatments of important rhetorical theorists and of philosophers and literary theorists who make substantial contributions to our understanding of language and rhetoric. In some cases, a book in this series is the first book-length treatment of the figure; in others, a book in the series is the first to examine a philosopher or theorist from the perspective of rhetorical theory.

The intended audience for books in the series are nonspecialists—graduate students coming to the study of a theorist for the first time and professors broadly interested in the rhetorical tradition. The series books are comprehensive introductions—comprehensive in the sense that they provide brief biographies, descriptions of the intellectual milieu, and discussions of the major scholarship on the figure as context for a detailed examination of the figure's contribution to rhetorical theory or history.

We envision these as the first books on their subject, not the last. While books in the series may exceed these modest aims, their focus is on achieving them. A complete list of books in the series can be found at the end of this volume.

Adam Smith

The Rhetoric of Propriety

STEPHEN J. MCKENNA

STATE UNIVERSITY OF NEW YORK PRESS

Published by
State University of New York Press, Albany

For information, address State University of New York Press,
194 Washington Avenue, Suite 305, Albany, NY 12210-2365

Production by Kelli Williams
Marketing by Anne M. Valentine

Library of Congress Cataloging-in-Publication Data

McKenna, Stephen J.
  Adam Smith: the rhetoric of propriety / Stephen J. McKenna
    p. cm. — (SUNY series, rhetoric in the modern era)
  Includes bibliographical references and index.
  ISBN 0-7914-9581-0 (alk. paper) — ISBN 0-7914-6582-9 (pbk.: alk. Paper)
  1. Smith, Adam, 1723-1790. Lectures on rhetoric and belles lettres.   2. English
language—Rhetoric—Study and teaching—Scotland.   3. English language—
Rhetoric—Study and teaching—History—18th century   4. English language—
Rhetoric—Study and teaching—Moral and ethical aspects.   5. Smith, Adam,
1723–1790—Knowledge—Language and languages.   6. English language—18th
century—Rhetoric.   7. Rhetoric—Moral and ethical aspects.   8. Smith, Adam,
1723–1790—Ethics.   9. Scots language—Rhetoric.   I. Title.   II. Series.
  PE1405.S26M38 2005
  808'.042'0710411—dc22
                          2005001023

10 9 8 7 6 5 4 3 2 1

Contents

Acknowledgments

Many people in many different ways helped to bring this book to fruition. My first debt is to Jean Dietz Moss, scholar, teacher, mentor, colleague, friend, who kept prodding when I barely took seriously her first suggestion that I investigate Smith's rhetoric lectures, and who guided me as my interest first deepened into a dissertation, and later took shape as a book. I hope she won't regret the suggestion; I'm simply grateful. Christopher Wheatley and Jerry Z. Muller also read parts of this in its earlier form; both corrected errors and made valuable suggestions. Thanks are owed as well to Fr. Robert Sokolowski, who taught me much of whatever I know about how to read philosophy; his insight and encouragement have meant a great deal. Lynee Lewis Gaillet, who must have seen something promising in a very early (and very rough) conference presentation on Smith's rhetoric lectures chose to publish that paper in her excellent collection, *Scottish Rhetoric and Its Influences*; my thanks go out to her. I also owe a debt of gratitude to Art Walzer, who likewise heard a conference paper and encouraged me to write on Smith for this series. Priscilla Ross, Director of SUNY Press, was patient almost beyond reason as I wrote and rewrote. Her good will and enthusiasm for the project helped enormously. Russell Wyland made excellent structural and stylistic suggestions on drafts of several chapters; I know the book is better because of him. Many other people listened patiently as I held forth on various parts of this project: Larry Green, Gary Hatch, Harvey Yunis, Jeroen Bons, Beth Manolescu, and Linda Ferreira-Buckley are particularly to be mentioned. Of course, any and all errors or shortcomings in this book are mine alone.

My parents, Stephen and Lolita McKenna, have always supported me in my decisions, academic and otherwise; there is no way to thank them adequately. My children, Grace, Claire, and Max McKenna are a source of inspiration and hope. Finally, my wife Anne, who has been an exemplary model of patience and love, and who has shown me in ever deeper ways the meanings of propriety, has been a force behind this book from beginning to end. I dedicate it to her.

Abbreviations

The following abbreviations are used to refer to the works of Adam Smith as contained in the *Glasgow Edition of the Works and Correspondence of Adam Smith*.

Corr.	*Correspondence of Adam Smith*
EPS	*Essays on Philosophical Subjects*
LJ(A)	*Lectures on Jurisprudence, Report of 1762–3*
LJ(B)	*Lectures on Jurisprudence, Report dated 1766*
LRBL	*Lectures on Rhetoric and Belles Lettres*
TMS	*The Theory of Moral Sentiments*
WN	*An Inquiry into the Nature and Causes of the Wealth of Nations*

CHAPTER 1

Smith and the Problem of Propriety

T hose who regard rhetoric as merely the verbal manipulation of an audience may be forgiven for supposing, from its title, that this book is about an abuse of method by Adam Smith—that it would show how propriety, a key idea in Smith's rhetorical and ethical thought, is craftily deployed in his sociological system to advance the twin causes of free market capitalism and genteel morality. It is true that we need look no farther than the first extant lecture of Smith's early *Lectures on Rhetoric and Belles Lettres* (*LRBL*) to learn that rhetorical propriety—the stylistic virtue that wins audience sympathy by communicating correctly, clearly, and appropriately—is best acquired by imitating "the better sort," by whom Smith means those who bear "the character of a gentleman." In his ethics treatise, *The Theory of Moral Sentiments* (*TMS*), propriety as the mode of action that wins the approval of an internalized audience—the "impartial spectator" of conscience—is similarly constructed in ways that might all too easily be dismissed as hegemonic. In *LRBL*, Smith makes rhetoric the genus to which all communication is species and singles out prose as the natural language of commercial society. Though he does not explicitly say so, we must assume he would hold the kind of rhetorical effectiveness he recommends to be beneficial to such a society. Indeed, Smith is clearly attuned to the importance of communication and persuasion in his economic thought, assigning the origin of the division of labor to our human propensities to speak and persuade. It is not unreasonable then to suppose that for Smith propriety mediates virtually all forms of social interaction. Such a view would my title herald, and the importance of propriety within Smith's vision for what Jerry Z. Muller has aptly called a "decent society" will be weighed. But the book might as justly be titled *Adam Smith and the Propriety of Rhetoric*, for it will argue that Smith's approach to the study of human society was fundamentally rhetorical in conception, that this was for him an approach more fruitful than others he might have taken, and that we may only judge the ideological content of his work once we have reckoned with this rhetorical undercurrent.

Smith and propriety: the intertwining subjects of this book have been relatively neglected in the history of rhetoric. As to the latter, across the twenty-five hundred year history of rhetorical theory, perhaps no single concept so widely recurs—variously surfacing as *to prepon*, *aptum*, *decorum*, seemliness, and still other terms—yet has so resisted theorizing as propriety. In his discussion of *deinotês*, the unifying force in style that requires the adaptation of every element of the speech to every contingency of the speech situation, the second century rhetorician Hermogenes of Tarsus addresses the daunting problem:

> Anyone who has tried to deal with this topic will know what an overwhelming task it is. To treat all the problems involved in this subject in a systematic way seems almost beyond human ability and to require some divine power. One would have to deal with times, characters, places, causes, manners and other such topics and to discuss all the possible cases, as well as the various forms they can take, and the ways in which they can be presented, and what kinds of sentiments are appropriate in each part of the speech . . . (107)

Smith read Hermogenes and surely would have been interested in his promised separate work on the subject, but if Hermogenes was ever able to tackle it, none survives.

The problem is a decisive one for rhetoric. Any attempt to theorize the appropriate as a norm would seem to go to the heart of the historical debate over rhetoric's status as an art, begging the premise assumed by all theory, namely, that rhetoric is neither a mere "knack" (an *empeireia*, as Socrates held it to be in the *Gorgias*), nor a solely innate gift, but a learnable methodology. But defining the appropriate has always been a key problem for rhetoric. Even from a historicizing perspective that would recognize and accept this, abandoning any theoretical conception of appropriateness in favor of an a posteriori description and criticism of successful practices in manifold situations, there is the problem that propriety can be seen as consisting in any number of forms of action. Evidence of this rests in the history of the concept of rhetorical propriety, wherein a variety of terms have pointed to a constellation of sometimes hazily defined ideas ranging from correct diction to decorous behavior. Perhaps as a consequence of this untidiness, relatively few treatments of propriety by either theorists or historians of rhetoric rival in depth the development and analysis that has been devoted to rhetorical concepts such as the enthymeme, the *topoi*, the artistic proofs, or figuration, even while these ideas themselves have been fraught with ambiguity at times.

This neglect is understandable. On the one hand, the concept may seem so obvious and intuitive, so rooted in the very nature of human experience, as to be pre-theoretical. This view is exemplified by Craig La Drière: "Perhaps its repugnance to specification is evidence that the idea of fitness is specific enough without reduction to any more concrete formula, and directly applicable to experience without being made less abstract. Perhaps its very obdurate abstractness, its resistance to assimilation by any particular context and its consequent elasticity in application to all contexts, explain its hardy persistence, and its permanent value, as a principle for aesthetic judgment" (quoted in Kinneavy, 356). Even theories treating the concept more fully (Aristotle's, Smith's) may at times seem to imply that propriety in praxis is as much a product of intuition or insight as it is a result of conscious application of rules. On the other hand and usually in opposition to this "intuitive" view of propriety is the view that responds to the problem of propriety by seeing it as groundable only on ideological or foundational premises. In this essentially Marxist view, the task of the rhetorician in regard to propriety is not to theorize it but to puncture it, exposing the ideology of which it is a symptom. Roland Barthes's scathing objection to prestructuralist criticism addressed not only its supposed pretense to objectivity and its insistence on clarity of language, but its conversion of social taboos against the use of certain language into what he saw as hollow criteria of "good taste":

> What shall we call this group of interdictions which belong to both ethics and aesthetics and in which classical criticism invests all those values which it cannot claim to be knowledge? Let us call this system of prohibitions *good taste*. . . . As a servant shared by ethics and aesthetics, it allows us to have a convenient turnstile connecting the Beautiful and the Good, discretely merged in the form of a simple measure. However, this measure has all the disappearing power of a mirage. . . . (42–43)

In a similar mode, the reader-response critic Stanley Fish ironically embraces propriety, but only after it has served as the insight that leads to the radical contextualization of meaning. On the basis of J. L. Austin's "discovery" that constative speech acts (utterances susceptible to judgments of truth, falsity, or verisimilitude) are really a subtype of performative speech acts (utterances that "do things" and are thus only susceptible to judgments of "felicity" or appropriateness), Fish concludes that "the formal core of language disappears entirely, and is replaced by a world of utterances vulnerable to the sea change of every circumstance—the world, in short, of rhetorical (situated) man"

(213). Contemporary treatments of propriety have ever tended toward this sophistic view, according to which rhetoric constitutes reality and thus takes on the character of wrangling.

So for Richard Lanham propriety is "a pious fraud, the 'social trick' par excellence" (46). Far from elaborating a theory of propriety as a norm or criterion, the poststructuralist rhetorician is concerned with dissolving the very notion of discursive norms, for in them presumably reside the devices of social injustice. Leaving aside for the moment the problems this creates for rendering *any* judgment, this view can be seen as a genuine response to the conundrum posed by the concept of propriety: the very will or need to make judgments of propriety seems to be either a tautological presupposition of that judgment's object, or, conversely, an indication that its object does not exist (that is, that the like-mindedness, tradition, usage, or common opinion required to arrive at conclusions about propriety must already be lacking, else why even mention them?).[1] In the case of the former, judgments of propriety are superfluous; in the latter, they are a form of violence, a forcible maneuver suiting one's own political agenda in the sheep's clothes of consensus. To put it another way: Where propriety exists, it need not be discussed; where it does not exist, it cannot be discussed, at least not honestly. The commonplace *de gustibus non disputandum* expresses the problem as well, if to it is appended Kant's comment that

> even though the basis determining a judgment of taste may be objective, that basis still cannot be brought to determinate concepts; and hence even proofs do not allow us to *decide* anything about such a judgment, although we can certainly *quarrel* about it. . . . One can quarrel about taste (though one cannot dispute about it). (210–11)

Lanham sees some affinity between the idea of propriety and the position of some contemporary theorists that reason itself is rhetorical, or, as it is usually phrased, that rhetoric is epistemic.[2] The universal and omnivorous quality of such a rhetoric would hold obvious problems for any theory that would support a usable methodology:

> [A]s a stylistic criterion [it] finally locates itself entirely in the beholder and not in the speech or text. No textual pattern is decorous or not. The final criterion for excess, *in*decorum, is the stylistic self-consciousness induced by the text or the social situation. We know decorum is present when we don't notice it and vice-versa. Decorum is a gestalt established in the perceiving intelligence. Thus the need for it, and the criteria for it can attain universal agreement and allegiance, and yet the concept itself remain without specifiable content. (46)

In at least one sense of "content" this is true of all rhetorical concepts, if rhetoric is conceived of as an art: as a methodology, rhetoric is applicable to all subjects and thus has no particular "content." But in Lanham's view, propriety directly implicates rhetorical education in the process of acculturation; accordingly, the concept appears to be less a true rhetorical norm than an anthropological fact—one that is *all* "content"—yet content needing no specification by or to one socialized into it. To the extent that it is taken as a rhetorical norm, propriety can only be a dictum of "piety." As such it has hidden from view what Lanham takes to be a central task of rhetorical theory: "Rhetorical theory has spent endless time discussing how to adjust utterance to this preexistent social reality without reflecting how that reality has been constituted by the idea of decorum" (46).

Adam Smith's treatment of propriety, both in his rhetoric lectures and his moral philosophy, is original and extensive, offering an innovative approach to many of these issues. His theory, as we shall see, has implications not only for understanding his thought, but for conceptualizing rhetoric's own interdisciplinarity as well as its relevance for conceptualizing the discursive embeddedness of many contemporary political and social problems. But Smith's rhetorical theory, like propriety itself, has been relatively unstudied. Even scholars trying to interpret Smith's own rhetorical practices have often put aside his theory as inapposite to their analyses. This is a curious omission, for it is hard to overrate the historical importance of the new Scottish belletristic rhetoric instigated by Smith and later taken up by followers such as Hugh Blair. In the succinct estimation of David Daiches, it was "a rhetoric for the literati of the Scottish Enlightenment, bent on exploring and clarifying their views of man and nature, as it was for the men of the American revolution, bent on explaining and clarifying and justifying the objectives of their revolutionary activity" (48). It is little exaggeration to say that it became the dominant rhetoric of liberal, enlightened modernity.

A variety of factors have contributed to the comparative neglect of Smith as rhetorician: his eclipsing fame as an economist; the fact that his rhetoric lectures survive only in the form of student notes; and the consequently far greater direct influence of other eighteenth-century rhetoricians such as Blair (who heard Smith's rhetoric lectures and partly modeled his own after them). When Smith's importance as a rhetorician is cited, the case is usually referred to the opinion of one scholar, Wilbur Samuel Howell, who argues in his seminal *Eighteenth Century British Logic and Rhetoric* that "Smith may confidently be called the earliest and most independent of the new British rhetoricians of the eighteenth century" (1971, 576). Howell devotes forty pages to an explication of Smith's rhetoric, a considerably longer and deeper analysis than he gives to most other rhetoricians in the volume. But to appreciate fully why so few have given Smith his due as a rhetorician, we should perhaps begin not by weighing the influence of Smith's rhetoric in his own day, but by looking back for a moment from the succeeding century.

The nineteenth century is not supposed to have been especially propitious in the history of rhetoric. The usual story is that the Enlightenment and Romanticism killed off the classical rhetorical tradition, and that the accomplishments of eighteenth-century innovators yielded dwarf fruit. Many nineteenth-century rhetorics—devoted heavily to rudimentary composition and elocution—do appear as fairly anemic derivatives beside either the great works of the classical tradition or the ambitious new rhetorics of the eighteenth century, both of which they drew upon. This interpretation has been under revision, but certainly it has some validity.[3] Yet it is countered by the pervasively oratorical culture of the American nineteenth century, upon which the Scottish new rhetorics were an important influence.[4] This apparent incongruity between theory and practice is a reminder, however, that while theories evolve and change, appearing to us more or less apposite to their moments—and more or less intellectually satisfying in our own—rhetoric never goes away. When rhetorical theory seemingly atrophies, we ought to seek it out in other places.

As it happens, the twilight of the classical rhetorical tradition in the nineteenth century coincides with the rise of the modern social sciences—political economy, psychology, sociology, anthropology, linguistics—and these are conspicuous as places to look for rhetoric's afterlife. If this in part explains the seemingly diminished importance of nineteenth-century rhetorical theory—rhetoric's traditional theoretical work now being done in these various new fields—it begs all the more for a reexamination of Smith the rhetorician, the theorist as well as the practitioner, for Smith is one of the founders of the modern social sciences, and his view of them was fundamentally interdisciplinary. In all likelihood this partly explains his interest in rhetoric, the original interdisciplinary field that alloys elements of logic, grammar, ethics, politics, epistemology, psychology, and poetics into a single practical art. It also suggests that to read Smith on rhetoric, we ought to read not simply within the boundaries of some unpublished reports of his rhetoric lectures, but across the range of disciplines in which he worked. An understanding of this interdisciplinarity in Smith's work—one which, as we shall see, gives rhetoric a key position—should not only advance our understanding of Smith the rhetorician, but also illuminate our own conceptions of rhetoric as architectonic within a range of contemporary disciplines and practices.

Scottish Enlightenment

A first step toward this greater appreciation of Smith as rhetorician is to survey the life and circumstances amid which his thought arose and developed. One common thread in Smith's main works in rhetoric, ethics, and economics is the charting of large-scale historical transformations in human society, an area of interest that makes perfect sense when we consider that the Scotland into which he was born was in a remarkable period of transformation itself. The Act of Union of 1707 had fused Scotland and England as Great Britain, ultimately bringing greater economic prosperity to both—indeed, by 1780 Scotland had moved from comparative backwardness to achieve a level of agricultural, industrial, and commercial strength unthinkable without the Union's having put an end to the mercantilist rivalry between the two countries.[5] But in the meantime Scotland was without a sovereign and had lost its parliament, as well as its right to a militia, with the Union affording it little in the way of power in London. Although Scotland had retained a separate legal system and national religion—both sources of power, prestige, and cultural identity—there was significant turmoil. Jacobite opposition to the house of Hanover, combined with various dissatisfactions with the Union, as well as political and economic conflict between highland and lowland Scots, led to rebellions, most notably in 1715 and 1745 (both failed). Political power and influence was largely in the hands of large landowners, who had to balance authority with both the Kirk session (Presbyterian assemblies) and a growing class of town-dwelling merchants, bankers, and lawyers. Increasingly the gentry managed their affairs from the distance of the major towns and cities—not only Glasgow and Edinburgh but London. To complicate matters further (and of particular relevance to this study), Scots found themselves speaking what they now perceived to be an orphaned dialect of English. As the Moderate minister Alexander Carlyle explains in his *Autobiography*:

> To every man bred in Scotland the English Language was in some respects a foreign tongue, the precise value and force of whose words and phrases he did not understand and therefore was continually endeavoring to word his expressions by additional epithets or circumlocutions . . . (quoted in Berry, 17).

Given these extensive dislocations (which are but crudely sketched here, and which in truth had been going on since at least 1603, when James VI had vacated the Scottish Court to inherit the English crown), it should not be surprising if something of an identity crisis in Scottish national culture came to a head.

Smith himself opined in a letter of 1760 that the Union had been an economic success for Scotland; but he knew only too well that economic improvement necessarily brings cultural change (*Corr.*, 50). By the time Thomas Boswell and Samuel Johnson made their famous visit to Scotland in 1777, they were disappointed not to find the "system of antiquated life" they had come to see. Even the highlanders were unexpectedly modern and urbanized; of them Johnson wrote, "There was perhaps never any change of national manners so quick, so great, and so general" (73). Johnson found the shift in language particularly remarkable:

> The conversation of the Scots grows every day less unpleasing to the English; their peculiarities wear fast away; their dialect is likely to become in a half century provincial and rustic, even to themselves. The great, the learned, the ambitious, and the vain, all cultivate the English phrase, and the English pronunciation, and in splendid companies, Scotch is not much heard, except now and then from an old lady. (151)

Smith himself was reported to have spoken without trace of accent or Scotticism, though the shift in dialect had evidently left "peculiarities" in his pronunciation—which in turn were reputedly unmockingly imitated by his students and followers (*EPS,* 276).

Likewise, Scottish assimilation had some peculiar repercussions of its own, as a sense of cultural inferiority was answered with an ethos of national pride and an optimism, particularly among leaders in the arts and sciences, that new methods of inquiry and applications of science and technology could solve problems in fields as diverse as rhetoric, law, ethics, historiography, epistemology, chemistry, architecture, medicine, agriculture, geology, and others still—all for the improvement not just of Scottish reputation, but of the human condition. This great upwelling of intellectual activity, often said roughly to begin (though somewhat for the sake of convenience) with the 1725 publication of Francis Hutcheson's *Inquiry into the Original of our Ideas of Beauty and Virtue* and ending with (or being superannuated by) the French Revolution, has since become known as the Scottish Enlightenment. At its highpoint just past mid-century, David Hume would remark,

Is it not strange, that, at a time when we have lost our Princes, our Parliaments, our independent Government, even the presence of our chief Nobility, are unhappy in our accent & Pronunciation, speak a very corrupt Dialect of Tongue which we make use of; is it not strange, I say, that in these Circumstances, we shou'd really be the People most distinguish'd for Literature in Europe? (Hume, *Letters,* 1:255)

This rich and complex moment in social and intellectual history can be but roughly sketched here, and the discussion will necessarily skirt some thorny questions of precisely what the "Scottish Enlightenment" was.[6] Still, even at a requisite level of generalization, a few points will be useful in situating Smith's work. The work of the Scottish literati in developing what David Hume called "the science of man" (Henry Home, Lord Kames called it "the culture of the heart") was aided by an atmosphere of religious tolerance that prevailed in the latter half of the Scottish eighteenth century.[7] "Moderate" Presbyterianism, though tending to be politically conservative (ministers were appointed by lay patrons who were for the most part controlled by the nobility), had moved away from strict Calvinist doctrines such as predestination and election in favor of a relatively de-theologized social morality.[8] As compared to the orthodoxy of the Scottish Kirk's "High Flyers," some moderates approached Deism in appearance. For his part, Smith was more than a little circumspect in stating his own religious convictions, which must be speculatively reconstructed at least as much from what he did *not* say as from what little he did. Though wary of arousing attention from conservative defenders of the Kirk (and in this, as we shall see, he was not completely successful), his essentially Christian deist position, and his concomitant interest in such themes as natural liberty and non-revealed foundations of morality met with far less opposition than they might have were it not for the buffer of Moderatism.

Religious liberalization as well as new pressures from an increasingly industrial society made way for reform in the Scottish universities, which subsequently earned a reputation as being as fine as any in Europe. Though retaining as their principal mission the teaching of young men bound for the ministry, room was made for other subjects such as medicine and law, which had previously been the domain of Continental universities. This expansion was made easier by decreased lecturing in Latin and the increased use of specialist teachers for separate subjects (inaugurated at Edinburgh). Notwithstanding such diversity, philosophy remained a central subject in the curriculum at Scottish universities, as it was a major concern in the Enlightenment as a whole. "The Scotch Metaphysics," as it was derisively called by George III, kept alive the subjects of the old trivium—grammar, rhetoric,

and logic—joining to them epistemology ("pneumatics") and moral philosophy (Davie, 7). This educational program was aided by the fact that prior
to the Union the Scottish parliament had created an extensive system of
grammar schools, and had sponsored as well the publication of university
textbooks that aimed to present a balanced picture of the contrast between
modern philosophy and the Aristotelian scholasticism it opposed. The hefty
subtitle of Hutcheson's *Inquiry* provides a convenient snapshot of Scottish
philosophy's general ambition, if not its entire agenda: *In Which the Principles
of the late Earl of Shaftesbury are explain'd and defended, against the Author of the
Fable of the Bees: and the Ideas of Moral Good and Evil are establish'd according to
the Sentiments of the antient Moralists, With an Attempt to introduce a Mathemati-
cal Calculation in Subjects of Morality.* Such eclecticism is endemic to both the
thinking and writing of the Scottish enlightenment, a phenomenon further
evident, for example, in George Campbell's influential *Philosophy of Rhetoric*
(1776), which draws both on elements of Hume's skeptical epistemology and
Thomas Reid's realist "common sense" foundationalism. Indeed, that
thinkers as different as Hume and Reid are both central figures in the Scottish enlightenment sufficiently indicates its intellectual breadth.

Interests were diverse and intertwined. Moral philosophy was an abiding
concern as, in response to the thought of Descartes, Hobbes, Mandeville, and
Locke, philosophers sought new foundations for moral conscience in sociological or psychological terms. Smith had his own unique answer to this
problem, and, as I will argue in chapter 4, it is an answer uniquely rhetorical
in character. History, too, was of extensive, almost obsessive interest among the
Scottish intellectuals, not only as they attempted to understand their own tu-
multuous past, but as they engaged in the kind of sociological analysis called
for by their pursuits in moral philosophy. This caused them to engage in a remarkable self-consciousness about the rhetoric of historiography itself—one
of Smith's central rhetorical interests, as we shall see. Many writers (Smith
among them) were led to undertake what Dugald Stewart labeled "speculative history"—that is, anthropological hypotheses about the "origin and
progress" (an oft-repeated phrase) of various human phenomena and institutions, such as language, law, and commerce. Another important vector in eighteenth-century Scottish thought, again connected with the new urgency in
moral inquiry, was an interest in aesthetics (as even Hutcheson's title indicates), the foundations of which were similarly challenged by developments in
modern philosophy. Smith, Blair, Kames, and others were led to consider the
concept of taste, to articulate norms for the criticism of art and writing, and
to investigate the relation of "sentiments"—emotions that issued as aesthetic

and moral judgments—to both the social and individual passions from which they sprung. In doing so, they created a language of social and political values in a period of shifting class identity and diminished political opportunity.

The universities offered an education that was both deeper and more specialized in this range of subjects, but this did not dampen the pervasive spirit of interdisciplinarity. There was lively interest in and exchange between all the arts and sciences, as well as between men of power and standing, professional philosophers and teachers, and men of merely "amateur" interests.[9] Symptomatic of this were the many clubs and learned societies that thrived as the media for the circulation of ideas among artists, physicians, professors, merchants, landowners, lawyers, scientists, philosophers, politicians, ministers, and military men. Smith was an active member of many such organizations, including Glasgow's Political Economy Club, the Literary Society (a debating society he co-founded in Glasgow in 1752), the Philosophical Society (which may have sponsored his Edinburgh lectures), the highly influential Select Society, and the Poker Club (established after The '45 to press for a Scottish militia, but which later took up varied social and political causes). Alexander Carlyle's telling remark about his experience in the Select Society— "[It] was in these meetings in particular that rubbed off all corners, as we call it, by collision, and made the *literati* of Edinburgh less captious and pedantic than they were elsewhere"—may be fairly generalized to describe the effect of many of the clubs.[10]

If the flavor of Scottish intellectual life was identifiably "Scotch" (particularly to the English), among the literati themselves, devoted as they were to Scottish improvement, the dominant ethos was seen as being just as cosmopolitan as it was national. The Enlightenment's leaders were well traveled on the continent, corresponded with the intellectual luminaries of Europe, and understood their work to be contributing to progress in European, not simply British, arts and letters.

Smith's Life

Today it may seem that the biography of a writer is not particularly germane to understanding the "texts" that writer produces. In the case of Adam Smith, this problem is largely obviated by three factors: He was generally retiring in nature; he was a poor correspondent; and, decisively for our knowledge of his life, he had many of his papers burned upon his death. Our knowledge of his life is therefore relatively limited; indeed, Ian Simpson

Ross's 1995 *Life of Adam Smith*, the first major biography in a century, reveals relatively little new information about Smith, though it adds significantly to the overall contextual picture. Nonetheless, some facts of Smith's life help are helpful in understanding the place of rhetoric in his thought.

Smith was born in Kirkcaldy, Scotland, a port town across the Firth of Forth from Edinburgh, in 1723. His father, for whom the younger Smith was named, had made a good living as the port's Comptroller of Customs but died before his son was born. Smith's mother, Margaret Douglas, raised the boy along with a stepbrother in relatively comfortable circumstances. Smith was something of a sickly child, but his was an attentive and indulgent mother; Smith would return her affection throughout his life. As a boy he attended the burgh school, part of a successful national system of local schools that was a source of pride to the Scots. The schoolmaster, David Miller, was of good reputation, and records suggest that Smith followed a curriculum of reading, translating, and writing of Latin, and had instruction in English composition, basic Greek, as well as training in mathematics. Smith was well liked among his schoolmates, despite his habits of frequently talking to himself and appearing to become lost in thought while in the company of others (*EPS*, 270). It was a trait that would follow him into adulthood. Wrote Dugald Stewart, in an early account of Smith's life: "Even in company, he was apt to be engrossed with his studies; and appeared at times, by the motion of his lips, as well as by his looks and gestures, to be in the fervour of composition" (*EPS*, 229–30).

In 1737, Smith moved on to the University of Glasgow, where he began a three-year curriculum most marked by his encounter with Professor of Moral Philosophy Francis Hutcheson. Hutcheson was a founding figure of the so-called Scottish Enlightenment, most known for his *Inquiry* (noted above), a work that drew eclectically on Shaftesbury, Locke, Addison, and Cicero's *De Officiis* to argue for an autonomous moral sense analogous to the sense of beauty. Although Smith would ultimately differ with Hutcheson on the matter of human benevolence, he was no doubt inspired by his teacher's insistence on the fundamentally social quality of the human condition, and also by his connecting of aesthetics and morality (if not by the specific connections Hutcheson made), a relation comparable in some ways to the associations Smith would make between rhetoric and moral conscience. All his life, Smith spoke admiringly of Hutcheson.

Then as now, promising students at Glasgow were given the Snell Exhibition to Balliol College, Oxford, and Smith was awarded this scholarship in 1740. His experience at Oxford, however, was significantly worse than he must have hoped for. His disappointment is evident in a letter to his guardian William Smith, a cousin and academic at Marischal College, Aberdeen, who had apparently offered advice to his cousin not to overwork himself. Replied the younger Smith, "[I]t will be his own fault if anyone should endanger his health at Oxford by excessive Study, our only business being to go to prayers twice a day, and to lecture twice a week" (*Corr.*, 1). If a similar judgment supplied many years later in *WN* is accurate, the academic situation was rather bleaker than even that: "In the University of Oxford, the greater part of the publick professors have, for these many years, given up even the pretense of teaching" (*WN,* 5.1.f.8). But while Oxford had no Hutcheson to inspire him, Smith was not one to have his time wasted: Taking advantage of Balliol's relatively good library, he read extensively on his own in both classical and modern literature and philosophy, further honing his abilities with classical languages, teaching himself Italian and French, and submitting himself to translation exercises, believing this to be the most valuable way of improving style in composition. Smith must have been an adept autodidact, for he would ultimately enjoy a reputation for having uncommonly precise and extensive knowledge of his other languages, particularly Greek and Latin. His aim in such study, speculated Stewart, was not to gain "a vain parade of tasteless erudition," but "a familiar acquaintance with every thing that could illustrate the institutions, the manners, and the ideas of different ages and nations" (*EPS*, 272). Whether the strange malady that afflicted Smith—"a fit of laziness which has confined me to my elbow chair these three months" he wrote his mother in November 1743—was induced by the strain of his self-imposed course of studies cannot be said, but, like the "inveterate scurvy and shaking in the head" that troubled him the following year, it suggests that his time at Balliol was anything but easy (*Corr.*, 3).

The Snell Foundation intended for its beneficiaries to study for the ministry, but if Smith ever had such inclinations, they unraveled at Balliol. What little teaching occurred at Balliol was reputedly bent on defending Aristotelianism against the onslaught of the scientific revolution and Enlightenment, subjects that no doubt held great appeal for Smith. His independent work apparently aroused the suspicions of his superiors, who caught him in the act of reading David Hume's *Treatise on Human Nature*, reprimanded him, and confiscated the book. To add to his difficulties, the Scottish Exhibitioners at Balliol were treated badly by their schoolmates and by college authorities, both of whom tended to regard the Scots—some eight among the hundred or so students at Balliol—as an "alien and intrusive faction" (Rae, 26). These discriminations were abetted by a suspicion of Hanoverian sympathies among the lowland Scot students, who must have felt all the more ill at ease with the predominating Jacobite sentiment at Balliol at the time of the failed Jacobite uprising known as The '45. Years later, in a letter discussing Scottish universities, Smith would lament that such institutions "all contain in their very nature the seeds and causes of negligency and corruption" (*Corr.*, 143). Whatever the cause, in 1746 Smith left Balliol, quite likely in disappointment, though not without at least some profit.

Smith spent the next two years living at home with his mother, and about this period in his life almost nothing is known. It is all but certain that he continued the independent study he had undertaken at Balliol, and perhaps he even wrote some of the shorter essays, referred to by Smith as juvenile works (*Corr.* 137) and posthumously published under the title *Essays on Philosophical Subjects* (*EPS*). (Some of these, however, were clearly written later.) The essays are on an array of topics, including a study of the "principles which lead and direct philosophical enquiries," illustrated by the histories of astronomy, physics, ancient logic, and metaphysics; as well as essays on the five senses, imitation in the arts, similarities between music, dancing and poetry, and comparisons between English and Italian verse. Of particular interest to rhetoricians is his "History of Astronomy," which, despite its title, begins by stating that its aim is to examine the nature and causes of the sentiments of wonder, surprise, and admiration. Wonder is a response to novelty; surprise, to the unexpected; and admiration, to the beautiful. Through an examination of the histories of astronomy, physics, ancient logic, and metaphysics, Smith argues that these effects, mutually interacting with one another, have had a greater influence on the course of philosophical investigation and literature than is ordinarily thought. This is in part because these responses are not simply raw passions, but "sentiments"—that is, they are emotions that also function as judgments. He approvingly quotes Malebranche (as Hutcheson had before him, and as he would again in *TMS*): "Our passions . . . all justify themselves; that is, they suggest to us opinions which justify them" (*EPS*, 48). If this work hints of an early interest by Smith in matters of affective response and rhetorical efficacy, it should not be surprising, for when Smith finally found a regular position, it was as a lecturer in rhetoric.

In 1748, a prominent member of the Edinburgh bar, Henry Home, later Lord Kames, perhaps inspired by the continuing need after the Union of 1707 to direct young Scots to the kind of polite learning that would further advance Scottish culture but also abet its assimilation to English, invited Smith to offer a series of public lectures on rhetoric. Precisely how and why

Kames chose Smith is unknown, but it would have to be surmised that Smith had some reputation as being interested and capable in the subject. And Kames must have been pleased at his choice. Shaped by an enlightened ethos of empiricism and yet nourished, albeit subtly, by the classics, Smith's lectures offered a fresh approach to literacy based on the suitability of style to the discursive context in which it is situated and focused on understanding the psychological effects of various forms of discourse. The librarian of Glasgow from 1750–1754, James Wodrow, recalled the lectures in a letter:

> Smith delivered a set of admirable critical lectures on Language, not as a Grammarian but Rhetorician—on the different kinds or characteristics of style suited to different subjects, *simple*, nervous, etc., the structure, the natural order, and proper arrangement of the different members of the sentence., etc. (quoted in Campbell and Skinner, 31)

Smith's surviving work on rhetoric—the lectures themselves were apparently among those papers burned upon Smith's death, but a set of student notes was uncovered in 1958—will be the subject of close analysis in chapter 4. He delivered his lectures to audiences of law and theology students at least three times between 1748 and 1751, adding lectures on civil law during the third year. The audience included Alexander Wedderburn (later editor of the *Edinburgh Review* and eventually Lord Chancellor), John Millar (later a prominent professor of law at Glasgow), and Hugh Blair, among other important Edinburgh figures.

The considerable success of the Edinburgh lectures earned for Smith an appointment to the Chair of Logic at the University of Glasgow in 1751, and a year later, to the Chair of Moral Philosophy, and they would continue to be of use to him in his work in those fields. (Meanwhile, Smith's success in Edinburgh is suggested by the fact that the lectures were carried on by Robert Watson, and that Hugh Blair modeled on Smith's parts of his own lectures later given at the University of Edinburgh as first Regius Professor of Rhetoric and Belles Lettres.) John Millar reported that in the logic post Smith found it necessary to abandon the old syllabus of Aristotelian logic and metaphysics. In its place Smith delivered studies of a "more interesting and useful nature": his "system" of rhetoric and *belles lettres*. His motive for such a drastic curricular shift was not simply fashionable antischolasticism. As Millar reported, Smith thought that "[t]he best method of explaining and illustrating the various powers of the human mind, the most useful part of metaphysics, arises from an examination of the several ways of communicating our thoughts by speech, and from an attention to the principles of those literary compositions which contribute to persuasion or entertainment" (*EPS*, 274).

As Professor of Moral Philosophy, Smith lectured on ethics, politics, jurisprudence, and natural theology, and continued to give his rhetoric lectures as well. Ethics and rhetoric were intimately related subjects for Smith, a matter I will take up in detail in chapters 4 and 5. As a teacher he was well liked, particularly for his lecturing style. As Stewart reports, he appeared to speak extemporaneously, offering in a "plain and unaffected" manner a number of propositions that would initially seem counterintuitive; gradually he would lose his hesitation, and his speech would become more "easy and fluent," his manner "warm and animated" as he proved his argument. Stewart's characterization paints Smith as equal parts orator and polite moral actor, as if Smith acted on his own complementary rhetorical and ethical principles in the practice of teaching:

> In points susceptible of controversy, you could easily discern, that he secretly conceived an opposition to his opinions, and that he was led upon this account to support them with greater energy and vehemence. By the fullness and variety of his illustrations, the subject gradually swelled in his hands, and acquired a dimension which, without a tedious repetition of the same views, was calculated to seize the attention of his audience, and to afford them pleasure, as well as instruction, in following the same object, through all the diversity of shades and aspects in which it was presented, and afterwards in tracing it backwards to that original proposition or general truth from which this beautiful train of speculation had proceeded. (*EPS*, 276)

As we shall see, Stewart's image of Smith providing his students pleasure as well as instruction by internalizing his audience and offering them a vehement and richly described account of the subject at hand is virtually an enactment of the intersection of rhetoric and ethics in Smith's thought.

During this period Smith wrote his major ethics treatise, *The Theory of Moral Sentiments*, first published in 1759. The book was well received in Britain and on the Continent, both on the merits of its argument that moral consciousness originates in the human propensity to sympathize with the situation and judgments of an idealized other, as well as for its lucid style. Edmund Burke equally admired the book's "solidity and truth" as its style of "painting of the manners and passions" (*Corr.*, 46–47). In an abstract of *TMS*, David Hume quibbled with Smith's analysis but similarly praised Smith's rhetorical skill in deploying such a "lively, perspicuous, manly, unaffected stile" (Ross, 180). Smith had apparently intended to develop the jurisprudence part of his moral philosophy lectures into a book on natural justice, government, and law, but his thinking on these matters, which subsumed some areas of economics, gave way to a fuller consideration of the economic principles that would eventually become the *Wealth of Nations*.

Smith also published two items in the *Edinburgh Review* during this period, and both are germane to his work as a rhetorician. Intended by its founder, Alexander Wedderburn, as a biannual review of Scottish publications, the *Review* was dedicated to the spirit of Scottish self-improvement, a cultural ethos marked, as J. C. Bryce has put it, by a "curious mixture of national pride and a sense of inferiority, (especially in the matter of language)" (*EPS*, 230). To the first issue (August 1755), Smith contributed a mostly positive review of Dr. Johnson's *Dictionary*. His lengthy quotation of Johnson's entry for the word *but* gives a good indication of Smith's close interest in grammar. Although he voiced several reservations about the dictionary, they tend to say more about Scottish anxiety over propriety in speech than about Johnson's book. His review laments that Johnson had neither "passed his own censure upon those words which are not of approved use," nor categorized meanings with enough hierarchical rigor, and he begs for finer distinctions between synonyms. Nonetheless, Smith's review is generally admiring, and he commends it as particularly useful to Scots, who have "no standard of correct language in conversation" (*EPS*, 241).

The second issue of the *Review* (January 1756) printed a letter from Smith urging against Scottish parochialism and recommending that its editor and readers look especially to Continental works of literature and philosophy as models of achievement. English literary and philosophical accomplishment is primarily in "imagination, genius and invention," writes Smith, but these are often as fleeting as they are striking. The French, on the other hand, are to be prized for their penchant for "just arrangement, an exact propriety and decorum, joined to an equal and studied elegance of sentiment and diction." Smith clearly relishes the French mode, which, though less flashy, has several distinct advantages from which Scots can learn:

> [I]t never revolts the judgment by anything that is absurd or unnatural, nor even wearies the attention by any gross inequality of the stile, or want of connection in the method, but entertains the mind with a regular succession of agreeable, interesting and connected objects. (*EPS*, 244)

Smith goes so far as to say that while he is flattered "as a Briton" by the Encyclopedists' esteem for English thinkers such as Bacon, Boyle, and Newton, he is "mortified" at the idea that those thinkers probably will be better known (or so he supposes) through their French interpreters, whose style imparts a useful "natural and simple order" to their ideas.

The *Edinburgh Review* lasted only two issues, but it was widely read and reprinted later. Smith's contributions shed valuable posterior light on the "improving" motive behind his earlier rhetoric lectures, but, perhaps more importantly, they also demonstrate that even as he was writing *TMS* he was still thinking deeply about matters rhetorical—and of rhetorical propriety in particular—not just as a social nicety but as critically requisite for lucid communication. Smith even goes so far as to suggest that waning English interest in moral epistemology (or "metaphysics") may be partly attributable to the discursive tendencies he sees in English writing, whereas the French, with their interest in propriety and order, retained an interest in the subject (*EPS*, 250). English "imagination, genius and invention" are unequal either to writing or prolonged thinking about such subjects; French naturalness, balance, and cohesion, on the other hand, are not only more suited to communicating such thought, but to directing it. In evidence Smith cites not only the *Encyclopédie*, but Levesque de Pouilly's Shaftesburian *Théorie des Sentimens Agréable* (1747). Presumably, Smith thought his own *Theory of Moral Sentiments* would remedy the neglect of moral epistemology in British letters, not simply in a return to the subject, but by applying a new, more appropriately rhetorical approach to it.

Charles Townshend, a prominent London politician (now principally remembered for the restrictive measures he sponsored against the American colonies), was impressed enough with *TMS* to seek Smith out as a private tutor for his stepson, Henry Scott, the Duke of Buccleuch. Smith accepted the invitation, resigning his Glasgow post in January 1764 to attend the young duke in an extended European tour. This seemingly drastic move is explained by two factors: the generosity of Townshend's offer, which, at £500 a year, plus a post-tutorship annual pension of £300, substantially exceeded Smith's pay at Glasgow; and by Smith's disapproval of the practice of professors taking extended leave. Lest his departure be seen as unseemly, Smith not only insisted on paying from his own pocket the substitute he hired to finish his teaching duties for the term, but he refunded to his students the additional fees that they had paid, even over their objection. Smith was always scrupulous in such matters. It is doubtful that he ever regretted the departure, though later in life he would reflect back upon his time at Glasgow as "by far the most useful, and, therefore, as by far the happiest and most honourable period of my life" (Rae, 405).

The ensuing tour, which also included the duke's younger brother, Hew Scott, was spent mostly in France and lasted two and one-half years, affording Smith at least as valuable an experience as it did his young charges. In

Geneva he met and conversed with Voltaire several times; at Paris, his friendship with David Hume purchased him access to salon life there; and he became acquainted with a group of influential economic thinkers, the Physiocrats, led by the physician François Quesnay. Their analysis of the centrality of agriculture to economic health differed from Smith's, but the antimercantilism this position entailed comported with his own views. He took full advantage of any opportunity to learn about economic practices in France, and many of these observations were added to a work he already had in progress, later to be *The Wealth of Nations*. The tour came to a sad end in 1766 when Hew Scott fell ill and died; Smith accompanied the body to London and remained in Britain ever after.

Smith stayed in London for several months, overseeing revisions to a new edition of *TMS*. Among other things, this included adding an appendix titled "On the first Formation of Languages," which had been developed earlier as part of his rhetoric lectures. When the duke married in 1767, Smith returned to live with his mother in Kirkcaldy, and he remained there most of the next six years while continuing to hone *WN*. In a letter to Hume he wrote:

> My Business here is Study, in which I have been very deeply engaged for about a Month past. My Amusements are long, solitary walks by the Sea side. You may judge how I may spend my time. I feel myself, however, extremely happy, comfortable and contented. I never was, perhaps, more so in all my life. (Corr., 103)

It is not known to what extent that sense of tranquility was disrupted over the next several years, as his apparent expectations that the book would be done quickly were frustrated, probably by a combination of the sheer massiveness of the project and Smith's own meticulousness in research and writing. Lord Kames commented to a correspondent in 1773 that he was "afraid the delicacy of [Smith's] taste exceeds his powers of execution" and that the book, though long overdue, "may be yet at a distance" (Ross, 245). Smith's own correspondence during this period, even more slight than usual, would suggest great absorption in the project, as would the story that one of his walks took him—wearing only a dressing gown—some fifteen miles to Dunfermline, where he was awakened from his thought by church bells (Rae, 259). A letter of January 1768 reports less progress than he had expected (*Corr.*, 113); another the following year seems to show him buried in financial papers and reports, which were "in a very great disorder" (*Corr.*, 115). He worked on *WN* in Kirkcaldy for another three years, and then for three years more after a move to London.

A letter from David Hume suggests another possible reason for the delay: the deepening crisis in American affairs, which centered on England's trade protectionism. Hume hoped that Smith was not holding up his work pending an outcome (*Corr.*, 149). But it was a matter that greatly interested Smith, and he was compelled to include an analysis of the economic aspects of colonial policy in his still-developing work. Aside from the interest he evidently took in the news, Smith periodically attended the House of Commons to listen first hand to speeches on the American question.

The Wealth of Nations was finally published in 1776, and was very well received, despite its concluding argument, advanced on the weight of its free trade doctrines, that England allow the colonies to go their own way, and that the colonial power "endeavor to accommodate her future views and designs to the real mediocrity of her circumstances" (*WN,* 5.3.92). Hume wrote approvingly of it, but thought that a book of such detail would be slow to reach a public indisposed to giving the requisite attention. Still, it had "Depth and Solidity and Acuteness, and is so much illustrated by curious facts, that it must at last take public Attention" (*Corr.*, 150). Hume must have been surprised, as was Smith's publisher, when in fact *WN* was very popular: the first edition sold out in six months. Perhaps this was all the more to be unexpected in that, as commentators have since noted, *WN* contained very little which was particularly new. What was new, and quite likely a significant cause of this surprising success, was the style of Smith's writing, which was, like that of his previous book, widely remarked to be lucid and compelling. John Millar, in a letter to Hume, remarks on some complaints Hume apparently had about the style of the book, but the nature of Hume's criticism is not known, and such a view would have been in the minority. For his part, Millar found the style "original," and "exceedingly well adapted" to the subject (Ross, 291). Hugh Blair concurred:

> One writer after another on these Subjects did nothing but puzzle me. I despaired of ever arriving at clear Ideas. You have given me a full and Compleat Satisfaction and my Faith is Fixed. . . . You have done great service to the world by overturning all that interested Sophistry of Merchants, with which they had Confounded the whole Subject of Commerce. . . . Your arrangement is excellent. One chapter paves the way for another; and your system gradually erects itself. Nothing was ever better suited than your Style is to the Subject; clear and distinct to the last degree, full without being too much so, and as tercly [*sic.*, probably "terse," meaning concise, polished] as the Subject could admit. Dry as some subjects are, it carried me along.

Blair's major reservation was that the book was not quite dry *enough* in places: he thought that the material concerning measures to be taken with

America was "too much like a publication for the present moment" and that Smith's views on universities and the Church were likely to "raise up formidable adversaries" (*Corr.*, 151). Edward Gibbon, the first volume of whose *Decline and Fall of the Roman Empire* was published the same year, also applauded, calling *WN* "an extensive science in a single book, and the most profound ideas expressed in the most perspicuous language" (Rae, 287).

On reading *WN*, Adam Ferguson wrote Smith, "You are surely to reign alone on these subjects, to form the opinions, and I hope to govern at least the coming generations," and indeed, the effects of *WN* were not merely literary (*Corr.*, 154). New taxes imposed under the leadership of Lord North in 1777 and 1778 drew on Smith's book, and various statesman sought Smith out for advice—in 1778 concerning policy for ending the war with America, the next year on handling trade issues with Ireland. William Pitt the Younger was a strong partisan of Smith's views on free trade and revenue, doctrines that were evident under his leadership as Chancellor of the Exchequer and First Lord of the Treasury in the 1780s and after. Of course these were merely the proximate effects of a work that has since been seen (if not read) as the bible of laissez-faire capitalism. Further discussion of *WN* and its rhetorical significance will follow in chapter 6.

1776 was a momentous year for Smith: it saw not only the publication of *WN*, but the death of Smith's "never to be forgotten" friend, David Hume (*Corr.*, 220). The event raised some problems for Smith that occasioned him to consider questions of rhetorical propriety. Hume had made Smith his literary executor, and among the things Hume wished to have published was his *Dialogues on Natural Religion*, a work likely to stir up many more adversaries than those Blair feared would be irked by Smith's preference for Presbyterianism in *WN*. Though a codicil to Hume's will ultimately left the matter to William Strahan (Hume's and Smith's mutual publisher), a copy of the *Dialogues* was sent to Smith in case either Strahan or, next, Hume's nephew, should fail to bring the work out. Notwithstanding the great affection Smith had for Hume, he was quite wary of being associated with his friend's work, not just because its skepticism was at odds with both his deism and his philosophical realism, but because he feared the clamor it would raise, and that the clamor would be directed at him. He wrote to Strahan: "I am resolved, for many reasons, to have no concern in the publication of those dialogues" (*Corr.*, 172). Hume also wished Smith to see to the publication of a short autobiographical piece. Smith was happy to comply in this task, even volunteering to add a postscript describing Hume's stoic valor in the face of the two years' illness leading up to his death. After writing the piece, Smith apparently altered his plan somewhat and decided that "there is a propriety in addressing it as a letter to Mr. Strahan" instead of adding something to Hume's autobiographical sketch. It is a telling remark in that, as we shall see, Smith viewed propriety, both in rhetorical and moral terms, as involving indirection. By writing the piece as a letter to Strahan, Smith probably hoped for a softened response to his praise for a dear friend who was yet regarded by many as an "infidel." He took the indirection a step further: when he sent the account to Strahan, he asked that it not be attached in any way to the *Dialogues*. Strahan found Smith's reticence overanxious; on his inspection, the *Dialogues* contained nothing more "exceptionable" than he had already published in Hume's other works, though he was businessman enough to delay publishing the *Dialogues* lest it harm sales of the new edition of Hume's complete works (*Corr.* 173).

Smith's account of his friend's death is quite a moving eulogy; its conclusion is modeled on that of Plato's *Phaedo*. But his apology for Hume's razor wit and rhetorical attacks, his admiring testimony as to the great skeptic's peace of mind before death, and his final judgment of Hume as "approaching as nearly to the idea of a perfectly wise and virtuous man, as perhaps the nature of human frailty will permit," was more than Hume's many enemies could stomach (*Corr.*, 221). Smith would later reflect, in a sentiment dually revealing as to his regard for the rhetorical quality of *WN* as well as to his rhetorical miscalculation in publishing the letter to Strahan: "A single, and as, I thought a very harmless Sheet of paper, which I happened to Write concerning the death of our late friend Mr Hume, brought upon me ten times more abuse than the very violent attack I had made upon the whole commercial system of Great Britain" (*Corr.*, 251).

For one who viewed himself as such a severe antagonist to the British mercantile system, it is perhaps rather curious that Smith's next major move in life would be to secure a rather important post as an official of that system. After Hume's death he returned to Kirkcaldy, undertaking work on an essay on the imitative arts (now collected in *EPS*), probably foreseeing it as part of the first of two "great works" he mentions, in a letter of 1785, as being "upon the anvil": namely, "a sort of Philosophical History of all the different branches of Literature, of Philosophy, Poetry and Eloquence." The second was to be "a sort of theory and History of Law and Government"—clearly an expansion of those aspects of his earlier lectures on jurisprudence not addressed in *WN* (*Corr.*, 248). Smith was returning, in other words, to the material of his early days as lecturer at Edinburgh and professor at Glasgow, and evidently he had made significant progress in developing and synthesizing it into these major works. But in 1778, on his reputation as an economist and through the influence of the Duke of Buccleuch, he was appointed Commissioner of Customs at Edinburgh, a position that came with the considerable annual salary of £600. Added to the £300 he received (over his protest) as pension from his tutorship of the duke, and Smith was quite well-off. Although he lived in some comfort with his mother and his cousin, Janet Douglas, he anonymously gave large sums to charity. Nonetheless, he would have more than enough in financial support to undertake his remaining "great works," though the valuable commodity of time would now be put in short supply.

As a customs official, Smith was quite competent and dutiful, though he was sometimes absent for periods, due both to health problems, which increasingly plagued him in later years, as well as to a desire to pursue "my literary pursuits." This latter included not only the two aforementioned "great works," but subsequent editions of *WN* and *TMS*. Gibbon was probably voicing the sentiments of many when he expressed surprise at the "strange reports" that a philosopher had taken such a post (*Corr.*, 187), but the Custom House job afforded Smith a certain comforting regularity and even "relaxation," as he found it "a much easier Business" than research and writing, which had always been a slow and laborious process for him (*Corr.*, 287). "I am a slow a very slow workman," he wrote, "who do and undo everything I write at least a dozen times before I can be tolerably pleased with it" (*Corr.*, 276). In 1780 he expressed regret at the interruptions caused by his new occupation; of the "two other great works," he wrote in 1785 that " the indolence of old age, tho' I struggle violently against it, I feel coming fast upon me, and whether I shall ever be able to finish either is extremely uncertain" (*Corr.*, 248). He managed to produce substantially revised and expanded editions of *WN* (the third) and *TMS* (the sixth) in 1784 and 1790 respectively, the latter including, among other additions, several elements probably designed to dissociate his views from those of the French revolutionaries; such insinuations had been, and would continue to be made. His two major projects, however, would never be completed. Apparently sensing that the end was near, in early 1790 he instructed his literary executors to destroy his papers, and they did—some sixteen folio volumes. Smith died a week later, on June 17.

Perhaps nothing would be of greater value to those interested in Smith the rhetorician than to know what he read at Balliol and during those two years back in Kirkcaldy prior to giving his rhetoric lectures in Edinburgh, but of this there is no record. Nevertheless, it is quite likely that his reading dealt extensively with rhetoric, else how could Kames have had the confidence to ask him to lecture on the subject? From the catalogue of his library it is quite evident that Smith's interest in rhetoric was extensive and life-long.[11] Rhetorical works weighed heavily in his collection of classics: he owned volumes of speeches by Aeschines, Demosthenes, Lysias, Isaeus, and Isocrates; in rhetorical treatises he owned Aristotle's *Art of Rhetoric* (in Latin and French, in addition to a complete works of Aristotle and two separate editions of the *Poetics*), Dionysius of Helicarnassus's *On Composition*; Demetrius of Phaleron's *Peri Hermeneias*, two editions of Hermogenes of Tarsus's *Peri Idean*, the pseudo-Longinus's *Peri Hypsous* as well as a separate volume anthologizing Hermogenes, Longinus, and Aphthonius; he owned three sets of the complete works of Cicero and Quintilian's *Institutio Oratoria*. Smith clearly kept up with modern publications on rhetoric as well: his library included George Campbell's *Philosophy of Rhetoric* (1776), Joseph Priestley's *Lectures on Oratory and Criticism* (1777), Thomas Sheridan's *Lectures on Elocution* (1762); Du Marsais's *Traité des Tropes* (1757), and a synopsis of William Barron's lectures on rhetoric and belles lettres given at the University of St. Andrew's. But for Du Marsais, the latter works all postdate Smith's lecturing on rhetoric, but they do demonstrate his abiding interest in the subject. Pairing this extensive interest with the central importance of propriety in both Smith's rhetoric lectures and his moral philosophy, it will be worth considering, if even in a necessarily hypothetical mode, what he may have encountered in his reading of those early works. Chapter 2 will be devoted to this subject. Chapter 3 will examine the subsumption of questions of rhetorical propriety into broader eighteenth-century developments in science, epistemology, and aesthetics. Chapter 4 conducts a close analysis of Smith's rhetorical theory in view of the centrality of his concept of propriety. Chapter 5 examines the relevance of this interpretation of his theory to *TMS,* arguing that Smith's notion of rhetorical propriety functions architectonically within his moral philosophy. The final chapter begins with an examination of some implications of this interpretation for our understanding of the social system Smith was attempting to promote in his works, including *WN*; the chapter then reassesses Smith's contribution to rhetorical theory, arguing not only for its uniqueness in the history of rhetoric, but for its relevance to both contemporary moral philosophy and some problems surrounding contemporary rhetorical controversy.

CHAPTER 2

Smith and Propriety in the Classical Tradition

T hough steeped in knowledge of classical literature, Smith rarely parades his learning, nor does he always explicitly draw upon it. When mentioning classical rhetoric in *LRBL*, he is often dismissive, as when he derides rhetorical works obsessed with categorizing schemes and tropes as "generally a very silly set of books, and not at all instructive" (1.59), and one might easily mistake this for his attitude toward of all of ancient rhetoric (in fact, he is referring to modern rhetorics as well here). We can pardon but also learn from the reaction of C. R. Fay, who, upon examining a catalogue of Smith's library half a century ago found himself surprised to realize that Smith's thought "issued from the womb of the classics" (1). Smith scholars today widely recognize that his deep knowledge of classical literature inevitably shaped his thought. Gloria Vivenza's work, showing Smith in some cases reproducing passages from classical texts nearly verbatim, should fully dispel any lingering surprise contemporary readers might have. Vivenza, however, makes little reference to the classical rhetorical tradition which Smith knew well. Smith's contribution to the theory of rhetorical propriety came in the context of twenty centuries of development in the history of the idea, and there can be little doubt that he was aware of and drew upon that tradition in ways both conscious and unconscious. A survey of this history is doubly useful then, not only as suggesting possible influences on Smith, but as an opportunity to examine some of the philosophical issues that theorizing about propriety involves. Two of the perspectives that come under analysis in this chapter—sophistic skepticism and platonic idealism—have direct analogues in two thinkers influential in Smith's time, Hume and Shaftesbury respectively. As we shall see, Smith's deployment of propriety in rhetoric and ethics was fully in accord with philosophical issues already well framed in the classical rhetorical tradition.

Pretechnical Hellenic Propriety

In the earliest Greek literature Smith read, he would have found pervasive the idea of propriety in speech and action, and it is almost certain that the first rhetoricians drew on the concept as it had surfaced in early poetry. These earliest formulations are a possible influence on Smith given the close relationship he articulates between propriety in rhetoric and ethics. As Hermann Fränkel has noted, "In [the Homeric epics] factual report of what men do and say, everything that men are, is expressed, because they are no more than what they do and say and suffer" (79). *What they do and say*: in oral cultures, word, deed and identity are not so distinct as they have become for us. Not surprisingly, appropriateness in Homer has been linked to characters' capacities for the discovery of both speech and action, in social settings as well as in internal dialogue (Enos, 5). Even centuries later, after the concept of propriety is artificially lodged under the canon of rhetorical style, it will retain heuristic overtones. Smith too, as we shall see, will reassign such functions to propriety.

The disparate effects of Telemachos's famous speech to Penelope in book one of the *Odyssey* are an instructive first example of archaic propriety. They are due as much to his youth as to any particular quality of his speech. Antinoös mocks him: "Why Telemachos, you must have gone to school with the gods! They have taught you their fine rhetoric and bold style!" (1.384). Though the speech induces wonder in Penelope, Telemachos fails to dislodge the suitors, for he lacks the requisite ethos, and his grand style ill-suits his youth. The appropriate was thus apparent in the suitability of speech (or lack thereof) to the age and character of the speaker, to the subject matter and to the audience—in short, to the speech situation as a whole.

Eventually several Greek terms came to signify appropriateness, including *to prosêkon* (that which is fit, beseeming), *harmozein* (to fit, suit), *to oikeion* (that which belongs to, is suited to, one's own), and, most commonly where stylistic propriety was intended, *to prepon*. The origins of *to prepon* extend to Homeric poetry, where the verb *prepein* means "to appear before the eyes," or "to be seen conspicuously." For example, in the Homeric Hymn *To Demeter,* Metaneira tells the goddess that "truly dignity and grace are conspicuous upon your eyes [*prepei ommasin*] as in the eyes of kings that deal justice"

(2.214–15). This visual meaning is often linked to propriety in speech, a relevant connection to follow here, as Smith also closely associates propriety and seeing.[1] Thus, Odysseus remarks that men are gifted unequally: One is comely, yet ineloquent, another ugly, yet gifted in speech. As for the latter, "God crowns his words with beauty, so that all may listen to [or gaze upon, *leussousin*] him with delight; he speaks in a steady voice with winning modesty, he is notable where men gather together [*meta de prepei agromenoisin*] and as he walks through the streets, all gaze upon [*eisoroôsin*] him as one inspired" (8.172) A noteworthy aspect of *prepein* here and elsewhere in Homer is that it is entangled in the archaic phenomenology of sight and appearance. As Raymond Prier has shown, the deployment of sight-related language in Homer indicates that the archaic mind did not register a whole set of modern cognitive dichotomies best summarized as "subjective" and "objective"—distinctions that do not emerge sharply until Plato and Aristotle.[2] Homeric seeing emanates from the eyes as much as it is the observation of external objects; sight is then both passive and active, both inwardly receptive and outwardly projective, both self-motivated and other-directed, balancing attributes of microcosm and macrocosm, human and divine. This noctic experience of seeing in Homer is abetted by its frequent expression in the Greek middle voice, which carries a sense of something being seen at once both for itself *and* for oneself. The seer thus participates in a kind of spatiotemporal intermediateness that even the standard English translation of *prepein* latently suggests: "to appear conspicuously" is to be objectively apparent, but in a manner shaded with subjective judgment. It is possible that Smith, with his keen knowledge of Greek, may have been at least sensitive to this. As Prier amply shows, though this holistic phenomenology of sight in archaic Greek may be impossible to translate neatly into any modern language and thus is somewhat difficult for us to grasp, it is not in the least bit subtle in Homer. Particularly interesting for the history of rhetorical propriety, it is implicated in the disclosure of appropriate and just action (Prier, 70), the revelatory power of speech (56, 107, 110, 115), and the power of both speech and sight to induce wonder (81–97).[3] In *LRBL*, Smith sees Homeric poetry precisely in terms of a historiography of "the marvelous" written in "the language of wonder" (2.45).

Although it can be perilous to assert neat analogies between ancient and modern minds, a radical cognitive disjuncture between the two is less likely than differences, even significant ones, of degree. Some eighteenth-century pre-Romantic reanimations of the ancient concept of sublimity (e.g., Edmund Burke's) were in part an attempt to grasp a phenomenology of experience that would undercut the radically individualized subject demanded by Enlightenment epistemologies (hence was Burke roundly criticized by associationists). As we shall see, Smith's notion of propriety in both speech and action has qualities somewhat reminiscent of such a phenomenology: It is intimately related to the visual; in referring to correct diction, it is object-directed; yet in also referring to emotional appropriateness, it is subjectively shaped; in being refracted though a theoretical spectator, it involves a kind of intermediation, a seeing-with. Yet discursive propriety does not induce stupefied wonder, nor does it bring about the submersion and disappearance of the speaker into a background of convention. (Smith held in his *History of Astronomy* that wonder, a response to novelty, is one of the key principles driving philosophical enquiry.) Lastly, one important quality of Smith's work in rhetoric and ethics is the way he often avoids much of the language of empiricism and its mechanistic psychology, which together entailed rigid dichotomies of internal/external, self/other, subject/object.

Already in these earliest instances of rhetorical propriety, several characteristics occur which will continue to typify theories of appropriateness in speech: (1) its origins are in the cosmic or natural order; (2) it is associated with clear perception through the senses, especially vision; (3) it occasions a pleasurable aesthetic response in hearers; and (4) it results in conspicuous social appearance for the speaker. Use of *prepein* in both Pindar and Aeschylus (both of whose works Smith refers to in *LRBL*) is revealing about subtle connotations that may have surrounded *to prepon* by the time it entered rhetorical theory in Aristotle, for in these texts *prepein* is regularly used with both the Homeric meaning, "to appear clearly," along with the later meaning, "to suit." Hence *prepein* could involve making something evident through vision, as in *Agamemnon* (30), when signal fires "indicate" (*prepei*) the fall of Ilium; or through hearing, as in the same work, when "there sounds clearly [*prepei*] within the town a clamor of voices that will not blend" (321); or even more generally to the understanding, as in Pindar's tenth Pythian ode, where "gold showeth forth (*prepei*) its nature when tried by a touchstone" (67), or in *Agamemnon* again, where the truth is said to be "not clear" (*ou prepei*). The verb can also mean "to become like" (we might say "to appropriate the form of") as in *The Suppliant Maidens*, when Zeus "likens his form [*prepei*] to a bull." Propriety thus tends to disclose experience in a manner not merely arbitrary and metaphoric, but indexical and synecdochic. That these other meanings were in simultaneous use with the more common and later meaning reinforces the idea that to the early Greek mind, awareness of the appropriate involved the clear perception of some defining characteristic of an object, but with an aspect of subjective judgment often closely attendant. Consciousness of the appropriate thus appears to have arisen through analogical thinking, as a correlation between objects and qualities through sensed resemblances or agreements. Propriety as such had aesthetic, emotional, and cognitive features.

When *prepein* and its related grammatical forms are used in connection with fitness, it often bears these nuances. Pindar writes that "Mortal aims befit mortal men [*Thnata thnatoisi prepei*]" (Isthmian Ode 5.16), and that the poet "may fittingly [*prepontos*] blend the varied melody of the lyre and air of the flutes with the setting of the verses" (Olympian Ode 3.9). In Aeschylus's *Suppliant Maidens* (195–203), *prepein* occurs twice in a passage associating clear and appropriate speech, disclosure in the eyes, and the character and situation of the speaker when, in an early scene, Danaüs instructs his daughters in how to act before the princes:

> Reply to the strangers, as is fitting for aliens [*hôs epêludos prepei*], in piteous and plaintive language of necessity, telling them clearly [*torôs legousai*] of your flight, how it was unstained by deed of blood. Above all let no arrogance accompany your speech, and reveal nothing impious in your peaceful eyes, from your respectful face. In your speech neither interrupt, nor hesitate [*mê proleschos mêd epholkos*]—for this would offend these people. And remember to be submissive: you are an alien, a fugitive, and in need. Bold speech does not suit [*ou prepei*] the weak.

Thus, to the four characteristics of appropriate speech listed above may be added: (5) appropriateness may involve a mean, seen here in "*mê proleschos mêd epholkos*"—literally "neither forward nor lagging" (though this mean aspect of propriety is perhaps already apparent in Odysseus's uncomely speaker's "sweet modesty" [*aidoi meilichiêi*]); and (6) propriety is constrained by the circumstances of the specific situation, especially the disposition of the audience. The fifth characteristic is significant for adumbrating a link between propriety in speech and the Aristotelian conception of virtue. The last characteristic is potentially at odds with the first one listed above (i.e., that propriety originates in the divine or natural order), thus placing the problem of defining propriety squarely in the middle of the ancient dispute over *nomos* (law, custom, convention) and *physis* (nature).

The Sophists: Propriety and Skepticism

The sophists' concerns over propriety in speech emerge as part of the larger *nomos-physis* controversy. Not surprisingly, given the itinerant nature of the sophists' profession, propriety was an important element of their teaching, and it appears to have been seen as derived mainly from *nomos* (Miller 1993, 224). As such it bears comparison to the efforts of some eighteenth-century writers who, in the absence of realist epistemological suppositions, derive standards of aesthetic taste from social situatedness. Hume's skeptical epistemology generally echoes these sophistic views. Furthermore, as outsiders to Athenian culture, the sophists bear some resemblance to the position of the Scots, who would similarly craft a rhetorical propriety apposite to their own alien status with respect to English culture.

Less known than Protagoras's view that "man is the measure of all things" is his doctrine of *orthos logos*—literally "straight," "true," or "correct" discourse. These would seem to be opposed teachings—one subjectivist, one objectivist (see Untersteiner, 34; Schiappa, 163–64)—unless *orthos logos* is taken to mean not representational correspondence but "appropriateness for a context also consisting of language" (Donavan, 46). Whether such propriety would be the expression of the speaker's virtue of justice (*dikê*), or whether that justice may simply imply respect for conventional audience expectations is probably impossible to say for Protagoras.[4] It is worth noting, however, that taken together, the four possibilities suggested here—grammatical correctness, stylistic appropriateness, speaker character, and regard for audience—anticipate the later development of *to prepon* in Aristotle as a concept denoting a harmonic response to all the exigencies of the rhetorical situation.

It is less difficult to be certain that propriety was a key part of Gorgias's rhetorical practice; quite possibly it was an explicit element of his theory as well. Little is known of the rhetorical handbook he is purported to have written, but given his renown for virtuosic extemporizing, he may well have treated appropriateness in connection with *kairos*, the timely or opportune.[5] *To prepon* for Gorgias has been described as "the formal element of the epistemological reality expressed by *kairos*": namely, "that which is fitting in time, place and circumstance" (Untersteiner, 197–98). As such it is not fully susceptible to art: Various specific elements can be learned, since they are strictly conventional, but because they must be enacted in the unfolding field of temporal exigency, they cannot be reduced to method. *To prepon* would be mastered predominantly by instinct or past experience.

Propriety was not merely a rhetorical concept for Gorgias, but, like *kairos*, it was consistent with a skeptical epistemology that extended to his ethics and aesthetics as well (Untersteiner, 198). The tenets of his *On Nature*—that (1) nothing exists; (2) if it did it would be unknowable; and (3) if it were, it would be incommunicable—fit with a theory of rhetoric as the use of nonlogical and/or nonlinguistic aspects of emotional appeal, style, rhythm, delivery, and the adaptation of these to both conventional mores and the situation at hand. Paradoxically, this anti-epistemology would further imply the need to act rhetorically *as if* the tragic incoherence of reality were not the case: to act, that is, as if speech were persuasive precisely because it *is* widely held to be an accurate means of communicating things about reality. In other words (and irrespective of Gorgias's actual epistemological commitments, which may even be intentionally parodic), Gorgianic rhetorical power would always be tempered by convention and situation. Gorgias's few extant texts employ precisely this strategy. In the *Encomium of Helen*, he argues that speech is a "powerful lord, which by means of the finest and most invisible body effects the divinest works"; it has the force of necessity; it affects the soul comparably to the "power of drugs over the nature of bodies." And yet the *Helen* is structured and subdivided as a piece of logical argument designed to persuade.[6]

Scott Consigny's interpretation of Gorgias is instructive here: opposing on the one hand a "mimetic" view (in which Gorgias's style is taken as reflecting the inherently antithetical or "tragic" nature of reality); and on the other hand an "expressive" view (in which Gorgias's language is endlessly creative, innovative, forcefully inventing its own domain, a sphere of relief from the incommensurability of physical reality and mind), Consigny reads Gorgias as rejecting both views, instead being radically "adaptive." His style is neither unique, nor self-contradictory; each of his works is utterly conventional within its genre. Thus, Gorgias practices a "stylistic opportunism" wherein "each discourse presents a distinct way of seeing and thinking" (48). The Gorgianic hermeneutic "treats understanding as a project of learning to speak effectively in new styles, using new vocabularies and new forms of reasoning." The residuum left to Gorgianic theory after this elimination of epistemology is nothing but propriety:

> [T]o speak effectively or successfully in any one instance, one must speak "fittingly," adapting to the constraints of the discourse at hand and speaking appropriately from moment to moment. . . . Gorgias implies that the success—and truth—of one's remarks is determined neither by the essential nature of a putative "reality" lying beyond every discourse, nor in an individual speaker's arbitrary inspiration or whim, but rather through the recognized protocols and criterion of the specific discourse being spoken. (50)

This point may seem far afield until we realize that Gorgias's position resembles that of David Hume on taste: Hume's skeptical epistemology constrains him to present taste not as a norm or set of norms, or even as a capacity, but as a behavior of adapting discourse to "a certain point of view." The sensationalist-emotivist ethics entailed by Hume's philosophy of human nature would in turn make rhetoric purely a matter of emotional appeal (as it largely was for Gorgias). Smith certainly knew Hume's portrait of taste as analogous to the need of the rhetorician to conciliate an audience's affections and "place himself in the same situation as the audience" (Hume 1965, 15). It may well have influenced Smith's ideas about rhetorical propriety, as well as his idea that the development of moral conscience involves the ability to put oneself imaginatively into the position of a spectator.

Borrowing a phrase from Richard Rorty, Consigny suggests that Gorgias is "willing to refrain from epistemology" (49). As we shall see, Smith too refrains from epistemology in the *TMS*, a work which yet implicates the theory of rhetorical propriety adduced in the *LRBL*. Enos has further pointed out that "Sophists such as Gorgias illustrate how heuristic techniques are grounded in stylistic modes of arrangement" and that "knowledge can be invented indirectly through 'heuristics' of style and arrangement" (88). As we shall see in chapter 4, Smith's theory of propriety, by taking on heuristic tasks typically handled by invention, effectively illustrates the same thing. Yet Smith's formulation will not imply the radical skepticism inherent in Gorgias's thought.[7]

Plato: Propriety and Idealism

If propriety was central to Sophistic rhetoric, it is unsurprising to find it near the heart of Plato's reticence to confer upon rhetoric the status of art. Plato's is important in the history of propriety, however, for he clarified aporia with which later theorists, notably Aristotle, would contend. And if Gorgias is in some ways a classical precursor of Hume, Plato is something of an analogous precursor for another of Smith's influential near-contemporaries, Shaftesbury.

From a casual look at some Platonic writings, one might not easily see that propriety posed nearly a theoretical impossibility for Plato. Take Socrates' famous strategy announced in the proem to his main argument in *Apology*: "It would hardly be suitable [*prepontos*], gentlemen, for a man of my age to address you in the artificial language of a schoolboy orator" (17c). Pleading old age, he asks for the deference given to foreigners who don't know the local ways. Here we meet a seemingly full cognizance of *to prepon*: Socrates knows that certain types of speech are thought to be appropriate to certain character types, ages, and origins, and he even draws on the alliance in pre-Socratic thought between *kairos* and *dikê* in tying his will to extemporize to the justice of his cause. But his position actually parodies that ideology. In distancing himself from the mode of discourse used by his accusers, even while going through the motions of a standard exordial apology for his style, Socrates knowingly commits a grave insult and impropriety, precisely because he was *not* a foreigner. High rhetorical style was the Athenian form of discourse par excellence, and given the verdict in the *Apology*, it is reasonable to conclude that the judges did not see that form as independent from content.

Scattered throughout the Platonic oeuvre are passages that seem to admit the legitimacy of propriety as a rhetorical norm—or at least as a valid human experience—but never is that recognition put into the mouth of Socrates. As Pohlenz points out, *to prepon*, as connected with individual appearance, has no place in Plato's transcendental idealism (55).[8] When a Platonic character remarks on propriety of speech, Socrates is usually quick to problematize matters.[9] For instance, Protagoras bridles under Socrates' demand that he refrain from giving speeches, and a dispute about propriety follows. "What do you mean, make my answers short? Am I to make them shorter than the subject demands?" asks Protagoras (*Protagoras* 334d). When Socrates answers no, Protagoras asks whether length is to be determined by the speaker or hearer; Socrates answers that if a speaker can speak either way, he ought to concede to his audience and be brief. Protagoras responds that his success in speech-making did not come from doing what opponents demand. Plato here suggests that propriety is thus symptomatic of speakers who aim to win arguments rather than engage in the dialectical search for ideals. The dispute nearly implodes on these incommensurable views of discourse, and the question of propriety is left unresolved.

When propriety explicitly comes up in reference to aesthetics, ethics, poetry, or rhetoric, Socrates seeks to undermine it.[10] The only extended discussion of *to prepon* in Plato is in the *Greater Hippias*, where Socrates asks Hippias, who has identified the beautiful (*kalon*) with the appropriate (*prepon*), whether the appropriate causes things to appear beautiful or to be beautiful (293e). When Hippias first answers that the appropriate makes things appear beautiful, Socrates responds that it is then a fraud in relation to beauty. Hippias tries arguing that the appropriate causes things both to be *and* to appear beautiful, to which Socrates readily responds that if that were the case, everything that is beautiful would appear so. Accordingly, people would be univocal in their perception of what is and what is not beautiful. Socrates concludes that they cannot find the cause of beauty in the appropriate.

In Platonic ethics, propriety is equally unwelcome. Meno, for instance, cites Gorgias's argument (presumably in his inextant work on *kairos*) that there are virtues specific to different places in life—those for a man, a woman, children, the elderly, the slave, and the free person (*Meno* 71e). But Socrates sees this as simply various designations of the *appearance* of virtues without knowledge of the essence of virtue. Without first securing a definition of virtue, Socrates will not allow any statement of what virtues might be appropriate to different individuals.

Discussing poetry, Socrates takes on Ion's assertion that the rhapsode will know "[t]he kind of thing . . . that a man would say, and a woman would say, and a slave and a free man, a subject and a ruler—a suitable [*prepei*] thing for each" (*Ion* 540b–c). Here Socrates argues that poetry is no art, because the poet has only inspiration, not true knowledge. If he knows how a general speaks, it is not because of his knowledge of poetry, but because of some acquaintance with the strategic art. Here we have a suggestion that poetic appropriateness exists for Socrates then, but its content cannot be apprehended other than as ideal knowledge; it certainly cannot be exploited by the art of the poet, because poetry is not concerned with this kind of knowledge.

The same picture emerges with regard to rhetoric. In a memorable passage in the *Gorgias*, Callicles uses the idea of propriety to criticize Socrates' chosen way of life. Here we still encounter close connections between seeing and propriety as a conventional Athenian notion:

> When I see [*idô*] a little child, for whom it is still proper [*prosêkei*] enough to speak in this way, lisping and playing, I like it and it seems to me [*phainetai*: appears] pretty and ingenuous and appropriate [*prepon*] to the child's age, and when I hear it talking with precision, it seems to me disagreeable and it vexes my ears and appears [*dokei*] to me more fitting for a slave [*douloprepes*], but when one hears a grown man lisping and playing the child, it looks [*phainetai*] ridiculous and unmanly and worthy of a beating. . . . [Likewise] when I see [*horôn*] philosophy in a young lad, I approve of it, I consider it suitable [*prepein*]. (485b–c)

Socrates probably still has this jibe in mind when he raises one of the central issues of the dialogue: namely, whether orators should speak with an aim to perfect or merely gratify their hearers (502e). As Socrates had earlier explained, in his view rhetoric is not an art, but a "knack" (*empeireia*) akin to cookery, because, unlike legitimate arts, it "can produce no principle in virtue of which it offers what it does, nor explain the nature thereof, and consequently is unable to point to the cause of each thing it offers" (465a); instead, it "preserves by mere experience and routine a memory of what usually happens" (503a). Socrates argues that practitioners of other arts order their materials with a certain view of their products in mind and compel each "to fit and harmonize with the other [*prepon te einai kai harmottein*]." Rhetoric would do this only if its practitioners acted upon the hearers' souls with a view toward ordering them according to justice and temperance (504d). Being able to construct oratory in such a way that it harmonizes with the variegated needs of a diverse audience (rather than simply gratifying them collectively) is one of the tasks of propriety, but it is no simple matter, and no solution as to how this might be accomplished is offered in the *Gorgias*. The dialogue leaves the subject of rhetorical propriety as a kind of hopeless ideal, with the reality being that few if any orators do have the good of their audiences in mind.

In the *Phaedrus*, we similarly find Socrates punching "holes in the fabric" (268a) of the recommendations in rhetoric handbooks, particularly those related to propriety, such as Prodicus's boast that he alone had discovered what the art requires—"to make neither long [speeches] nor short, but of fitting length [*metrión*]" (267b). Socrates again applies the analogy of other arts, asking Phaedrus what should be thought of the teacher of doctors who teaches only which treatments to give for which ailments but then expects students to manage for themselves which patients ought to be treated how and when. Phaedrus says such a doctor would be regarded as mad. Socrates then asks if one could become a tragic poet simply by knowing how to make long speeches about little matters, and short ones about important issues without knowledge of the soul. Phaedrus replies: "I imagine that they too would laugh at anyone who supposed that you could make a tragedy otherwise than by so arranging such passages as to exhibit a proper relation to one another and to the whole of which they are parts." Nor would one who simply knew how to produce the lowest and highest possible notes be a musician, for he would only have knowledge of a few basic elements of harmony. Similarly, the rhetoric handbooks are concerned with technical trifles, says Socrates: "[T]hey don't bother about employing the various artifices in such a way that they will be effective, or about organizing the work as a whole. . . ."[11] One can become a "finished performer" (269d) by studying "mere empirical routine" (270b), but "the art itself, as distinct from the artist" (269d) requires what Pericles had: not only practice in speaking, but "high flown speculation" (270a). From his knowledge of human nature, Pericles "applied to the art of rhetoric what was suitable thereto" (270a).

Socrates elaborates, admitting that the only legitimate form of rhetoric would be one based on sound knowledge of the types of human soul. This might suggest a rhetoric based in a large way on at least one sense of propriety, for the speech would have to be adapted to the nature of the hearers.

[The types of soul] are of a determinate number, and their variety results in a variety of individuals. To the types of soul thus discriminated, there corresponds a determinate number of types of discourse. Hence a certain type of hearer will be easy
to persuade by a certain type of speech to take such and such action for such and
such reason, while another type will be hard to persuade. (271d)

The entire passage expresses a hypothetical power of propriety, yet one that
seems well-nigh unattainable, short of divine intervention. Such propriety
would ultimately be derived not from experience of the way people themselves generally are but from a dialectical inquiry into the ideal realm of
knowledge. And propriety in oratory is only indirectly for the sake of persuasion: The wise person will pursue such things first and foremost in order
to "speak what is pleasing to the gods." This is a more difficult route than
simply discovering what techniques generally work in persuasion, but it is
necessary "because the goal is glorious" (274a). Needless to say, this is not the
goal usually thought to be the object of rhetoric.

Even Plato's idealistic theory of propriety, however, remains at the level of
a fairly undeveloped assertion: one should address "a variegated soul in a variegated style," a "simple soul in a simple style" (277c). At the same time, this
propriety is fairly rigid in nature: it assumes a close, one-to-one fit between
speech and audience. Neither Socrates nor Phaedrus moves to explain how
the problem of even a slightly diverse audience should be handled. Nonetheless, Plato did later theorists the service of demonstrating that a legitimate art
of rhetoric and a functional theory of rhetorical propriety would have to include a practical study of character types and passions. This challenge was directly answered by Aristotle, who included an extensive treatment of
characters and emotions in his *Rhetoric*. Smith's rhetoric provides a similar
approach, particularly if we read *TMS* as a work based in part on the theory
of propriety adduced in *LRBL*. Indeed, if we take these two works together
as comprising a philosophy of rhetoric, Smith is remarkable among eighteenth-century rhetoricians for his discussion of character types, the nature
of the passions, and their dynamic influence on the effectiveness of all types
of communication.

Aristotle: Propriety and Realism

Rather than look to a realm of ideal knowledge for the sources of persuasion, Aristotle takes rhetoric as it is—a practice of human social and political
experience wherein people use their faculties of reason and emotion to con-

front matters about which there is less than apodictic certainty. His definition of rhetoric as "the faculty [*dunamis*] of discovering the possible means of persuasion in reference to any subject whatever [*peri hekaston*]" (1355b28) answered Plato's challenge to rhetoric's claim to artistic status and to a legitimate theory of propriety. As a *dunamis*, rhetoric can be studied theoretically, apart from the necessary situatedness of practice, yet this study always keeps in view the circumstances of practice "in each case" (*peri hekaston*).[12] Aristotle examined "what gives things themselves their persuasiveness" [1403b19], and accordingly he constructed a theory of persuasion based on both the psychological and the social nature of human beings as he found them in life. This is reflected in his designation of the three "artistic proofs" (*entechnoi pisteis*)—*ethos* (moral character), *pathos* (emotion), and *logos* (intellect). Propriety functions in relation to all three. [13]

When Aristotle theorizes style in *Rhetoric* book three, he names two primary and closely interrelated virtues: clarity (*saphêneia*) and propriety (*prepon*). Clarity is a more basic concept as the sine qua non for accurate verbal transmission of thought; propriety on the other hand is a more complex and developed rhetorical concept permeating nearly everything Aristotle has to say about style. He begins by noting that while clarity is prerequisite for crafting language appropriate to the emotions and character of both speaker and audience, clarity is itself produced by using language appropriate (*prepousa*) to the subject matter (1404b5). This two-way relationship is not as paradoxical as first it may seem: Clarity is achieved through correct diction; diction itself is affected by the type of discourse being conducted. Thus, "foreign" words and ornate phrases are more suited to poetry than to prose, because the subject matter of poetry tends to be more extraordinary than that of prose. This idea is extended when Aristotle notes that different styles are suitable to written and spoken prose, as well as to each of the three fields of rhetoric—deliberative, judicial, and epideictic (1413b3ff). Where language is used metaphorically, propriety is of even greater consequence. Lack of propriety in the creation of metaphors is a chief source of stylistic frigidity, for lack of proportion between analogous elements in a metaphor makes the language ridiculous or obscure (1406b5).[14] In either case, frigidity results because the intelligibility of the language and the object to which it refers is impaired.

The interconnection of clarity and propriety is significant in Smith's rhetoric as well; Smith similarly demands a close correlation between propriety and correct and clear diction. In an intriguing parallel with Aristotle's notion that inappropriate metaphors occasion ridicule, Smith also holds that inappropriate actions—those out of proportion to that with which a (metaphorical) impartial spectator could sympathize—similarly generate ridicule. Smith, again like Aristotle, sees language as a product of thought about the real world. Aristotle's linguistic realism, as set forth in *On Interpretation*, explains why clarity is not a theoretical problem for him: "Spoken words are symbols of mental experience and written words are symbols of spoken words. Just as all men have not the same writing, so all men have not the same speech sounds, but the mental experiences, which they directly symbolize, are the same for all, as also are those things of which our experiences are the images" (16a4–8). The mutual inextricability of clarity and propriety means that these stylistic virtues together have complementary roles to play in presenting reality to the mind. By requiring style to be suited to the subject matter, propriety abets the intelligibility of the message and with it the intelligibility of the reality the message is about.[15]

In his next major statement on propriety in the *Rhetoric*, Aristotle involves the three artistic proofs: "Propriety of style [*to prepon*] will be obtained by the expression of emotion and character, and by proportion [*analogon*] to the subject matter" (1408a12). He then expounds a highly developed theory of propriety:

> Style is proportionate [*analogon*] to the subject matter when neither weighty matters are treated offhand, nor trifling matters with dignity, and no embellishment is attached to an ordinary word; otherwise there is an appearance of comedy. . . . Style expresses emotion, when a man speaks with anger of wanton outrage; with indignation and reserve, even in mentioning them, of things foul or impious; with admiration of things praiseworthy; with lowliness of things pitiable; and so in all other cases. Appropriate style also makes the fact appear credible; for the mind of the hearer is imposed upon [*paralogizetai*—will draw a wrong conclusion or logical error] under the impression that the speaker is speaking the truth, because, in such circumstances, his feelings are the same, so that he thinks (even if it is not the case as the speaker puts it) that things are as he represents them; and the hearer always sympathizes with one who speaks emotionally, even though he really says nothing. This is why speakers often confound their hearers by mere noise. (1408a10–25)

This passage is critical for implicating propriety in the three proofs, further suggesting that propriety is an essential element of Aristotle's entire theory. The rational nature of propriety supports Aristotle's view that rhetoric is an *antistrophos* of dialectic; propriety's integration of style with Aristotle's teaching on emotion and character (treated in book two of the *Rhetoric*) further demonstrates the indispensability of these subjects to rhetorical study. Because Smith, like Aristotle, makes propriety central to his rhetoric, Aristotle's theory merits further analysis here.

The key idea expressed in the passage above is that relating *to prepon* to *logos*: appropriate style "makes the fact appear credible." It does so in a way that will resonate with Smith's treatment of propriety: facts are made credible by virtue of the speaker's stylistic adaptations, because appropriateness signifies a sympathetic correlation between emotional states in the speaker and hearer, the disclosure of which leads the hearer to think that things are indeed the way the speaker represents them.[16] It would be a mistake to think that since the mind of the hearer may not draw a logically conclusive inference from appropriate style, the perception and mental processing of the appropriate are simply irrational. Aristotle's insight is quite the opposite. The implication of his remark is that appropriate style is a kind of proof from non-necessary or fallible sign.[17] His use of the verb *paralogizomai* (to misreckon, miscalculate) in the context of this passage is meant not to indicate irrationality but to indicate that signs of pathetic appropriateness are more fallible than those of ethical or pragmatic (i.e., subject-matter-determined) appropriateness. He is not implying that all such inferences are false; even the drawing of an invalid inference implies that reason has been engaged.

When Aristotle treats ethical appropriateness a few lines later, he in no way implies that the hearer's mind runs quite the same risk of being "imposed upon":

> Character also may be expressed by the proof from signs, because to each class and habit there is an appropriate [*harmattousa*] style, I mean class in reference to age—child, man, or old man; sex—man or woman; to country—Lacedaemonian or Thessalian. I call habits [*hexeis*] those moral states which form a man's character in life; for not all habits do this. If then anyone uses the language appropriate to each habit, he will represent the character; for the uneducated man will not say the same things in the same way as the educated.[18] (1408a26–31)

Êthos as Aristotle explains it is not the reputation that precedes a speaker, but the speaker's moral character "due to the speech itself" (1356a9). Thus, appropriate style must play a significant role in disclosing the speaker's *êthos* to the audience.[19]

It is perhaps tempting to think that this occurs simply by mere knack or instinct, but in fact reason plays a role in the functioning of style with regard to *êthos*. In effect, fitting style serves as a latent minor premise of an enthymeme whose universal premise is something such as, "All speakers whose speech exhibits X style are of X character."[20] The sign of appropriateness is not necessarily propositionalized in hearers' minds, but then neither are many of the unspoken premises underlying enthymemes. As this does not make the enthymeme less rational in nature, it need not imply that ethical propriety is irrational. Inference drawn from a sign of appropriateness is fallible, but then that is simply endemic to all rhetorical discourse.[21]

A notable consequence of Aristotle's emphasis on the rational, pragmatic quality of the aesthetic elements of speech thus unifies two audience types he had distinguished earlier in his treatise. These were the judge (*krites*), the term he uses generically for jurors or legislators, and the spectators (*theoroi*) of epideictic speech, who are also judges, but principally of speakers' ability in the present (1358b1). As we shall see, propriety in speech and action for Adam Smith will consist of the ability of the speaker/agent to act in such a way as to win the approval of and please an audience that is in the roles of both the admiring spectator and the approving judge.

Propriety for Aristotle is thus a powerful rhetorical tool, serving to support and strengthen persuasion through the artistic proofs. Aristotle will later explicitly refer to "persuasiveness resulting from propriety [*ek tou prepontos*]" (1414a35). Propriety is most useful in substantiating *êthos*, "the most effective means of proof (1356a). But even as an element of ethical proof, appropriateness extends itself to the other *pisteis*: *êthos* consists not only of moral virtue (*arête*), but of good will (*eunoia*) toward the audience, and practical reason (*phronêsis*) in regard to the subject matter (1378a9). *Eunoia* will be disclosed in part by the use of style indicating the appropriate emotion; *phronêsis* will be made evident in part by the speaker's use of language appropriate to the type of rhetoric and its subject.

Phronêsis, which Aristotle more fully identifies in the *Nicomachean Ethics* as "a reasoned and true state of capacity to act with regard to human goods" (1120b20–21), is not only a virtue but, as the capacity to make moral choices, requisite for the achievement of all the other virtues. The connection between *to prepon* and *phronêsis* is highly suggestive, then, and directly relevant to the rhetorical-ethical matrix in Smith's thought. The choice of the appropriate means of persuasion is not a morally neutral matter for Aristotle. Propriety will require that the rhetor have the virtue of practical reason; the speaker who is seen to have acted in a rhetorically appropriate way will be one who has the intellectual virtue of *phronêsis*, the primary habit of virtuous character.[22] Smith too will establish an integral connection between appropriateness in rhetoric and moral virtue, although the connection, as we shall see, will not principally involve reason.

Even if cultural and conventional influences can be admitted as shaping propriety, the phenomenon itself—style's ability to indicate rhetorically purposive emotion and character—is taken by Aristotle to be elemental to human nature. He indicates, for example, that specific emotions and character types will be made apparent by the use of particular stylistic devices suited to each: "Compound words, a number of epithets, and 'foreign' words especially are appropriate [*harmottei*] to an emotional speaker" (1408b10). Elsewhere he notes that it is inappropriate (*aprepes*) for older speakers to use hyperbole, because the vehemence of hyperbole seems youthful (1413b2). These examples reflect inevitable aspects of the human condition: Strong emotional states disturb ordinary speaking patterns; youth's lack of experience inclines it to rash speech and exaggerated statement.

An orator can try to exploit this, of course: one can attempt to appropriate the style whose correlative character or emotion may contribute to effecting persuasion. But audiences may have an advantage over the potential deceptions of unethical orators in two ways. First, *êthos*, as quoted in the passage above, denotes a moral state formed by habit (*hexis*).[23] Habits are not mere behavioral adaptations to or accidents of culturally stipulated moral convention, but the outcome of having exercised the activity (*energeia*) of virtue (1103a33)—deliberate, moral choice (*proairesis*). Were this not the case, authentic rhetorical character might be easily imitable. But "using the language appropriate to each habit" is no simple matter. Auditors who themselves have observed and/or experienced the habit in question for themselves are likely to be astute in identifying its misappropriation. This may be one reason why Aristotle regards the true and good as "naturally always easier to prove [*eusyllogistôtera*] and more likely to persuade" (1355a38). Second, audiences have an advantage in knowing that virtuous orators generally *do* style their speeches fittingly. As Aristotle notes in an earlier discussion of the good, among the things that humans deliberately, prudentially choose are "things which are appropriate [*harmottonta*] to them." Thus appropriate style is a (non-necessary) sign of ethical character, which in turn results from *proairesis*, and as such indicates a speaker capable of exercising practical reasoning toward the production of good and useful things.[24] This accords with what Aristotle says at the outset about *êthos*: "The orator persuades by moral character when his speech is delivered in such a manner as to render him worthy of confidence" (1356a5).

This interpretation is supported by the fact that propriety, like *proairesis*, also involves the choice of a mean. For example, different epithets are appropriate (*prepei*) to poetry and to prose (1406a14); still, prose may make use of poetic epithets to attain a "foreign" air, a desirable quality, so long as they are not used to excess. In applying them, "one must aim at the mean" (1406a18). Later, Aristotle reemphasizes the interconnectedness of clarity and propriety,

implicating the latter in seeking a mean:"If [style] be too diffuse, or too con-
cise, it will not be clear; but it is plain that the mean is most suitable [*harmottei*]" (1413a30). From this perspective, Aristotle's use of the phrase "virtues of
style" (*aretês tês lexeôs*) seems not metaphorical but a symptom of style's
imbeddedness in ethical reality. This connection between propriety and moral
choice is presumed as well by Smith, whose conception of moral propriety in
TMS entails enacting a mean—a "mediocrity" of passion with which a spectating audience can sympathize.

One last aspect of rhetorical propriety in Aristotle's thought merits our
attention, and that is the quality of the pleasure it induces. Aristotle specifically cites the quasi-syllogistic quality of antithesis as a source of the pleasure it induces; this makes sense, as the completion of enthymemes requires
one to "supply what is wanting" (1371b33) and can induce learning, two significant causes of pleasure; as we've already seen, propriety's functioning is
also quasi-syllogistic. [25] But there is a more elementary way in which style
causes pleasure. In *Rhetoric* I.11, Aristotle discusses the causes of pleasure as a
source of human motivation:

> Pleasure is a kind of movement of the soul and a collective and perceptible set-
> tling down into one's natural state. . . . [A]nything productive of the state just
> mentioned is pleasurable. . . . [C]onsequently it follows of necessity that both to
> pass into the natural state is, as a general rule, pleasant, and most especially is there
> pleasure when things done according to nature recover their own special nature.
> (1369b33–70a5)[26]

It may be extrapolated that propriety of style causes pleasure because it fulfills the audience's expectations of human character and emotion. Similarly,
Smith will present propriety as a way of bringing about a pleasing mental
"tranquillity" by fulfilling the expectations of spectators. For Aristotle this
produces pleasure for the hearer both as an experience of external things
meeting expectations, but also potentially as an occasion of learning and thus
a synchronic "settling down into one's natural state."

Aristotle's understanding of pleasure is such that it argues powerfully
against the poststructuralist tendency to dismiss propriety as gestaltic, merely
ideological, something recognized mainly by its absence. It is telling in this
respect that in his closing words on style, Aristotle argues that any requirement that style be pleasant or magnificent (*megaloprepê*) is superfluous:

> Why so, any more than temperate, liberal, or anything else indicating moral virtue
> [*êthous aretê*]? For it is evident that, if virtue of style has been correctly defined,

what we have said will suffice to make it pleasant. For why, if not to please, need it be clear, not mean, but appropriate [*prepousan*]. (1414a23)

One needn't struggle to aim at creating pleasure: it will be a natural by-product of the appropriate, and as such sufficiently perceptible to hearers. Aristotle's hesitancy in treating pleasure as style's sole aim is explained by his more extensive treatment of pleasure in the *Nicomachean Ethics*, where he holds that pleasure perfects an activity (*energeia*, 1174b14ff) and is thus an end (*telos*), not a process, means, or motion (*kinêsis*, 1153a9). It accompanies not the acquisition of moral capacity but its exercise. In accord with his statements on pleasure in the *Rhetoric*, he further calls pleasure an "activity of the natural state" that is "unimpeded" (1153b7). As such, pleasure may not be perceptible apart from the activity it accompanies, but as a completion of that activity—in this case the perception of propriety—pleasure must be perceptible. Those such as Richard Lanham who hold that propriety is merely a gestalt in the hearer's consciousness confuse appropriateness with the pleasure that accompanies it. For Aristotle, *to prepon* involves conspicuous appearance occasioning a conscious rational and aesthetic response from hearers.

One need not idealize audience here. In a discussion of the innate human response to *mimesis*, Aristotle notes in the *Poetics* that "[l]earning things gives great pleasure not only to philosophers but also in the same way to all other men, though they share this pleasure only to a small degree. The reason why we enjoy seeing likenesses is that, as we look, we learn and infer what each is . . ." (1448b). The *Poetics* generally supports the *Rhetoric*'s teaching on propriety, not only in making appropriateness an element of dramatic character and thus emphasizing its mimetic quality, but also in its teaching that character is the result of moral choice in discursive representations of life. It merits attention here especially in that Smith closely links rhetoric and literary discourse. Dramatic character, writes Aristotle, must be "good": "The play will show character if . . . either the dialogue or the actions reveal some choice [*proairesin*]"; and the character will be good if the choice is good (1454a16). As the *Rhetoric* makes clear, appropriate language is a sign of habituated character and hence of the speaker's capacity for practical reasoning. The *Poetics* also makes one use of *to prepon* that indicates that the oldest meaning of the word, that having to due with sight, still had resonance for Aristotle: he notes at 1455a25 that in plotting and constructing dialogue, the dramatist should "keep the scene before his eyes" [*enargestata*], for only then will he find what is fitting [*to prepon*].[27] Smith too will closely link propriety and vividness in verbal description.

As the foregoing analysis has shown, propriety for Aristotle has some modest relation to invention in that it is in part a response to the nature of the subject matter.[28] Propriety is primarily a virtue of style, however, denoting the coordination of stylistic devices and tone to character type, age, status, and gender.[29] In sum, Aristotle should be seen as having made a great contribution to the theory of rhetorical propriety. His treatment, prodded by the challenges posed by the sophists and Plato, gives a philosophical grounding to the major characteristics of Hellenic propriety discussed at the beginning of this chapter. I have noted the fact that this conception bears close parallels to Adam Smith's theory of propriety. Given Smith's familiarity with Aristotle's rhetoric, and his ownership of multiple editions of the text, it would be a mistake to overlook them. Both Aristotle and Smith fuse concepts of discursive propriety and clarity, echoing the early view of propriety as involving clear perception through the senses. Both Aristotle and Smith treat propriety as involving a mean with regard to action, hence insinuating propriety into ethical theory. Aristotle's rational configuration of the concept implicates the natural origins of propriety seen in early Greek literature by putting propriety within a teleological framework according to which the proper end of human beings is to exist in relation to their essentially rational nature. This is the most significant difference between Smith and Aristotle: Smith treats propriety as virtually excluding reason; he emphasizes instead its functioning within the psychology of the emotions. Propriety for Aristotle, as a sign of character and emotional state, is structured through the social conventions of discourse (which Smith also emphasizes), thus it is constrained by the exigencies of the rhetorical situation, not the least of which is the audience's capacity for emotion. The implication of this constraint for Aristotle, as for Smith, is that all rhetorical audiences must be conceived of as both spectators and judges who must be both pleased and persuaded. The most striking similarity between Smith and Aristotle is that the aesthetic component of style signifies a correlation between emotional states of the speaker and audience, which can stimulate a pleasurable response. This effect, for both Aristotle and Smith, not only reinforces the credibility of the speaker's character but lends credibility to the speaker's representation of reality. Smith may well have known these implications of propriety from his reading of the *Rhetoric* and *Poetics*; at the very least the similarities here suggest broadly similar tendencies of mind, and they place Smith's conception of propriety in closer proximity to the classical rhetorical tradition than is commonly thought.

Classical Propriety after Aristotle

Aristotle developed a nuanced theory of propriety, but it met with the same fate as his *Rhetoric* as whole, for not until at least Smith's time was rhetorical propriety to be given such a philosophical foundation. With the exception of Cicero's, no theory after Aristotle's treats propriety as a rational element of rhetorical proof. In addition, most treatments to follow (even Cicero's) blur the relationship between rhetorical and ethical propriety. After Aristotle, propriety tends to be absorbed into other concepts, such as the levels of style, or flattened into a wholly positive and thus theoretically empty prescriptive. These changes may in part be explained by the historical changes that overtook rhetoric as a whole. Rhetoric's drift from oral to written discourse as its domain (labelled *letturaturizazione* by George Kennedy) may have played a role in the diminishing of philosophical rigor in the theory of propriety as rhetoricians wrote handbooks thinking less and less of rhetorical praxis as involving face-to-face, spoken delivery (Kennedy 1980, 16). A more likely cause lies in the concomitant trend in rhetoric toward theoretical simplification as a part of its expanding institutionalization in education. Propriety would be particularly apt to atrophy. Since in practice it is culturally shaped, the philosophy behind propriety would naturally be seen as less strictly necessary, particularly for inexperienced students.

These trends are evident in Aristotle's student Theophrastus, whose lost *Peri Lexeôs* apparently sought to make Aristotle's theory more pedagogically useful, and thus stripped away such complexities as the rational relationship between clarity and propriety and propriety's relation to ethical character. Instead, Theophrastus offered a flat set of stylistic categories, a pattern followed in the first century BC pseudo-Ciceronian *Rhetorica ad Herennium*, whose author offers *elegantia* (clarity and Latinity), *compositio* (correct arrangement of words), and *dignitas* (varied ornament) as discursive values present in any style that is appropriate and finished [*commoda et perfecta*] (12.17). This reductive approach seems to have guided the development of the doctrine of style levels, which the *Ad Herennium* also features.[30] The grand (*gravis*), middle (*mediocris*), and simple (*attenuata*), each paired with a corresponding faulty style, are tonal registers carrying with them the implicit stricture of suitability. The levels of style offer a pedagogically simplified access to propriety, forgoing any philosophical justification.

The three levels of style in the *Ad Herennium* were a reduction from the four set out in *Peri Hermêneias*, a handbook on style in the Peripatetic tradition attributed to Demetrius of Phalereus. Demetrius (whose work Smith knew) is concerned with propriety throughout, delineating the manner of expression appropriate to each of four styles (*megaloprepês*, "the elevated," or, literally, "fitting the great"; *glaphyros*, "the elegant"; *ischnos*, "the plain"; and *deinos*, "the forceful") along with four corresponding defective styles. The author uses the terms *kairos* and *prepon* almost interchangeably to describe the relation of various phrases and devices to corresponding types of style (see sections five and six, for example). Though Aristotle is cited approvingly, his view that stylistic requirements beyond clarity and propriety are superfluous goes unheeded. Demetrius retains the idea that style must be appropriate to subject (120), but also says that subjects are suited to styles (190), indicating that the handbook was intended for exercises wherein a speaker would first choose a style, then look for a matching subject. Absent is any account of how these styles might be related to the emotions of the speaker and audience, as is any discussion of the probative values of these styles as signs of *ethos*.

The levels of style reached their apex with Hermogenes, whose *Peri Ideon* delineates seven "ideas" of style (with *twenty* subtypes), each of which was determined predominantly by subject matter. His discussion of each style begins with a consideration of content (*ennoia*) which thenceforth has a determinative effect on style. One of these styles merits separate discussion however: *deinotês*, translated "awesomeness" or "force," the last "idea" Hermogenes discusses, is "nothing other than the proper use of all the kinds of style previously discussed and of their opposites and of whatever other elements are used to create the body of the speech."

> To know what technique must be used and when and how it should be used, and to be able to employ all the kinds of style and their opposites and to know what kinds of proofs and thoughts are suitable in the proemium or in the narration or in the conclusion, in other words, as I said, to be able to use all those elements that create the body of a speech as and when they should be used seems to me to be the essence of true Force. . . . For if any speaker knows when he should use each particular style and when he should not and where he should use it and for how long and against whom and how and why, and if he not only knows but also can apply his knowledge, he will be the most forceful of orators and will surpass all others, just as Demosthenes did. (101)

In *Peri Ideon*, Hermogenes refers to another treatise, *Peri methodou deinotêtos*, which would take on the daunting task of fully explaining *deinotês*, a text now regarded as spurious.[31]

Hermogenes' concept recuperates some of the importance of *êthos* and *pathos* to propriety, for while four of the other six "ideas" are stylistic—clarity (*saphêneia*), grandeur (*megethos*), beauty (*kallos*), and rapidity (*gorgotês*)—one, character (*êthos*), is ethical, and another, sincerity (*alêtheia*), is (despite its name connoting "truthfulness") pathetic. In his discussion of *êthos*, he mentions "styles that reveal character" but then addresses not character revealed through style but styles and thoughts that give an impression of good character (70). He confines himself to simplicity, sweetness, subtlety, and modesty. Under sincerity, he gives examples of style evincing anger, pity, amazement, fear, irritation, confidence, indignation, and so forth. But if these characteristics in one way indicate a turn back toward Aristotle's fuller understanding of *to prepon*, in another way Hermogenes' theory of *deinotês* is more Platonic, for the "ideas" of style were really ideals reachable only by a rare Demosthenes, forms discovered through speculation on the characteristics of the ideal orator rather than through observation of the way the art typically functions.[32]

Another Hellenic text influential in eighteenth century transmutations of propriety was the *Peri Hypsous* written by an unknown author called "Longinus." Rediscovered in the Renaissance and widely known in Smith's time through many editions of a translation by Nicolas Boileau-Despréaux, *On the Sublime* addresses sources of verbal "sublimity"—a kind of awe-inspiring gravity and moral solemnity combined. While the author is thus relatively narrow in his concern for one type of style, he is consistently concerned with the import of *kairos* for success at achieving sublimity (16.3, 41.1), and frequently notes that sublimity is dependent on *to prepon* (9.7, 42.5).

Hermogenes, Demetrius, and Longinus were influential for later rhetorical theory (all were known by Smith), but none so much as Cicero, whose works evidence a pervasive if difficult interest in propriety. In *Orator*, his first mature work on rhetoric, Cicero seeks to describe the ideal rhetorician, but does so with far less specificity than Hermogenes; what emerges is not theory so much as a set of attitudes governed by an encompassing dictate of propriety. He makes a novel theoretical move by coordinating the three levels of style with each of three duties (*officiis*) of rhetoric: demonstrating (*probare*) demands the plain style, pleasing (*delectare*) takes the middle style, and moving the emotions (*flectere*) takes the grand style (69). But no philosophical principles seem to guide this: The ideal orator will simply know how to adapt to the demands of the case and to the audience's "opinion and approval" (24). "It is difficult," he writes, "to describe the 'form' or 'pattern' of the 'best' (for which the Greek word is *charaktêr*), because different people have different notions of what is best" (36). This surrender is made as well in regard to invention: the ideal orator will "select the loci that fit [*aptis*] the subject" (47). But the nature of the fitting is elusive:

> In an oration, as in life, nothing is harder to determine than what is appropriate. The greeks call it *prepon*; let us call it *decorum*. . . . For the same style and the same thoughts must not be used in portraying every condition in life, or every rank, position or age, and in fact a similar distinction must be made in response to place, time and audience. The universal rule, in oratory as in life, is to consider propriety. (70–71)

As Elaine Fantham has argued, in *Orator*, Cicero subsumes *aptum* (reserved more for coordinating practice to situational demands) under *decorum* ("an absolute standard of aesthetic merit at which the speaker should aim"), thus reviving the Greek aspect of *prepon* that involves the intermediation of extrinsic and intrinsic criteria (Fantham, 124). Cicero offers a few technical points—plain speaking should avoid far-fetched metaphors (82); in the middle style all forms of ornament are appropriate [*conveniunt*] (92)—but such prescriptions have no theoretical base in *Orator*. Cicero is as adamant about the importance of propriety as he is reluctant to elaborate:

> It is difficult to prescribe here how each of these parts is to be handled; as a matter of fact they are not always handled in the same way. But since I am not seeking a pupil to teach, but an orator to approve, I shall begin by approving of one who can observe what is fitting. This, indeed, is the form of wisdom that the orator must especially employ—to adapt himself to occasions and persons. . . . He . . . will be eloquent who can adapt his speech to fit all conceivable circumstances. (123)

The picture in Cicero's most mature work is much the same. Many of the statements in *De Oratore* on the nature of rhetoric would seem to require a theory of propriety, such as Cicero's introductory remark that unlike other arts, whose practitioners seek an excellence far above that of ordinary individuals, in rhetoric "the cardinal sin is to depart from the language of everyday life and the usage approved by the sense of the community" (1.13). In the dialogue, when Crassus introduces four virtues of style, declaring that language should be correct (*latine*), lucid (*plane*), embellished (*ornate*), and appropriate (*apte*) (3.37), he notes that the first two are easy enough, but the second two, which are interrelated, are more difficult (3.52).[33] Whereas Aristotle had linked propriety and clarity, Cicero defines appropriateness (*aptum*) together with the fitting (*congruens*) as the management of *ornatus* according to situation (3.53). But no theory follows; he simply notes of *aptum* and the decent (or suitable: *quid deceat*) only that no single kind of speech can be found to suit (*congruere*) every cause, audience, speaker, and occasion (3.210–211).

Different styles are required by deliberative speeches, panegyrics, lawsuits and lectures, and for consolation, protest, discussion and historical narrative, respectively. The audience is also important—whether it is the lords or the commons or the bench; a large audience or a small one or a single person, and their personal character; and consideration must be given to the age, station, and office of the speakers themselves, and to the occasion, in peace time or during a war, urgent or allowing plenty of time. (3.211–212)

At first glance this may seem as theoretically satisfactory as, say, Aristotle's teaching that certain arguments are more likely to be used in judicial rhetoric, others in deliberative. But then Aristotle had described at length the nature of those speech situations, the nature of the arguments they called for, and the characters and emotions that typify their likely participants. Cicero offers no such kairotic analysis, and he ultimately he gives up trying to take the matter further: "[I]t does not in fact seem possible to lay down any rules" (3.212). In a sophistic manner, propriety is left to the speaker's devices.

In *De Officiis* Cicero treats the subject of moral propriety, beginning with the premise that humans are distinguished from animals not only by their capacity for reason, but, as an entailment of this, by their possession of "a feeling for order, for propriety [*quod deceat*], [and] for moderation in word and deed" (14). This neo-Stoic position counters the sophistic current of Cicero's rhetorical works: from them one must conclude that propriety is a prescription to obey culturally determined convention. Here, at least, Cicero asserts that propriety is not *merely* a cultural construct, for it is an aspect of human nature knowable apart from the variation of cultural form. He first classifies propriety (*decorum*), as part of one of the cardinal virtues—temperance—and once again notes its origins in the Greek concept of *to prepon* (93). Propriety is not identical to temperance but is its outcome. But then Cicero corrects himself and says that propriety can only be understood in terms of all four cardinal virtues—wisdom, justice, fortitude, and temperance (94). If one comprehends the virtues, he says, there is no need for any further theoretical specification. Propriety, then, is "perfectly self-evident and does not require any abstruse process of reasoning to see it," for "there is a certain element of propriety perceptible in every act of moral rectitude; and this can be separated from virtue theoretically better than it can be practically" (95). Perceptibility for Cicero is elemental to the definition of propriety: It is virtue's sensible attribute, moral reality's mode of appearance to the mind. This again resembles the Homeric sense of *to prepon* as appearance of social distinction through speech; its connection to temperance shows similarity to propriety as involving a mean.

What relevance does this ethical propriety have for rhetorical propriety? Cicero would likely identify them. In *De Officiis*, Cicero proceeds to identify two kinds of propriety reflecting the lamination of intrinsic and extrinsic qualities in *Orator*: (1) general propriety, that which is related to moral goodness as a whole, an entelechial property "which harmonizes with man's superiority in those respects in which his nature differs from the rest of animal creations"; and (2) subordinate propriety, which harmonizes with other natural potentials in human nature that are yet socially cultivated, including self-control, temperance, and civilized deportment. This subordinate propriety is inferred through the mediation of speech. Cicero specifically analogizes poetic propriety (97), but whereas poets are concerned with what is suitable (*quid conveniat*) and fitting (*quid deceat*) for all types of character, the moral philosopher is concerned with the propriety "which shines out in our conduct, engages the approbation of our fellow men by the order, consistency and self control it imposes on every word and deed." Virtue is knowable, then, only through an apprehension of propriety, which is the sensible correspondence between character and deed, almost inevitably deeds spoken or accompanied by speech. Propriety can thus prescribe action consistent with nature—our universal nature as human, our social nature, and our individual natures (107, 125). Ethical propriety and rhetorical propriety are ultimately indistinguishable, and the same three basic rules apply to both: (1) Impulse must obey reason; (2) attention to the object to be accomplished shall be in accord with the importance of the object; (3) moderation must be observed (141).[34]

Cicero's adoption of *decorum* in the *De Officiis* has been read as a debt to the influence of later Stoic philosophers who sought to temper the severe adherence of early Stoics to *honestas*—moral worth—as the sole good (Seigal, 19–20). There can be little doubt but that this move by Cicero was also abetted by his practical experience of and inquiries into the art of rhetoric. It is a tempering that Adam Smith would have found warrantable, and one he may have emulated in *TMS* (though he explicitly rules out stoicism as an adequate philosophy of morality). As Gloria Vivenza has shown, the influence of stoicism on Smith is not insignificant, but it is likely that Smith drew on stoicism through this Ciceronian lens, which shows *decorum* as useful precisely because it was first of all a norm of speech that cannot be reduced to an absolute but must always be determined with the kind of imprecision endemic to speech situations. Ethical propriety's entanglement in rhetorical theory for Cicero was an admission that rhetoric is always concerned with the translation of ideas into action, a translation that cannot be formulaically regulated by universal and abstract rules, and yet which is not free from the influence of various conditions, be they cultural or arbitrary or invested with characteristics of extracultural human nature. What the Ciceronian theory of propriety lacked in philosophical rigor, then, it made up for in a sort of humane realism. As we shall see, Adam Smith similarly looked to the necessarily imprecise nature of the rules of composition (as opposed to the fixed rules of grammar) as a paradigm of the rules of moral virtue. He may well have had in mind the Ciceronian precedent of using rhetorical *decorum* as propaedeutic to the discovery of ethical norms.

Propriety would continue to be an important rhetorical concept after the classical period.[35] Quite notably it was a core classical idea that, along with *imitatio*, lent itself to the ends of the Renaissance humanists' program of cultivating virtuous civic character as an amalgam of practical wisdom and eloquence (Fumaroli, 22). As Hanna Gray has shown, *decorum* for the humanists was indivorceable from *imitatio* in humanist thinking, indeed, was its "exact analogue." This fusion was "not due to any particular philosophical conviction; it *was* their philosophy" (Gray, 506). In short, humanism made explicit the position implicit in Cicero. As a consequence, propriety was taken down one of two paths. It would in some cases be preserved as a technical concept, without much in the way of a philosophical grounding, as in Thomas Wilson's concept of "aptenesse" (187) or George Puttenham's "seemelynesse" (262); certainly the identity of decorum with imitation abetted this outcome. On the other hand, for some humanists, propriety was hypostatized as the core of a rhetorical ethics. Victoria Kahn has argued that these humanists pushed to its extreme conclusion the Ciceronian idea that ethical propriety is derived from discursive propriety (31). Thus, the fusion of ethics and rhetoric through *decorum* in much humanist thought was due not to anxieties about rhetorical propriety needing ethical grounding, but in fact it expressed precisely the reverse idea: a kind of rhetorical pragmatism writ large over morality. In this vein, Nancy Struever has shown that for Lorenzo Valla, rhetorical *decorum*, far from being an adaptation of classical ethical orientations, was the very tool to be used in puncturing Peripatetic and Stoic ideas of moderate virtue (191–202). This marks as clearly as any point in the history of rhetoric the arrival of the modern cast of mind as an inversion of the classical mind. Machiavelli would give it perhaps its purest expression in recasting prudence as *virtù*, the prince's prerogative to do what he must to survive. It marks a resuscitation of the sophistic attitude wherein propriety is coterminous not only with invention, but with reason itself.

CHAPTER 3

Rhetorical Propriety in Eighteenth-Century Theories of Discourse

W hile Smith's theory of propriety in rhetoric and ethics was undoubtedly influenced by his encounter with classical propriety, his thinking also clearly drew on and responded to a vigorous attention to propriety and related concepts by scholars and writers in his own time. The strands of interest in rhetorical propriety in seventeenth- and eighteenth-century Britain that influenced Smith flowed from a larger set of concerns dominating intellectual discourse, including a commitment to inductivism in science, complementary developments in epistemology, and, partly in response to developments in these areas, a new interest in criticism and aesthetics. Each of these merits some attention before we turn to Smith.

Propriety in Scientific and Philosophical Discourse

Francis Bacon's reorganization of human knowledge in *The Advancement of Learning* (1605) tasked rhetoric or "illustration" with transmitting the discoveries of science (3:409), signaling an elevation of *res* over *verba*. "The first distemper of learning is when men study words and not matter" (3:284). Consequently, rhetorical propriety for Bacon was largely a matter of coordinating words with the matter of which they are "but the images." If this indicates a new scientific emphasis on visual observation, it also suggests that rhetorical propriety, with its historical connection to sight and appearance, would have a role to play. Indeed, for Bacon, the new subject matter allows some stylistic latitude in the coordination of words and things: the widely accepted view of Bacon's attitude toward style is that he saw it as functional—that is, as determined by appropriateness to subject matter, audience, aim, and (to a lesser extent) speaker.[1]

But Bacon was a propagandist for science, not a practitioner. For the new scientists, style was to be rigidly plain and unadorned. A tempered Ciceronian style was much more in practice, however, so they had to make a case for plainness, and they did so on the basis of propriety. A year after co-founding the Royal Society of London, Robert Boyle, in a perhaps canny anticipation of the effort that would be required to instantiate the new plainness, published *Some Considerations Touching the Style of the Holy Scriptures* (1661), in which he defends the "flat" ineloquence of the Bible on the grounds that it perfectly meets the rhetorical dictum of "congruity of [embellishments] to our design and method, and the suitable accommodation of them to the various circumstances considerable in the matter, the speaker, and the hearers." Startlingly, he even pays homage to Machiavelli's famous defense of his own plain style in *The Prince*, arguing that Machiavelli had chosen a plain style because "*he thought fit either that nothing at all should recommend his Work, or that only the Truth of the discourse should make it acceptable, and exact its welcome*" (emphasis original). Boyle concluded: "If a meer Statesman, writing to a Prince, upon a meer civil Theme, could reasonably talk thus: with how much more Reason may God expect a welcoming Entertainment for the least Adorn'd parts of a Book, of which the Truth is a direct Emanation from the Essential and Supreme Truth, and of which the Contents concern no less than mans Eternal Happiness or Misery" (296).

With little alteration, Boyle's words could apply to the standards of scientific communication advanced by the Royal Society. Boyle employed his theory of propriety in all his works, writes John T. Harwood, in order to "create an audience" for his natural philosophy, wherein (note here the visual analogy) "clarity and eyewitness testimony were crucial to his *ethos*, his credibility" (Harwood, lxi). The stylistic standards of scientific discourse adopted by the Royal Society were famously described by Thomas Sprat in his *History of the Royal Society* (1667) as spurning ornament. "Who can behold," he asks, "without indignation, how many mists and uncertainties, these *Tropes* and *Figures*, have brought on our knowledge?" (112). The remedy was to "reject all the amplifications, digressions, and swellings of style; to turn back to the primitive purity, and shortness, when men deliver'd so many *things*, almost in an equal number of *words*" (113).[2]

This would seem to be a renunciation of rhetoric, and to the extent that he targets Ciceronian excess, Sprat was renouncing much of what was con-

sidered to be "merely" rhetorical.[3] Yet plainness is inescapably a style
nonetheless—the more so in a context where it is novel and understood to
be an entailment of the communicative situation.[4] In Boyle's essay, God's
plain style is explicitly said to speak in a way appropriate to His character,
aim, subject matter, and audience. This appropriateness is really rhetoric
entire for Boyle: "[R]hetorick being but an organical or instrumental art, in
order chiefly to persuasion, or delight, its rules ought to be estimated by their
tendency, and commensurateness to its rules; and consequently, are to be
conformed to by a wise-man, but so far forth as he judgeth them seasonable
and proper to please or persuade" (299). For Sprat and Boyle, subject matter
and "speaker" have become one in the form of Nature, and the character of
the new scientific audience is such that its members would feel "indignation" were speakers not allowed to deliver themselves in a fitting manner.

Once plainness becomes the predominantly appropriate style, propriety is
largely associated with correctness in diction. Propriety had not completely
disappeared—it was now chiefly a matter of fitting style to subject matter.
In the new scientific regimen, matters of ethos and pathos are generalized
or sublimated into the implied discourse community, and propriety no
longer explicitly encompasses appropriateness to individual speakers or audiences. Smith's first statements in the *LRBL* relating propriety, clarity, and
diction, though echoing Aristotle's treatment of these ideas and ultimately allowing more flexibility than Sprat, show a debt to this shift. Smith had studied Aristotelian logic at Glasgow, but also Locke's *Essay Concerning Human
Understanding* (1690), and probably no work did more to both propagate and
problematize the use and defense of plain, clear, and correct language in the
next century (Ross, 42).

As is well known, Locke's empiricist doctrine is that there are no innate
ideas: knowledge comes through sense experience and a subsequent reflective
association of ideas. Words are simply arbitrary markers of ideas as each individual has them, not of the reality of the things ideas signify (3.2.4). Ideally,
words would communicate and record thought, but language's imprecision
frustrates this end, particularly as words are called to stand for complex or abstract ideas that have no coordinate physical object in reality (3.9.4–5). Lockean communication aspires to telepathy: it succeeds only when words "excite,
in the Hearer, exactly the same Idea, they stand for in the Mind of the
Speaker." This is especially a problem for words compounded of multiple
ideas ("mixed modes"), such as moral terms, which involve aspects such as intention "not visible in the action itself" (3.9.6–7). Smith, as we shall see, was
directly concerned with the problem of clearly communicating "internal

invisible objects" such as sentiments, moral judgments, and intentions, and he looked to propriety as a way of overcoming this invisibility.

What Locke calls the "Rule of Propriety" (3.9.8)—by which he means adherence to common usage—is of some assistance, but only in common conversation, where matters are of no great import. But propriety is inadequate in philosophical discourse, or in any sort of communication about matters concerning "[t]ruths we are required to believe, or Laws we are to obey" (3.9.10). The only remedy is a Cartesian bid to minimize the "Abuse of Words." It should not be surprising, given Locke's nominalist account of language, that he sees the chief abuses as (1) using words without "clear and distinct ideas"; (2) using words inconsistently; (3) affecting obscurity; (4) confusing words for things; (5) using words to denote abstract things which cannot be denoted; and (6) assuming a necessary connection between words and the things they signify. It is rhetoric, of course—"that powerful instrument of Error and Deceit"—that has perpetuated such abuse: "But yet, if we would speak of Things as they are, we must allow, that all the Art of Rhetorick, besides Order and Clearness, all the artificial and figurative application of Words Eloquence hath invented, are for nothing else but to insinuate wrong *Ideas*, move the Passions, and thereby mislead the Judgment; and so indeed are perfect cheat . . ." (3.10.34). If this passage is notable as a denunciation of rhetoric, it is no less significant as evidence that Locke does not regard "Order and Clearness" as outside the realm of rhetorical art. They are called upon precisely because they answer the rule of propriety that style should suit subject matter, aim, and audience.

When Locke addresses antidotes to the abuse of words, among them is once again "Propriety of Speech," though what he now describes is less like familiar usage than an exacting diction generated though careful analysis of precedent: "The proper signification and use of terms is best to be learned from those, who in their Writings and Discourses, appear to have had the clearest notions, and apply'd to them their terms with the exactest choice and fitness" (3.11.11). Propriety here seems to demand a rigorous coordination of words and things, as if it were a computer language; the users of words, their audiences, and the exigencies surrounding their situations seem to be left out of the equation. This is almost the case, but not quite: propriety cannot be attained without the prior example of fitting adaptations of words to things by the "best" writers. This reverberation of Humanism's dialectical relationship between *imitatio* and *decorum* suggests a residual trace of ethical appropriateness lingering in Locke's notion of propriety. And indeed, there is an explicitly ethical quality to appropriate diction for Locke—he regards those who abuse words as "an Enemy to Truth and Knowledge" who corrupt their audiences into being "more *conceited* in their Ignorance, and *obstinate* in their Errors" (3.11.5).

Propriety, Taste, and Aesthetics

Partly growing out of these concerns over communication in science and philosophy, and to a lesser extent in reaction against them, was eighteenth-century Britain's expansive discussion of aesthetic judgment—most often under the rubric of "taste"—which intrinsically encompassed matters of rhetorical propriety. Interest in epistemology not only involved inquiry into how humans gain knowledge about the physical objects of science, but also led to speculations as to how humans ascertain knowledge about phenomena not immediately present to the external senses, such as beauty, morality, and religious feeling.[5] The skeptical tendencies endemic to empiricist epistemology, by seemingly threatening the grounds for such phenomena, gave impetus to both inquiry into their foundations and in some cases opposition to empiricist assumptions themselves. Ironically, often the response to this threat was to appropriate to nonscientific discourse the scientific idiom of using "natural" words to suit the things of nature.

The near obsession with questions of taste in this period has a complex etiology. Marxist interpretations relate it to post–civil war class conflict and the rise of consumer capitalism (itself spurred by scientific development); hence, taste became an issue when aesthetic experience and cultural discourse were reified as tokens of class membership (Dykstal, 46–48). Terry Eagleton, for example, names propriety and taste among the neoclassical aesthetic values that were pressed into service in the "reconsolidation" of a destabilized social order (17). This process is not always derided by Marxist critics—Eagleton confesses admiration for the English creation of cultural consensus through taste. Where there is broad cultural consensus on matters of taste, there will be little motivation to theorize it. When Shaftesbury and Smith contended that models for appropriate expression were to be found in men of "the better sort," they were implicitly (though not solely) referring to class difference.

Although theorizing taste was a way of consolidating or appropriating class knowledge and the power it commanded, this reductivist explanation is inadequate by itself, for the British theorists of taste were almost univocal in favoring simplicity, naturalness, and plainness in writing style—hardly the way to go about rarifying, secreting, or otherwise privileging access to a realm of discourse. Inquiry into taste must also be understood as a genuine attempt to understand some deep human innervations and their relation to the life of the individual in society. In part for these reasons, Timothy Dykstal has argued that taste as formulated by Joseph Addison in the *Spectator* "can serve as an organizing principle of the public sphere," a point to which I will return presently (48).

Locke did not venture the fuller analysis of propriety and its relation to moral knowledge that his philosophy begs for. His student Anthony Ashley Cooper, who became Third Earl of Shaftesbury, had more to say on these subjects, in part out of an objection to Locke's epistemology. Shaftesbury doubted that epistemological and metaphysical questions could be answered by force of reason alone, though reason had some role to play. Accordingly, he offered not a counterepistemology so much as he pursued epistemology by other means—mainly through an aesthetics that assigned a central place to discursive propriety. Through an eclectic mix of neo-Platonic, neo-Stoic, and yet some empiricist elements, he forged a humanistic but idiosyncratic alloy of rhetoric and ethics (see Klein, 29). Rhetoric's stock had fallen greatly by this time, particularly in England, yet Shaftesbury's innovations sublated elements of the rhetoric of the *polis* in the form of politeness, the discursive mode of the gentleman. His approach was of profound influence for later writers on criticism and ethics, particularly Smith, who was similarly suspicious of Lockean epistemology and refrained from setting explicit epistemological underpinnings for his moral philosophy.

In place of Locke's empirical-associationist model of thought, Shaftesbury assumed that there is a common sense—not as an innate idea, but as an innate capacity which, if properly nurtured and cultivated, is capable of knowing truth. Aesthetic experience, because it requires holistic understanding and collapses subject and object, is a kind of ideal propaedeutic model for the type of judgment exercised by this common sense (Grean, 40). At the center of Shaftesbury's thought was a defense of "true" religious enthusiasm, based in part on the premise that emotions and beliefs are closely related (Grean, 31). Though Smith was not interested in finding grounds for religious belief, Shaftesbury's approach to emotion and belief nonetheless stands as a precursor for Smith, who similarly would hold that the representation of emotion could convey knowledge about the objects of discourse. Shaftesbury treated emotion and belief in terms recalling classical propriety: if there are affections appropriate to beliefs, it followed that there are modes of communication appropriate to transmitting those beliefs to various audiences. Key to managing this propriety is a Stoic honesty in self-knowledge, which one develops through the self-conscious interaction of "natural affection" and social situatedness. Honesty is the key link in a kind of heuristic chain: It abets a form of sociability that is both congenial to others, yet true to self, clearing room for a self-interest that is yet not selfish (1:121); this social self-possession is in turn rhetorically significant, for it becomes beautiful, and beauty is elemental to the power of persuasion, the "mother" of all the arts, including rhetoric (1:237); study of the arts leads the gentleman to "discover" honesty in himself (1:135–36). The idea is aristocratic in a literal sense—perhaps unpalatably so for contemporary political taste—but it was also remarkably unconventional for its time. As Lawrence E. Klein has shown, Shaftesbury's entire project aimed at designing a culture of liberty that would disrupt traditional associations of genteel hegemony with monarchy and ecclesiastical authority (20–21; 154ff). There is at least a modest egalitarianism in his description of gentlemen, who achieve their status some by "genius," others by education. Some are "extravagant" or "irregular in the morals"; yet the cultivation of taste makes them "discover their Inconsistency" (1:135). "Men of cooler Passions and more deliberate Pursuits," on the other hand, are similarly persuaded by "the Force of *Beauty*," the "*Venustatum*, the *Honestum*, the *Decorum* of Things" (1:138–39).

Shaftesbury treats this "decorum of things" extensively in an essay titled "Soliloquy: or, Advice to an Author." Soliloquy, which he calls a "Powerful Figure of inward Rhetoric" (1:188), is the practice of self-criticism through inner dialogue with oneself, but it is not performed in a social vacuum; self-knowledge comes about in part through the discovery of requisite fitness in verbal representation.[6] The practice clearly adumbrates propriety in Smith, which similarly engages in an "inward rhetoric," self-regulating sentiments before an internal "impartial spectator." For both, the visual dimension of the process is strong: as Smith will do, Shaftesbury compares it to representation in painting (1:202). Cultivation of taste in the arts is important for both as well; for Shaftesbury, critics such as etymologists, philologists, grammarians, and rhetoricians do a great public service in this regard, empowering even common people with a discursive aptitude that is both morally and socially beneficial. So long as they do not "content themselves with the contemplation merely" of the arts, they can "[teach] the publick what [is] just and excellent in performances," thus disclosing "the hidden Beautys which lay in the Works of just Performers; and by exposing the weak Sides, false Ornaments, and affected Graces of mere *Pretenders*. Nothing of what we call *Sophistery* in Argument, or *Bombast* in Style; nothing of the *effeminate* kind, of the False *Tender*, the pointed *Witticism*, the disjointed *Thought*, the crouded *Simile*, or the mix'd *Metaphor*, cou'd pass even on the common Ear: Whilest the NOTARYS, the EXPOSITORS, and PROMPTERS . . . were everywhere at hand, ready to explode the *unnatural* Manner"(1:240–41). [7] This cultivation of taste not only abets public critical and rhetorical capacity, but prompts a meliorative reflectiveness in the individual: "If *Civility* and *Humanity* be a taste; if *Brutality, Insolence, Riot*, be in the Same Manner a TASTE; who if he could reflect, wou'd not chuse to form himself on the amiable and agreeable, rather than the odious and perverse Model? . . . If a natural *good* TASTE be not already form'd in us; why should not we endeavor to form it, and become *natural?*" (1:338). Thus, "inward rhetoric" is modeled on public discourse; in turn it structures moral character, which itself becomes both inwardly and outwardly persuasive. As Stanley Grean explains, the good, true, and beautiful are a teleological whole for Shaftesbury; accordingly, "An action is right if it is appropriate to the context in which it occurs" (1:250). This would hold for speech as much as any form of action. Ironically, however, just as it was for Sprat, Boyle, and Locke, "nature" is the master context, and the only one that really matters.

Where style is concerned, the consequence is clear: Shaftesbury champions a "natural" style and disdains high and sublime styles (an irony given his own stylistic extravagance, which Smith criticizes in *LRBL*). Not only does grand style corrupt criticism with "contemplation merely," but affected manner is the "easiest attained" and entertains children (1:242). The mature mode of expression is simple and plain, because it is closer to what is natural, even if it necessarily practices a form of *sprezzatura*: "*The Simple* manner, which being the strictest Imitation of Nature, shou'd of right be the completest, in the Distribution of its Parts, and Symmetry of its whole, is yet so far from making any ostentation of Method, that it conceals the Artifice as much as possible: endeavoring only to express the effect of Art" (1:257). This plain style is directly connected to self-honesty and propriety: "[T]here is no expression more generally us'd in a way of Compliment to great Men and Princes, than that plain one, which is so often verify'd, and may be safely pronounced for Truth, on most occasions 'That they have acted *like themselves*, and suitably to their own Genius and Character' " (1: 280).

In a later essay ("Miscellaneous Reflections"), he remarks that honesty is a passion "moving strongly upon the *Species* or *View* of the DECORUM, the SUBLIME of Actions." The honest man is one who, "instead of outward Forms or Symmetries, is struck with that of *inward* Character, the Harmony and Numbers of the Heart, and Beauty of the Affections, which form the

Manners and conduct of a truly *social* life." He identifies this beauty with classical "*Honestum, Pulchrum, to kalon, to prepon*" (3:34).

It may seem that Shaftesbury, like Sprat, Boyle, and Locke, takes the latitude out of propriety by not admitting a range of possible styles for the manifold permutations comprising communication events. This is partly because none of these writers is addressing a theory of rhetorical propriety in general; instead, they set parameters for propriety to their proximate aims. Boyle, Sprat, and Locke demand a plain style because they seek to reform the scientific and philosophical idioms. Shaftesbury demands a plain style because it will promote a socially beneficial and egalitarian self-knowledge. Shaftesbury in fact does allow some stylistic latitude within what is "natural": "Now whether the Writer be *Poet, Philosopher*, or of whatever kind; he is in truth no other than a *Copist* after NATURE. His *Style* may be differently suited to the different Times he lives in, or to the different Humour of his Age or Nation: His Manner, His Dress, his *Colouring* may vary. But if his drawing be uncorrect, or his *Design* contrary to Nature; his Piece will be found ridiculous, when it comes thoroughly to be examin'd. For Nature will not be mock'd" (1:354). For Smith as well, impropriety occasions ridicule, which thus functions to temper stylistic and moral incorrectness.

Alasdair MacIntyre has referred to Shaftesbury's thought as "philosophical antitheory," an apt description of his often circular argumentation, impressionistic prose style, and self-conscious eschewal of system (1988, 223). It was left to his follower Francis Hutcheson, Professor of Moral Philosophy at the University of Glasgow from 1729–1746 and Adam Smith's teacher there, to try to give Shaftesbury's ideas a more systematic treatment. Hutcheson was more explicitly empiricist than Shaftesbury and freely used Lockean terminology, but like Shaftesbury he opposed and sought to rectify the moral skepticism inherent in Locke's epistemology. Hutcheson specifically objected to what today we would call Locke's behavioristic account of abstract and complex experiences such as those of beauty and morality. His *Inquiry into the Original of our Ideas of Beauty and Virtue* (1725) was written in explicit opposition to Locke's position "'That all our Relish for Beauty and Order, is either from the Prospect of Advantage, Custom, or Education, for no other Reason but the Variety of Fancys in the World'" (52), as well as his contention that things are good or evil "only in reference to pleasure or pain" (2.20.2). As in Aristotle, pleasure and pain for Hutcheson are "joined" to these perceptions (16), but are neither constitutive nor determinative of them: "[T]he Ideas of Beauty and Harmony, like other sensible Ideas, are necessarily pleasant to us, as well as immediately so; neither can any

Revolution of our own nor any Prospect of Advantage or Disadvantage, vary the Beauty or Deformity of an Object: For as in the external Sensations, no View of Interest will make an Object Grateful, nor View of Detriment, distinct from an immediate Pain in the Perception, make it disagreeable to the sense" (8). Smith will similarly insist on the immediateness of aesthetic and moral perception against utilitarian explanations, but Hutcheson put this view to use in a way Smith will reject. From this observation of the immediate sensation of the pleasure of beauty, Hutcheson concluded that there are "senses fitted for perceiving it." Reason, custom, education, law, and advantage can give us more opportunities to experience beauty or work to "superadd" to our experience, but this presupposes that the experience itself is "antecedently" rooted in some internal sense (8–9; 57–59). "Taste" or "Genius" refers to a cultivated capacity for receiving such ideas of both the external (6) and internal (13) senses.

The moral sense is just such an internal sense, one fully analogous to the sense of beauty—Hutcheson even refers to the moral sense, after Shaftesbury, as "this Moral Sense of Beauty in Actions and Affections" (15).[8] Hutcheson explains the teleology of these senses in a way that demonstrates he had not only Locke in his sights, but Hobbes and Mandeville, whose egoism he reverses, "as the Author of Nature had determin'd us to receive, by our external Senses, pleasant or disagreeable Ideas of Objects, according as they are useful or hurtful to our Bodys; and to receive from uniform Objects the Pleasures of Beauty and Harmony, to excite us to the pursuit of Knowledge, and to reward us for it; or to be an Argument to us of his Goodness, as the Uniformity itself proves his Existence, whether we had a Sense of Beauty in Uniformity or not; in the same manner he has given us a Moral Sense, to direct our Actions, and to give us still nobler Pleasures: so that while we are only intending the Good of Others, we undesignedly promote our own greatest private Good" (84).

Smith, though rejecting the idea of a moral sense, will also be interested in the unintended consequences of human action, and will open his treatment of propriety in *TMS* by rejecting Hobbesian self-interest as the prime human motive. For Hutcheson, the moral sense is disinterested and benevolent. As it directs human action, so it is implicated in any activity having to do with directing human action, including rhetoric: "Upon this moral Sense is founded all the Power of the Orator. The various Figures of Speech are the several Manners, which a lively Genius, warm'd with Passions suitable to the occasion, naturally runs into, only a little diversify'd by Custom: and they only move the Hearers, by giving a lively Representation of the Passions of the

Speaker." All modifications of style, adds Hutcheson, "are but more lively Methods of giving the Audience a stronger Impression of the Moral Qualities of the Person accus'd or defended; of the Action advis'd or dissuaded . . ." (165). This passage reveals not just an analogy between aesthetic and moral sense, but a synecdochic relationship. Indeed, Hutcheson had earlier explained that the sense of beauty operates according to synecdoche: "Those objects of Contemplation in which there is Uniformity amidst Variety, are more distinctly and easily comprehended and retain'd, than irregular Objects; because the accurate Observation of one or two Parts often leads to the Knowledge of the Whole" (65). In the same way, the adaptation of style to "Moral Qualities" is perceived by the moral sense as a "Species of Morality" from which one can reconstitute knowledge of the whole moral character of the subject matter.[9] Hutcheson goes so far as to offer the fact that those untrained in rhetoric are most affected by it as proof that there is a moral sense: the "rude undisciplin'd Multitudes" would not be so moved by the appearance of moral qualities in oratory were there not "some Sense of Morality antecedent to Instruction" (167). Although there can be little doubt that Hutcheson's perspective was a formative influence on Smith, caution should govern our acceptance of assertions that Smith's notion of propriety was "derived from" Hutcheson (Teichgraber, 29–30). Smith admitted that benevolence bestows and "communicates" beauty in actions (*TMS*, 7.2.3.5), but he rejected the possibility of an autonomous, internal "moral sense" (*TMS*, 3.4.5) and he found fundamental human benevolence insufficient to explain many qualities humans approve of (*TMS*, 7.2.3.15). The important connection here is that like Hutcheson, Smith ascribed a strong probative value to the aesthetic dimension of speech as a form of moral representation.

At approximately the same time that Boyle, Locke, Shaftesbury, and Hutcheson were writing, a number of French authors—René Rapin, Dominique Bouhours, Charles Rollin, Bernard Lamy, François de Salignac de la Mothe Fénelon, Jean-Baptiste Dubos—were making contributions to rhetorical and aesthetic theory that would profoundly influence eighteenth-century British theories of discourse. English translations of Rapin's *Réflexions sur l'éloquence* (1670) and Bouhour's *L'manière de bien Penser dans les Ouvrages d'Esprit* (1687) helped solidify for British literary circles the belletristic conception of rhetoric and its fourfold division of discourse into poetry, oratory, didactic writing, and history, a division implicitly demanding strictures of generic appropriateness (Howell 1971, 524). Rollin's *De la Maniere d'enseigner et d'étudier les belles lettres* (1726–1728) had much the same influence, and had explicitly connected taste (*goût*) with Quintilian's requirement that the good orator have "that prudence, that discernment which apprehends for each subject and for each occasion that which one must do and how one must do it" (quoted in Conley, 202).

Though citing no textual evidence, Barbara Warnick finds a "very likely" French influence on Smith's rhetoric in Fénelon's *Dialogues sur l'éloquence* (1718), which makes *bienséance*, a natural and proportionate correspondence between subject and style, its central discursive criterion (57–62). Fénelon and Smith do have much in common: both had a distinctly modern, belletristic conception of rhetoric that encompassed appropriateness in literature, history, oratory, and didactic writing; both adhered to the need for speakers to shape discourse in response to the capacities of audiences; both advocated naturalness in style, and both dispensed with most of the topical apparatus of classical rhetoric. Warnick does note the difference, however, that Fénelon's concerns were driven more by neoclassical reverence for uniformity and order, while Smith's conception of propriety was aimed at explaining the way verbal representation functions in the operation of sympathy.

A key aspect of Smith's conception of this representational function of propriety is his treatment of description as "painting," a commonplace at least as old as Horace's *ut pictura poesis*, but which experienced an expansive new currency in eighteenth-century French aesthetic and rhetorical theory. Lamy's Port-Royalist *L'art de Parler* (1675, quoted here from an anonymous 1676 translation) had set up the analogy this way:

> A Painter will not lay on his Colors 'till he has formed in his imagination what he designs to draw. Discourse is the Picture of our thoughts; the Tongue is the Pencil which draws that Picture, and Words are the Colors. We ought therefore in the first place to range our Thoughts, and put such things as we intend to represent into natural order; disposing them so, that the knowledge of some few of them, may render the rest more easie and intelligible to the reader. (Hobbes and Lamy, 182)

Fénelon extended this advice to implicate the passions in making verbal descriptions intelligible. Dispassionate, enumerative description (what Smith will call "direct description") is generally inappropriate; to be effective, narrative representation calls for the mediation of imagery through the emotions of the participants in the scene: "It is necessary not only to acquaint the listeners with the facts, but to make the facts visible to them, and to strike their consciousness by means of a perfect representation of the arresting manner in which the facts have come to pass." It is not enough to say Dido grieved at Aeneas's departure; to give a true sense of the scene, the writer must "assemble all the surrounding features of her despair." The scene is then "put before your eyes" because "[y]ou enter into all the feelings which the actual spectators had as they looked" (93–94). This clearly foreshadows Smith's theory of "indirect description" in *LRBL*, the method by which "invisible internall objects" such as sentiments are conveyed by refracting them through a description of their effect on spectators. As we shall see in *TMS*, sentiments become moral when they are modified and communicated in anticipation of the way they will affect an "impartial spectator."

While French rhetorical theorists were turning to painting as an analogue of verbal representation, French aesthetic theorists were turning to classical rhetorical theory to explain the effects of art. Prominent among these was Abbé Jean-Baptiste Dubos, whose *Réflexions critiques sur la poésie et sur la peinture* (1719) is the only one of the French works mentioned above listed in the catalogue of Smith's library; Dubos is explicitly mentioned by Smith twice in *LRBL*. Dubos's main concern was with explaining how humans are moved to feel pleasure from painting and poetry, and he analogized this with persuasion, drawing frequently on Quintilian. His analysis put him in territory similar to that taken up by Smith in *TMS*, for to explain how humans are moved by art was "vouloir rendre compte à chacun de son approbation et de ses dégoûts; c'est instruire les autres de la maniere dont leurs propres sentimens naissant en eux" (8). Our natural ability to be moved by the objects of art and by persuasive speech, writes Dubos, is part of the propensity to sympathize with others' feelings generally, a power implanted in us by nature so as to keep us from degenerating into self-absorption.[10] The operation of sympathy, he wrote, "precedes all deliberation," requiring no intervention by reason.[11] A similar conception of sympathy is at the heart of Smith's theory of propriety in both *LRBL* and *TMS*.

This French discourse on description, taste, and sympathy was echoed resoundingly in British intellectual circles in the latter half of the eighteenth century. The number and breadth of texts in this discussion is too great to survey here; hence I will limit attention to just a few: Henry Home, Lord Kames (*Elements of Criticism*, 1762), who sponsored Smith's first lectures in Edinburgh; David Hume ("Of the Delicacy of Taste and Passion," "Of Simplicity and Refinement in Writing," "Of Refinement in the Arts," 1742, and "Of the Standard of Taste," 1757), Smith's close friend and correspondent; and Joseph Addison (main author of *The Spectator*, 1711–12), who was, along with Shaftesbury, demonstrably in Smith's thoughts as he wrote his rhetoric lectures. I will take them in reverse chronological order, coinciding with what I take to be their increasing order of importance for Smith.

Kames's *Elements of Criticism*, published a year before the date of the student notes of Smith's rhetoric lectures, probably had little influence on Smith; in fact, the influence may have been by Smith (whose *TMS* was first published in 1759) on Kames. Kames's book is often tedious—"It is easier to write that book, than to read it," Goldsmith is reputed to have remarked (Boswell, 415); and it is derivative—his chapter on taste, for example, draws heavily on Hume. Nonetheless, it is noteworthy as the only text under discussion to make frequent mention of "propriety" as a concept, although philosophically Kames's treatment is rather confused and impressionistic. Kames's treatise aims to increase cultivation of critical aptitude, or "taste," which in turn "furnishes elegant subjects for conversation, and prepares us for acting in the social state with dignity and propriety." Appropriately developed taste "envigorates the social affections"—particularly sympathy—and "moderates those that are selfish" (15). Propriety is a species of the more generic concept of "congruity" (165–66; the term is probably suggested by Cicero, *De Oratore* 3.53), which is a pleasant response to an object's suitability to or correspondence with the circumstances that attend it. Whereas congruity responds to all such correspondences, propriety has a strongly moral overtone—it is solely a response to voluntary acts, such as, Kames notes, the acts of an author.[12] By "author" Kames combines the meanings "writer" and "moral agent," and hence there is an obvious parallel with Smith's dual subsumption of propriety in rhetoric and ethics. Like Smith, Kames assigns a role to spectatorship in the development of moral conscience: "[A] generous action suited to the character of an author, which raises in him and in every spectator the pleasant emotion of propriety . . . generates in the author both self-esteem and joy; the former when he considers his relation to the action, and the latter when he considers the good opinion that others will entertain of him: the same emotion of propriety produces in the spectators esteem for the author of the action . . . (1:168). Thus, for Kames, as for Smith, speech action and moral action are elided, and propriety is central to both. But Kames's handling of propriety is loose: Sometimes it is a sense (1:165, 170), sometimes an emotion (1:168), yet at others a natural law (1:171).

Hume's treatment of propriety is more consistent, but also more wily. His essay "Of the Delicacy of Taste and Passion" marks his early interest in the relationship between a "cultivated taste in the polite arts" and the development of moral conscience. His thesis is simply that the cultivation of aesthetic sensibilities "improves our sensibility for all the tender and agreeable passions; at the same time it renders the mind incapable of the rougher and more boisterous emotions" (27). In similar terms, Smith will imply that the rhetorical reception of all kinds of representation is key to developing the sort of conscience that allows humans to sympathize appropriately—that is, morally—with others. In "Of Simplicity and Refinement in Writing," Hume recapitulates one of the key classical elements of propriety by arguing that "a proper medium" between the two extremes of tenderness and roughness should be sought. He observes that there is no way to determine precisely where this medium lies, but that it is preferable to err on the side of simplicity rather than refinement, which is bound to be both "less beautiful and more dangerous" (46). In "Of Refinement in the Arts," Hume takes his analysis further, arguing that cultivation of private taste in the arts leads to "industry, knowledge, and humanity," which together "diffuse their beneficial influence on the *public*" (51, original emphasis).

Perhaps with this public relevance in mind, Hume returned to the subject of taste some fifteen years later in his best-known work on the subject. In "Of the Standard of Taste," he notes the agreement people share about general terms for virtue and beauty even while they vary greatly in the particular things they consider virtuous and beautiful (4). This variety occurs because virtue and beauty are not qualities in objects, but are in the mind of the beholder. And yet, adds Hume, there *are* certain qualities in objects "which are fitted by nature to produce those particular feelings" (11). Hence, the standard of taste can be verified empirically: it is to be ascertained by "appeal to those models and principles which have been established by the uniform consent and experience of nations and ages" (12–13). Nowhere does Hume say what the standard is, because taste, as he presents it, is an activity, a practice. A critic of good sense, whose sensory organs are not impaired, who has had practice in judging, and who is free from undue prejudice, is able to praise and blame the objects of beauty and virtue suitably. Taste, then, is the competent critic judging.

Tellingly, Hume supports his argument with an analogy to the situated nature of rhetorical practice. Every work of art, he writes, successfully produces its effect only by conforming to "a certain point of view" in the same way that "an orator addresses himself to a particular audience and must have a regard to their particular genius, interests, opinions, passions and prejudices. . . ." If the orator differs in some way from the audience, "he must endeavor to conciliate their affection" by "[placing] himself in the same situation as the audience" (15). This critic enacting taste is similar to Smith's concept of an "impartial spectator" determining the grounds of rhetorical and ethical propriety: in both cases one determines propriety by imagining the situation from the point of view of a spectator.

No source exerted stronger influence over discussions of taste and prose style in eighteenth-century Britain than the essays by Joseph Addison, Richard Steele, and others published in *The Spectator*. Published daily in London between 1711 and 1714 to a large audience of readers (and listeners), the *Spectator* is well known as an important source or point of transmission for key ideas in British belletristic theory—taste, grandeur, novelty, beauty, wit, genius, the sublime, "criticism," and so on. Hutcheson, Smith, and Blair draw admiringly on Addison's "pleasures of the imagination" essays (numbers 411–22), and Smith and Blair both use Addison as prose model, in part because his style was suited so well to his character and circumstances.

To the extent that historians of belletristic rhetoric deal with the *Spectator*, it is exclusively to identify and analyze this important relation. But of course the *Spectator*, which touches on a vast array of topics, is far more diverse than Addison's contributions on the "pleasures of the imagination." Probably no subject is more pervasive in the essays than that of discursive propriety: Appropriateness of expression in political, forensic and pulpit oratory, prose, poetry, drama, conversation, song, and gesture features prominently in at least sixty of the essays; dozens of essays make analogy between visual and verbal communication. By accretion of these themes, the *Spectator* asserts a synaesthetic economy of visual and verbal worlds wherein propriety is the currency. Thus, the *Spectator* should be seen as an important, albeit nontraditional rhetorical handbook of the day. As such it supplied a ready and useful model for some aspects of Smith's manifold project in belles lettres and ethics. If we need proof that Smith read the *Spectator* beyond "the pleasures of the imagination" essays (and we probably don't, for the essays were nearly as canonical as the Bible by mid-eighteenth century) there is the oft-made suggestion that Smith drew the phrase "impartial spectator" from Addison's dedication to the first published edition of the collected essays: "I should not act the part of an impartial spectator, if I directed the following papers to one who is not of the most consummate and most acknowledged merit." The phrase is reprised by Mr. Elsewhere in number 564 (by Eustace Budgell): "I endeavor . . . to look upon men and their actions only as an impartial spectator."

A key part of the education in rhetorical propriety offered by the *Spectator* comes in its publishing of letters from a wide range of correspondents, often with praise for the grace and suitability of their expression. Mr. Spectator's reply is rarely direct; instead, his "reply" is usually just to publish the letters. These in turn supply him with topics for conversation, which, he reminds his readers, functions heuristically, "to furnish us with hints we did not attend to" when thinking on the subject alone (352). In one remarkable essay, Mr. Spectator (Steele) admits that he had rewritten some of the letters, "dressing them in my own stile, by leaving out what would not appear like mine, and by adding whatever might be proper to adapt them to the character and genius of my paper." Clearly, some writers wanted this. As one wrote, "If the following essay be not to [*sic*] incorrigible, bestow on it a few brightenings from your genius, that I may learn how to write better, or to write no more." Hardly could one express more decisively the question of presence and absence at stake in propriety of style. But then Mr. Spectator admits being "touched with pity," on realizing that his revisions deprived writers "who impatiently longed to see [their letters] in print, and who, no doubt, triumphed in themselves in the hopes of having a share with me in the applause of the public." He promises to revise no more, but to have them "appear rightly" in their own "native dress and colors," thus purchasing for them a place of appearance in the new social world, the "Republic of Letters" as Addison punned. For an exemplar, they had to look no further than Mr. Spectator himself, whose ease of movement between roles of silent, impartial observer and public rhetor was authorized by the propriety of his writing. Thus, rhetorical propriety is the architectonic art of a new form of social discourse. The function of aptly constructed metaphor and allegory as described in number 421, which is to "transcribe Ideas out of the Intellectual World into the Material," is more generally that of propriety itself.

Critics such as Habermas, Brewer, Dykstal, and others have often read this "transcription" as a focused rhetorical effort forging a new, distinctly modern political structure, a "public sphere," or what Hannah Arendt calls more simply and usefully "the social" as distinct from private or public. Driven by the changes wrought by early industrialism, this new society, already a kind of proto-mass society, was supplied by the *Spectator*, an early mass medium, with a revised hierarchy of class and gender roles, a modified, bourgeois catalogue of virtues and vices, and a subtle politics of moderate Whiggism. Moreover, the *Spectator* modeled a form of communication, namely "conversation,"—the term is virtually cognate with "society" in the *Spectator*— which, ideally and appropriately conducted, would both lead to the discovery and abet the dissemination of a serviceable moral code. Scholars who have thus interpreted the *Spectator* have focused predominantly on the explicitly practical dimensions of this project—consisting mostly in direct exhortation or epideictic treatment of various "decencies" or "enormities" of various characters and actions, both real and allegorical. But the *Spectator* was practical and theoretical, and the theory of propriety it models and explicitly offers is remarkably egalitarian.

Some essays take up the subject of propriety directly. *Spectator* number 407 is of particular interest because in it Addison praises the style typical of British oratory as appropriate to the national character, but then criticizes those who fail to match that style with an appropriate mode of delivery. Proper gestures by a speaker, he writes, "are a kind of comment on what he utters, and enforce everything he says," and "they show the speaker is in earnest, and affected himself with what he so passionately recommends to others." Hence gesture must be visibly "becoming," "suitable," and "agreeable." Quite possibly with this sort of visual suitability in mind, Addison's next entry is on taste, which he defines as "that faculty of the soul, which discerns the beauties of an author with pleasure, and the imperfections with dislike." Addison urges his readers to look for "specific qualities" of classical authors, such as Sallust's "entering into those internal principles of action which arise from the characters and manners of the persons he describes." Smith will describe moral propriety as sentiment modified and presented so that it can be "entered into" by a spectator. He will be particularly interested in the way propriety represents the causes of sentiments, which Addison calls here "internal principles of action." Addison's advice for cultivating taste is to be well read in the classics and the critics, and to engage in "conversation with men of polite genius." Similarly, Smith will recommend "society and conversation" as means of restoring one's mind to the kind of tranquility requisite for appropriate sentiments (*TMS*, 1.1.4.9).

Addison acknowledges that taste is a metaphor taken from the sense of flavor, but he is never far from a visual metaphor in his explanations: "[T]here is as much difference in apprehending a thought clothed in Cicero's language, and that of seeing an object by the light of a taper, or by the light of the sun"; in 416, he compares deficiency in taste to poor eyesight. Addison closes 409 promising a fuller explanation of the foundations of taste, a promise he fulfills in a series of essays (numbers 411–21) collectively titled "The Pleasures of the Imagination." The first of these begins with a lengthy discussion of the sense of sight, from which all of the pleasures of imagination derive. After discussing the ways that the imagination takes pleasure in grand, new, and beautiful sights in nature, Addison moves on to a discussion of "secondary pleasures" (number 416) which include all forms of representation, though he principally discusses the fine arts. Among these he discusses description, which will be a central area of concern in Smith's treatment of rhetorical propriety. A professed admirer of Locke's *Essay*, Addison nonetheless at times gives a remarkably un-Lockean account of propriety in verbal description: "Words, when well chosen, have so great a force in them, that a description often gives us more lively ideas than the sight of things themselves. The reader finds a scene drawn in stronger colors, and painted more to the life in his imagination by the help of words, than by any actual survey of the scenes which they describe." Although Addison is primarily discussing poetic description here, he says that the "talent of affecting the imagination . . . sets off all writing in general." Talent is a key term, as Addison asserts that the ability to use words this way is partially inborn and partially the result of extensive experience: "For, to have a true relish and form a right judgment of a description, a man should be born with a good imagination, and must have well weighed the force and energy that lie in the several words of a language, so as to be able to distinguish which are most significant and expressive of their proper ideas, and what additional strength and beauty they are capable of receiving from conjunction with others. The fancy must be warm, to retain the print of those images it hath received from outward objects, and the judgment discerning, to know what expressions are most proper to adorn them to the best advantage" (number 416).

It is perhaps easy to be distracted by the casual vacillation here between words as "expressive of their proper ideas" (as Locke, admitting the difficulty of this, would nonetheless ideally have it) and words as giving us "more lively ideas" than the things themselves (as Locke would have thought an abuse) from a more important argument underlying Addison's treatment of aesthetic taste, an argument implicit in Hutcheson's, Kames's, and Hume's treatments as well. For Addison, word choice and word arrangement are key "qualities" which indicate a certain type of character and as such answered implicit demands of rhetorical propriety. As Timothy Dykstal has put it, most of the essays in *The Spectator* "portray Mr. Spectator inhabiting a world where every utterance tells something about the inner person, every action makes 'visible . . . the inward Disposition of the Mind.'" (51, quoting number 86). It is easy enough to dismiss this as a consolidation of reified bourgeois values, but it can equally be seen, with Dykstal, as an attempt to recognize the function of taste in creating, cultivating, and circulating both shared standards of public discourse and grounds of ethical and political relevance. Taste from this perspective is not an ability to sense or judge grandeur, novelty, and beauty in cold abstraction, but to do so with rhetorical propriety—that is, in a way that will persuade others. Taste is always cultivated in anticipation of the need to communicate with others, and hence Addison's bourgeois aesthete always develops with the rhetorical *kairos* "in mind."

This aesthetic-rhetorical consciousness runs against the skeptical grain implicit in Locke's epistemology (and explicit in Hume's), for, as Hannah

Arendt explains, although taste is subjective, "it also derives from the fact that the world itself is an objective datum, something common to all inhabitants." Although Arendt made these observations primarily in reference to Kant's *Critique of Judgment*, her remarks are relevant to theories of taste and propriety in general:

> Taste Judgments . . . are currently held to be arbitrary because they do not compel in the sense in which demonstrable facts or truth proved by argument compel agreement. They share with political opinions that they are persuasive; the judging person—as Kant says quite beautifully—can only "woo the consent of everyone else" in the hope of coming to agreement with him eventually. This "wooing" or persuading corresponds closely to what the Greeks called *peithein*, the convincing and persuading speech which they regarded as the typically political form of people talking with one another. (222)

Arendt's analysis suggests that it is a mistake to take the commonplace about eighteenth-century writers such as Hutcheson and Smith aestheticizing ethics to mean only that they gave a purely subjectivist, emotivist, and/or reified account of morality. Similarly, it would be wrong to read aesthetic education in the period as an opiate for the masses, a wholesale "depoliticization of rhetoric" (T. Miller, 202). To the contrary, the translation of concepts of taste from the disciplines of aesthetics and rhetoric to the understanding of morality brings something useful and insightful to ethics and politics. The inherently socially situated component of taste, and propriety as a particular response to this situatedness, always points to the fact of shared social circumstances and, potentially, shared grounds of discourse. This interpretation of taste then tends toward the dissolution of the foundationalism-social constructionism controversy. It also suggests an explanation as to why so many rhetorical theorists across history have drawn a connection between propriety and the sense of sight: it is sight, after all, that most immediately makes the world-as-shared, and hence social and political reality, apparent. As will be shown in the next chapter, Adam Smith readily drew the analogy between propriety and sight, and it is precisely the social quality of this aesthetic-rhetorical judgment that made propriety a compelling and central concept in his rhetorical and ethical theories.

CHAPTER 4

Propriety in Smith's Rhetoric Lectures

The work published as *Lectures on Rhetoric and Belles-Lettres* comes not directly from Smith's hand—presumably it went up in smoke with the papers he had burned at the end of his life. We must settle instead for a set of student notes discovered in 1958, titled simply "Notes of Dr. Smith's Rhetorick Lectures." Given that Smith was reputed in one obituary to have discouraged student note taking (though other reports say he allowed it), we may well ask how reliably they reflect Smith's thought (Rae, 64). On the basis of a range of evidence, scholars have come to regard the student notes as being very close to Smith's words. The accuracy of the notes themselves is aided by the fact that they show the work of two hands collaborating to reconstruct Smith's lectures. The second scribe, who corrects errors and fills gaps left by the first, may have worked with the assistance of another set of notes (Bryce, "Introduction," *LRBL,* 4–5). Student marginalia in the notes for lecture 18—"I could almost say damn it" and "Not a word more can I remember"—indicate that that lecture, at least, was written down later, but also strongly suggests that the students were attempting not merely to record the gist of Smith's thought but were painstakingly trying to record the lectures word-for-word. This compulsion is a bit curious given that Smith generally did not read his lectures but delivered them *sine libro*, a fact noted in the manuscript for two lectures (21 and 24) and confirmed by Dugald Stewart in an early biographical essay on Smith (*EPS*, 275). Whether the students got every word or not, it can be said that they did capture Smith's prose style well, and that the notes are quite consistent with Smith's other published work.

The surviving notes are thought to have been made during Smith's fifteenth and last year presenting them (1763), which suggest the possibility of an archival motive by the transcribers. More importantly, the fact that the notes were made late in Smith's teaching career increases the likelihood that, however strictly faithful they are to his precise words, they reflect the refinement and development of thought and consideration that inevitably would have resulted from a decade and a half of teaching and writing. Smith was known as a scrupulous reviser of his own published work. The best evidence of this are the six editions that *TMS* went through between 1759 and 1790, the second and sixth of which contained substantial clarifications and additions.[1] What revisions the rhetoric lectures underwent cannot be known, though Smith's most recent biographer argues that the Glasgow version of the lectures reproduces the Edinburgh material "without much alteration." Tellingly, there are few references to texts later than 1751 (Ross, 87, 92), and none to major figures such as Hume and Voltaire as might be expected. After considering the difficulties attending the authority of the text, Howell concludes that the notes are "a substantial and largely accurate version of what he said" (1971, 18). Another useful piece of evidence is the fact that Smith did eventually publish an expanded version of the third lecture, first separately under the title "Considerations Concerning the First Formation of Languages," then, significantly, as an accompanying text to the third and subsequent editions of *TMS*. Although the published version is some six times the length of the student notes of the original lecture, a careful inspection shows that this difference is entirely due to the addition of examples and more detailed explanations of the main ideas. In argument and general outline, the two texts are virtually identical.

Though the notes do evince an attempt at the kind of systematic approach favored by Smith in his major published works, the structure of the lectures is both looser and more subtle than one would hope for in a published treatment of the subject. This is particularly true of the first eleven lectures, which deal most explicitly with propriety. Smith even casually skips over material he regards as "taedious and unentertaining" (*LRBL,* 1.14). While this complicates the task of analysis, this approach is also suggestive about Smith's view of the nature of propriety. Smith's tendencies to digress and to not follow through on promised trains of discourse are probably due to his extemporaneous delivery, and to the lectures' initially public nature, which may have required less rigor than a course given as part of a university curriculum. There is also Smith's professed attitude toward his subject: he clearly had little use for the elaborate systematizing that had typified so much prior rhetorical theory. To be sure, he makes approving references to classical systematic rhetoricians, but when Smith speaks of the rhetorical tradition as a whole, he usually disparages it. He regarded most modern and classical rhetorical textbooks given to elaborate classification of figures and tropes as "generally a very silly set of books and not at all instructive" (1.v.59). Similarly, when he treats the Aristotelian distinction between deliberative, judicial, and epideictic rhetoric, he notes that "[i]t is rather reverence for antiquity than any great regard for the beauty or usefulness of the thing which makes me mention the Antient divisions of Rhetorick" (1.152). He dismisses classical invention and arrangement as rather simple and obvious matters not requiring instruction. Instead, Smith mainly treats "propriety" in speech and writing, a diffuse enough concept to allow him to move through an array of subjects, including material traditionally seen as belonging to invention and arrangement. The apparent looseness of the lectures may thus indicate Smith's self-awareness of authoring a new approach. As I shall discuss in a moment, and as this chapter as a whole will amply demonstrate, the paucity of overt structure is more apparent than real, but it is also symptomatic of Smith's own rhetorical strategy, by which he seeks to dissociate his theory of propriety from any notion that it might be put into practice through the rote application of routine heuristic or stylistic formulae.

As was discussed in chapter 1, Smith initially gave the lectures in 1748–1751 to a public audience in Edinburgh, then continued them in connection with his duties as Professor of Logic and Rhetoric, and later Chair of Moral Philosophy, at the University of Glasgow. The most compelling reason for continuing the rhetoric lectures was, as Millar reports, that Smith held the study of speech communication and literary discourse to be the best means of explaining the powers of the mind. But Smith probably kept giving the lectures as well simply because they were highly original, compellingly delivered, and thus in demand; furthermore, continuing to teach them was a way of establishing domain over his intellectual property, something about which Smith may have been reasonably anxious. Continuing the lectures would have been quite natural, moreover, as Smith, like most of his contemporaries, did not rigidly compartmentalize the disciplines he taught: his moral philosophy curriculum encompassed natural theology, ethics, jurisprudence, and political economy, and he was known to make frequent and illuminating digressions into literary criticism during any of these lectures (Rae, 56).

That Smith viewed the study of communication in such an interdisciplinary way is a key presupposition of this study. Of course, there is ample precedent for this in the classical rhetorical tradition: Aristotle had put rhetoric into an overlapping relationship with dialectic, ethics, and politics; Cicero and Quintilian in particular made the study of rhetoric virtually coterminous with that of ethics. Smith was well aware of this interdisciplinary character of rhetoric, and he put it to good use. Rhetoric appears to have served a propaedeutic function within the curriculum Smith taught, at least in Millar's assessment of Smith's motives: "By these [literary and rhetorical] arts, everything that we perceive or feel, every operation of our minds, is expressed and delineated in such a manner, that it may be clearly distinguished and delineated. There is, at the same time, no branch of literature more suited to youth at the first entrance upon philosophy than [rhetoric and belles lettres], which lays hold of their taste and feelings" (*EPS*, 274). Dugald Stewart concurred in remarking that Smith's interest in the fine arts was driven "less, it is probable, with a view to the peculiar enjoyments they convey, (though he was by no means without sensibility to their beauties) than on account of their connection with the general principles of the human mind" (*EPS*, 305).

Smith's lectures, then, would have provided his students with preliminary insights into basic elements of human thought and action—a groundwork, as we shall see, conspicuously absent from his moral philosophy. Moreover, his treatment of rhetoric would have whetted the intellectual appetite of his audience for more advanced work, serving as well to establish epideictically a set of values without which any advanced study of morals would be impossible. It is quite significant that the thirteen-year period in Glasgow during which Smith gave his rhetoric lectures was also the period during which he wrote *TMS* and was germinating his first ideas on political economy. It should come as no surprise that his writings on rhetoric and other subjects, ethics in particular, are cross-pollinated with similar concepts.

Occasionally this fact has been noted, but never has it been studied in depth. Scholars writing on the relation between Smith's rhetoric and ethics have tended to read *LRBL* as derivative of *TMS*, a tempting approach given the far greater theoretical rigor of *TMS*. J. C. Bryce, for example, has sketched in his introduction to the Glasgow edition of the *LRBL* a few broad correlations between the *LRBL* and *TMS*. He finds that (1) the different forms of communication addressed in *LRBL* are illustrated with concepts from *TMS*; (2) the rhetoric lectures extend *TMS*'s treatment of sympathy; and (3) the lectures' treatment of propriety complements that presented in *TMS* (Bryce, "Introduction," *LRBL*, 10). Similarly, Vincent Bevilacqua remarks that Smith's "attention to the philosophical bases of style resulted . . . from his extension of the moral-aesthetic precept of propriety to rhetoric" (567). The assumption of both Bryce and Bevilacqua that the concepts in *TMS* provided Smith with the basic conceptual framework for his rhetoric lectures is repeated by Patricia Spense, who views Smith as having "evolved a belletristic rhetoric from his sentimentalist ethics" (95). Barbara Warnick, too, has noted that the speaker's need to effect sympathy in the audience is framed in terms supplied by *TMS*. However, Warnick also indirectly suggests that the reverse relationship merits examination: "Observance of [rhetorical] propriety is key to the workings of sympathy because propriety is what enables listeners to identify with the speaker and the experiences and responses the speaker seeks to promote" (Warnick, 58–59). Though Warnick does not follow through in investigating the implications of this observation, it is notable for its strong presumption that the kind of social interaction described in *TMS* as the source of moral conscience almost certainly involved speech, and hence is underwritten by Smith's theory of rhetorical propriety.

The orientation that puts *TMS* as the source of ideas in the *LRBL* is certainly suggested by the fact that the student notes of the rhetoric lectures postdate the publication of *TMS*. It has also proven a convenient arrangement for historians of the discipline of English literature who, often overestimating Smith's dedication to the study of English literature as a social panacea (by far Smith's criticism focuses on classical literature) want to portray the lectures as instigating a shift in rhetorical pedagogy purely in service to the polite mores conducive to laissez-faire capitalism and bourgeois ascendancy (Court, 20; Crawford, 41; T. Miller, 189). There is undeniably a shift in this period wherein notions of civic duty are translated into civil politeness, and Smith's rhetoric surely in part reflects this, but if it had succeeded as the manifesto it has been made out to be, English departments would be teaching Demosthenes, Vergil, and Tacitus as much as Swift and Addison. Despite the dates of the texts, however, assigning priority to the ideas in *TMS* introduces some curious circumstances, particularly if Ross is right in his assessment that the extant lecture notes closely represent Smith's 1748 lectures. The chronology of Smith's intellectual activity strongly suggests that his ideas about communication influenced his ethical thought at least as much if not more than the reverse, and the peculiar methodology of *TMS* (to be addressed in chapter 5) also gives precedence to rhetoric. If *TMS* were the source of Smith's ideas about discursive propriety, as has generally been thought, one would have to wonder, given the pervasiveness of the concept in the rhetoric lectures, what *LRBL* would have contained in 1748. Neither Stewart nor Millar in their reports mention any significant development or change in the content of the rhetoric lectures between 1748 and 1763, and certainly any radical evolution of *LRBL* in response to *TMS* would have been strikingly noteworthy to these keen observers of Smith's teaching.

The precise antecedence that these ideas had in Smith's mind is of course impossible to trace. It could be that the rhetoric lectures were crafted around ethical concepts Smith had already developed, but there is no evidence to suggest this. Furthermore, to view *LRBL* as essentially an outgrowth of or illustrative appendix to Smith's ethical thought overlooks Smith's evident awareness that communication is prior to ethical thought, and that the study of communication is therefore prior to the study of ethics. Smith believed— in a rather Aristotelian manner[2]—that just as humans cannot become fully developed moral agents without communicating with others, so must they have some practical knowledge of communication before they can have theoretical knowledge of ethics: "Were it possible that a human creature could grow up to manhood in some solitary place, without any communication with his own species, he could no more think of his own character, of the propriety or demerit of his own sentiments and conduct, than of the beauty or deformity of his own face" (*TMS* 3.1.3). Only one Smith scholar, his most recent biographer, has seen the obvious parallel between this priority of communication to ethics and the chronology of Smith's work: Ross notes in passing that Smith's interest in epideictic rhetoric in *LRBL* contains the "seeds of the *TMS*" (92).

If more Smith scholars have failed to take this into account, it is likely because the seedstock presents some immediate challenges to analysis, beginning with the apparently loose organization of the work as a whole. Yet if we assent to Ross's view, the apparent lack of structure appears at once to be strategic on Smith's part. First, the broadly ranging subject matter of the first lectures simply provides an entertaining introduction to rhetoric and belles lettres. But more importantly, these first lectures allow him to establish through gradual accretion the pervasiveness of propriety—the main conceptual thread holding these lectures together—yet in a manner that does not empirically formulize the concept.

In *TMS*, Smith provides some retrospective explanation for this seeming anti-method. Discussing the moral jurisdiction of duty, he comments that in the practice of virtues other than justice, "our conduct should rather be directed by a certain idea of propriety, by a certain taste for a particular tenor of conduct, than by any regard for a precise maxim or rule" (3.6.10). Later he repeats the point, likening the rules of justice to the "precise, accurate, and indispensable" rules of grammar, whereas the rules of other virtues (by contrast "loose, vague and indeterminate") are akin to those for "attainment of what is sublime and elegant in composition." These latter rules "present us rather with a general idea of the perfection to aim at, than afford us any certain and infallible directions for acquiring it" (7.4.1). Just as "language wants names" to mark the limitless permutations in moral action "according to every possible variation in circumstances" created by time and contingency (7.4.3), so is compositional theory limited in its ability to state precisely the rules that would govern practice in the complex kairotic web of rhetorical action. Thus, in *TMS* Smith approves of the ancient Peripatetics and Stoics who in discoursing on the virtues "wrote like critics," rather than those casuists who wrote "like grammarians" (7.4.2). Analogously, in the first eleven rhetoric lectures, Smith elucidates stylistic propriety by writing more like a critic than a formal rhetorician, thereby dispelling any suggestion that effectiveness in composition may be acquired simply through the application of abstract rules.

This is not to suggest, however, that the lectures lack a readily perceptible order or logical progression. On the contrary, while Smith adduces little metadiscourse on his arrangement of the lectures (though the missing first lecture may well have contained commentary to this effect), he is keenly attuned to the relationship between arrangement and subject matter, and he unfolds his treatment in a deliberate way, beginning at the level of elementary semantics (lecture 2), building on this to develop an emotive theory of grammar (lectures 3–5), and only then proceeding to larger-scale discursive matters such as figuration (lecture 6), ethos (lectures 7–11), and description (12–16). He saves for last his treatment of propriety in different genres of discourse (lectures 17–30). The close reading of *LRBL* that follows in this chapter will parallel that structure (excepting a brief digression on the role of vision in Smith's theory of description). It will become apparent that all of the main sections have the issue of rhetorical propriety running through them as a pervasive theme.

Propriety and Perspicuity (Lecture 2)

Besides possibly supplying a division mapping the full set of lectures, the missing first lecture may well have contained some introductory remarks by Smith on the general nature of the relationship between the study of communication and other fields of inquiry such as logic, ethics, and politics. Nevertheless, his awareness of the close relationship between rhetoric and ethics is already well apparent in the second lecture, which begins with the subject of perspicuity or clarity on the word level. Smith appears at first to hold fairly typical empiricist ideas about semantics: Words stand for things; good style eschews ambiguity; communication aims at the efficient and successful transmission of meaning, largely through the reduction of "defects" endemic to language generally and English in particular. Yet he is aware that clear communication involves a great deal more than this rather narrow approach might suggest; indeed, on close examination, Smith's notion of propriety appears to be rooted in his very understanding of language itself, and so it necessarily plays a primary role in clarity.

Smith begins in seemingly good Lockean fashion by noting that perspicuity is achieved if the rhetor avoids the ambiguity created by synonyms. He then also advises that perspicuity follows from using "native" English words. He combines these two dicta in several examples, showing that older words of Anglo-Saxon origin signify more strongly than Latin terms imported by the French. "Unfold" is superior to "develope"; "unravell" to "explicate." (Note that the preferred words denote visualizable actions, and that they even latently refer, through the reversing prefix *un-* to a more remote and original action.) "Insufferable" and "untollerable," though deriving from synonymous Latin roots, have distinct uses in English turning on the degree and quality of emotion expressed: "We say that the cruelty and oppression of a tyrant is unsufferable, but the heat of a summer's day is untollerable" (1.3). The graver import of the first word, "insufferable"—its ability to convey emotion and moral indignation as opposed to merely physical discomfort— is due to its having been in English usage longer. "Untollerable" is indeed a relative neologism. Older words, it seems, have greater affective impact because they are closer to some kind of originary experience, one that is intriguingly analogous to the sort of "original experience" that all communication from one mind to another strives to convey. In a very un-Lockean fashion then, far from being something that obstructs clarity, this affective function is utterly necessary to it.

Smith here is already foreshadowing questions of propriety in what might otherwise appear to be a narrow discussion of semantics: "We may indeed naturally expect that the better sort will often exceed the vulgar in the propriety of their language but where there is no such excellence we are apt to prefer those in use amongst them, by the association we form betwixt their words and the behavior we admire in them. It is the custom of the people that forms what we call propriety, and the custom of the better sort from whence the rules of purity of style are to be drawn" (1.7). The stylistic virtues of propriety and perspicuity, then, are as integrated for Smith as they are for Aristotle, but they are so in quite different ways: whereas for Aristotle, a relatively objective clarity of speech largely suffices for rhetorical appropriateness, for Smith, proper deployment of affective connotation abets clarity. For Aristotle, if you are clear, you will be appropriate; for Smith, if you are appropriate, you will be clear.

It would be fairly easy to explain this away as bourgeois hegemony at work. There is no denying that Smith was clearly a product of his age and class, and, moreover, as a Scot (who at Oxford had suffered all too keenly the awareness of his Scottishness), he seems to have been anxious about a sensed inferiority of Scottish culture and dialect. Though he does refer here to "behavior we admire," when he writes of "the better sort" he seems to mean "men of rank and breeding"—more specifically English and Continental men of rank and breeding—as much as he means those of excellent character. This view would have been in harmony with the ethos of enlightened Scottish improvement in general and with the agenda of the *Edinburgh Review* in particular. Later in life, Smith will revise his position, noting in the sixth edition of *TMS* (1790) that the propensity to admire those of rank and wealth over those of wisdom and virtue is "the great and most universal cause of the corruption of our moral sentiments" (*TMS*, 1.3.3.1). To limit analysis along solely ideological lines is a mistake if it blinds us to the more important insight that occurs here, for Smith was obviously beginning to work out, albeit in rough terms, the mimetic economy of communicative action and moral agency. In this interactive relationship, admiration of virtue is the focal point. Noteworthy is the important visual metaphor lurking here recalling *to prepon* in its oldest sense denoting "conspicuous appearance": *to admire* is literally to look approvingly upon someone or something. In the same paragraph Smith notes that "manner of language" and the appearance of dress are analogous in their ability to signify character, and it is the visual character of the comparison here, rather than its relation to class, that is most significant. Admiration is followed by an association between character and the words that attend it, words which one then can and presumably should appropriate to one's own lexicon as a way of purchasing, as it were, the character that caused them.

This relationship between style and character is purely arbitrary: Smith often refers to character as a "cause" of sentiment and style (e.g., 1.162, 1.183). Indeed, in Smith's view, style and character are closely laminated together. Without virtuous character, there would be no virtue of style; but, as will become evident in *TMS*, without the model of appropriate speech, virtuous character would be inaccessible to both the agent and the moral philosopher. This clearly parallels, consciously or unconsciously, Aristotle's notion of *to prepon's* relationship to moral character, as discussed in chapter 2. Neither virtue nor style is really prior to the other, and yet Smith is treating deeper matters of moral philosophy through the prior consideration of appropriate speech. His approach is unique in rhetorical history. It may seem superficially comparable to sophistic conceptions of propriety, or to the approach taken by Lorenzo Valla, in that it seeks moral worth through the norms of decorous speech. Yet Smith's aim, as we shall see in the next chapter, will not be to eviscerate Stoic and Peripatetic notions of temperate, mean-based virtue, but to support them.

So despite the lectures' informal and seemingly unsystematic surface, there is a serious philosophical idea germinating below, an idea that is crucial for understanding Smith's insistence on perspicuity as the foremost element of propriety. Seen as playing a necessary part in the both the development of moral character and the advance of ethical thinking, perspicuity is neither a schoolmarmish stricture nor simply a bid for the mantle of social power; it is an absolute necessity if there is to be any such thing as morality or moral authority within society. For to "exist" socially, morality must first be sensed—that is, "seen"—in language (both perspicuity and clarity are visual metaphors). Smith goes on in this second lecture to recommend, in scattered fashion and with reference to both ancient and contemporary sources, some of the means to perspicuous language. He approves of "natural" word order for easy comprehension, and advises that sentence length and transitions be suited to genre (brevity and concision suit history writing, or fact-narrating, which Smith calls "didactic," but it is not appropriate for orators, who are seeking to arouse emotion). He further counsels avoidance of figures of thought and speech, and overuse of pronouns, which generally cause obscurity (*LRBL,* 1.13). All of these recommendations must be understood as more than superficial pointers on how to become discursively institutionalized. They are discursive adaptations to a complex of circumstances attending the communicative situation that imply a dialectical relationship between style acquisition and the formation of moral character.

An Emotive Grammar (Lectures 3–5)

Instead of simply continuing to itemize factors contributing to perspicuity, however, Smith takes an unexpected turn in the third lecture: he presents a speculative history of the "origin and progress" of language. The function of this lecture may be understood in a number of ways. As we shall see, the lecture provides him with an opportunity to segue from lexical to syntactic semantics, with a convenient symmetry between the binary pair of primitive/modern languages and that of single-word/larger-discursive-unit semantics. In a rhetorical sense, it is simply entertaining—an appealing introduction to the somewhat drier grammatical matters of lectures 4 and 5. In terms of intellectual fashion, Smith appears to have been following a trend set by such works as Condillac's "Essai sur l'origine des connaissances humaine" (1746), a copy of which Smith owned, and Rousseau's "Discours sur l'origine et les fondimens de l'inégalité parmiles hommes" (1755), from which Smith quoted in a letter to the *Edinburgh Review* a few months after its appearance (*EPS,* 250–54). Smith claims in a letter of 1763 to have been first set to thinking about these subjects after reading Abbé Gabriel Girard's *Les vrais principes de la Langue Françoise, ou la parole réduite en methode conformément aux lois d'usage* (1747) (*Corr.,* 86). Structuralists or deconstructionists will no doubt ascribe this chapter to a typical Enlightenment yearning for a functional standardization of language, a desire already to some degree implicit in the call for perspicuity but now sought through knowledge of the "original," natural "design," and "genius" of language itself. Again, this would not be entirely wrong: Smith does evince an almost scientistic discomfort with the connotative power of language and clearly hopes that his lectures will, if not wholly eradicate connotation, at least help his students to control it.[3] Smith probably saw this conjectural genealogy as a helpful step in understanding the nature of the highly cultivated language used in civilized societies, "from whence the rules of purity of stile are to be drawn," and as a means of introducing the way in which rhetorical propriety is an aspect not just of diction but of syntactic construction.

Dugald Stewart wrote in his early memoir of Smith that this "theoretical or conjectural history" of language was significant less "on account of the opinions it contains, than as specimen of a particular sort of inquiry" and as evidence of an intellectual work ethic that gives check to "that indolent philosophy, which refers to a miracle, whatever appearances, both in the natural and moral worlds, it is unable to explain" (*EPS,* 292–93). Smith's implicit methodology here parallels the explicit approach he will describe in *TMS:* moral philosophy, he writes, has two main areas of inquiry: First, what is virtue? Second, by what power of the mind do we become aware of the moral (*TMS,* 7.1.2)? The first question is of the utmost practical use, but the second is of speculative interest only (*TMS,* 7.3.intro.3). Similarly, Smith provides this conjectural history of language as an introduction to the question, How do we become aware of that thing we call style? This lecture suggests that he is as interested in the philosophy of style as he is in handing down guidelines for eloquent composition. It is likely too that Smith understood this endeavor in terms of his broader philosophical project, for as already noted, he reworked and extended this lecture and published it separately, first in *The Philological Miscellany* (1761) as "Considerations concerning the first formation of Languages, and the different genius of original and compounded Languages," then again, significantly, as an appendix to the third edition of *TMS* (1767).

Still, one might easily overlook this chapter as an oddity, for it is apt to appear somewhat humorous today, an allegory in which "two savages" bearing a remarkable resemblance to a couple of reasonably sensible Scottish gentlemen go about the polite business of discovering linguistic effectiveness. But we should not let this obscure its essential lesson, which is that language, as Smith sees it, operates according to a phenomenological hierarchy organized in terms of cognitive and psychological proximity. In his genealogy, Smith always hypothesizes that words came into being according to how common and "interesting" (to use the eighteenth-century term) their objects were to primitive people. Substantive concrete nouns, then, are among the first words to be contrived, followed by more abstract categorical nouns, adjectives, and prepositions.[4] At some points his discussion of this hierarchy hints as to how emotional representation could bring the subjects of discourse closer to our awareness and understanding. His analysis of verbs is revealing in this regard. All verbs, he speculates, originated in impersonal form (*pluit, ningit*), which expresses a complete action—really a substantive *and* an event—in one word. All of the examples he gives are concretely connected to immediate and pressing human concerns. The latin *venit,* for example, may have first designated the approach of "some terrible animal as a lion"; only later would it be transferred to signify the approach of any fearful animal, then any fearful object, then any object at all. Note how *venit* loses emotional urgency. The implication of this, when read in the context of his theory of propriety, is that the emotional contextualization achieved by propriety and perspicuity helps restore to words the originary force of their more primitive meaning.

This primitivism may seem at first blush to run counter to the spirit of propriety's socializing function in Smith's ethics; unless, that is, we revise the standard estimation of what propriety does in *TMS*. It does, of course, result in the inculcation and perpetuation of what Deirdre McCloskey has aptly called the "bourgeois virtues," but from Smith's point of view, this would only be incidental to its main function, which is to reconnect ethics to a naturalistic account of the human condition—without the mediation of metaphysics or epistemology. The use of rhetorical propriety as the infrastructure for his moral philosophy resembles philosophy's so-called linguistic turn, though predating it by a century and a half. We shall return to this subject in the next chapter.

By examining one of Smith's observations on the invention of adjectives, we can further see how emotional expression would be crucial in the perspicuous disclosure of meaning. Adjectives had to be discovered after nouns, he notes, because "[t]he quality denoted by an adjective is never seen in the abstract, but is always concreted with some substance or other, and the word signifying such a quality must be formed from it by a good deal of abstract reflection" (1.5.19). We are now in a position to see that for Smith, language that does emotional adjectival work—modifiers expressing the "sentiment or affection" of a rhetor toward the subject—far from being merely a matter of arbitrary and subjective coloration, are potentially indexical of that subject matter. As part and parcel of the rhetor's cognition of the subject matter, they bear an existential connection to it, one which the audience, through sympathy (a concept he will presently introduce), can share.

In lecture 4 Smith builds on these insights by examining the elements of propositions. His taxonomy is fairly standard and brief—subject, copula, and predicate are "Subjective," "Attributive," and "Objective" respectively. There are then four categories of auxiliary elements: (1) "terminatives" and (2) "circumstantials," which are restrictive modifiers denoting how a proposition is to be understood, and there are (3) "conjunctives." A final category of terms, however, receives deeper consideration: These are (4) "adjunctives," metadiscursive, clausal modifiers such as those that function to "point out what particular opinion the speaker has of [the proposition.]" Apparently, the adjunctive was of special interest, because the second student-scribe repeats the first student's notes but adds detail (something that occurs throughout the manuscript almost exclusively at critical theoretical junctures): "The adjunctive is that which expresses the Habit of the Speakers' mind with regard to what he speaks of or the sentiment it excites." Curiously, the adjunctive class of clausal elements also comprehends terms that name an addressee, presumably because an addressive (e.g., "Sir") discloses a disposition (here respect). This pairing of functions is not as odd as it may at first seem, for it is consistent with Smith's view that the very use of language to communicate presumes the necessity of emotional contextualization.

Smith's very first practical rhetorical advice follows upon this essentially emotive analysis of grammar. In lectures 4 and 5 he will offer means to remedy what he takes to be one of the main problems of communicating effectively in

English, namely the "prolixity" that results from it being noninflected and compounded from multiple sources. Inflected languages and those that are lexically "purer" are grammatically more complex, but for Smith they allow the advantages of greater harmony in sound, greater flexibility in arrangement, and implicitly, a greater proximity between words and their originary contexts. He likens the grammatical simplification of language that results from cultural intermingling to the simplification of machines through technological advances, though unlike machines, languages are not improved by being simplified—they lose their appealing sonority, syntactic variety, and, most importantly, contact with their circumstances of origin. That is, loss of inflection strips nouns of their verbal, event-contextualized aspect. (Hence, literary translations, which alter both lexicon and word order, "from the beginning of the world to its end will be unsufferably languid and tedious" (1.5.48). Notice "unsufferably." Such translations arouse indignation because they tyrannically refuse concession to the author's or the audience's orientations to the world.)

Native English speakers have overcome some of this by adapting a "ringing" and "melodious" pronunciation. Writers, of course, cannot avail this, but they can pay close attention to word arrangement, which has some potential to remedy these defects. The most obvious word order, of course, is subject-verb-object, but, says Smith, "thus would a man always speak who felt no passions. But when we are affected with any thing, some one or other of the Ideas will thrust itself forward and we will be most eager to utter what we feel strongest" (1.5.46). To illustrate, he quote's Pope's "Eloisa to Abelard": "In vain lost Eloisa weeps and prays / Her heart still dictates and her hand obeys." Had Pope instead moved "in vain" to the center of the clause—"Lost Eloisa weeps in vain and prays"—the line would have lost not only metrical balance but emotive force. The example has a telling double appropriateness, with its situation of emotional urgency and its dramatization of writing as a means of overcoming psychic and physical separation.

This directive—to put the strongest, most "interesting" element of the sentence to its fore—may be puzzling by the best modern compositional standards, according to which, as Joseph Williams has shown, a host of writing problems are avoided by moving emphatic material to the ends of sentences. But Smith is not concerned here with emphasis; he uses "interesting" in its prevailing eighteenth-century meaning—that is, tending to affect us, or demanding an affective response from us." He means that adjunctives—modifiers that clarify our emotive or attitudinal disposition toward our subject (e.g., "In vain") ought to initiate sentences: Words ought to "arrange themselves in the order of ideas," but not out of some Lockean demand for objective *res-verba* correspondence. Ideas are first formed in a primary dispositional context. To relate that context at the end of sentences is to "drag a tail" as Smith puts it: it potentially alters, revokes, or edits the idea or image already established in a prior clause.

Propriety and Figuration (Lecture 6)

It is only after Smith has established this rule, grounded in his emotive account of grammar, and just before he moves into a discussion of figuration, that he makes his central and programmatic statement in the rhetoric lectures. The position is not happenstance. He has already done much to establish it by implication: word arrangement is important, as we've seen, in making sentences "express our sentiment with suitable Life"; effective style thus communicates "the spirit and the mind of the author" (1.5.47). Still following his hypothetical evolution of language, he argues that the attempt to name grammatical rules led to the discovery of many expressions—tropes and figures—that seemingly violated them, and he unfairly berates the Greek and Roman rhetoricians for having supposed that real eloquence consisted in the use of these. The numbering and naming of all the figures was thus an attempt by the ancients to overformulize style, indeed to grammaticize rhetoric. Quite naturally Smith objects (as even Quintilian had done). In one of his extended analogies in *TMS* between justice and grammar and between the other virtues and composition, he notes: "A man may learn to write grammatically by rule, with the most absolute infallibility; and so perhaps, he may be taught to act justly. But there are no rules whose observance will infallibly lead us to the attainment of elegance or sublimity in writing, though there are some which may help us, in some measure, to correct and ascertain the vague ideas which we might otherwise have entertained of those perfections" (3.6.11). Likewise, in *LRBL* Smith argues that ancient rhetoricians had incorporated the figures of speech into their grammatical systems, so that they could "[stick] close to their old scheme" with "the greater appearance of justice" (1.5.54–55).

   Smith finds this approach entirely wrong; the figures have "no intrinsick worth of their own." He then enunciates his central rhetorical tenet: "When the sentiment of the speaker is expressed in a neat, clear, plain and clever manner, and the passion or affection he is possessed of and intends, *by sympathy*, to communicate to his hearer, is plainly and cleverly hit off, then and then only the expression has all the force and beauty language can give it" (1.5.56, original emphasis). It would have been quite natural for Smith to include in his formula the concept of sympathy, a central idea in Hume's *Treatise*, which indeed Hume had made essentially synonymous with "communication." In analyzing the imagination's relation to the passions in book two, Hume writes that "Nothing is more capable of infusing any passion into the mind, than eloquence, by which objects are represented in their strongest and most lively colors." Yet Hume here means eloquence in a highly stylized, figured sense. Such eloquence, in fact, is not always necessary: "The bare opinion of another, especially when inforc'd with passion, will cause the idea of good or evil to have an influence upon us, which wou'd otherwise have been neglected. This proceeds from the principle of sympathy or communication . . ." (2.3.6).[5]

Hume's influence on Smith here is likely, yet Smith's formulation grants the name of eloquence to the appropriately passionate and clear discourse that Hume regards as something other than eloquence. Smith's central doctrine is repeated in nearly identical words in lecture 8 (1.96), and with some variation in many other places (e.g., 1.5.57, 1.73, 1.76, 1.135). The second student-scribe here restates the point in only slightly different language: "When your Language expresses perspicuously and neatly your meaning and what you would express, together with the Sentiment or affection this matter inspires you with, and when this Sentiment is nobler or more beautiful than such as are commonly met with, then your Language has all the Beauty it can have, and the figures of speech contribute or can contribute towards it only so far as they happen to be the just and natural forms of Expressing that Sentiment." Clearly, Smith's position is that it is not the uncommonness of the diction or phrasing but the uncommonness of the sentiment and appropriate expression that accounts for eloquence. Smith's idea that the intention to communicate a given passion or affection originates in sympathy is an entirely new contribution to the theory of rhetorical propriety. Though he does not define sympathy in *LRBL*, it is the central concept in his theory of ethics, where it refers to a correspondence or agreement of sentiment among agents resulting from a natural human disposition to be affected by the emotional conditions of others. Human beings, Smith assumes, have an instinctual desire both to enter into the sentiments of others and to have others enter into their sentiments approvingly. Beauty and effectiveness in language result from successfully transacting this sympathy; conversely, as we shall see, we are only made aware of sympathy as an ethical concept through experience of the discursive adaptations of rhetorical practice. Although sympathy is clearly a prior condition for eloquence, and although it conditions propriety in language, it is likely that Smith only arrived at his notion of sympathy after considering what happens in effective human communication.

The single most important aspect of effective communication, Smith repeatedly urges, is the appropriate expression of sentiment. Even technical aspects of the figures of speech are governed by this. For example, Smith treats metaphor as the paradigmatic figure of speech: the rule that governs it is "equally applicable" to the other figures. A metaphor, he says, will have "justness or propriety" if it gives "due strength of expression to the object to be described" (1.66–68). Smith's pairing of the terms *justness* and *propriety* may seem wrong given the connection cited above which links justice with precision and propriety with imprecision. But there is a way in which this description is consistent. By "due strength of expression" he means that metaphors must maintain a reasonable proportionality in the comparison between the tenor and vehicle: If the vehicle is too far-fetched (e.g., calling a soldier a tornado) the result is bombast; if the vehicle is too understated, the result is burlesque. Hence, metaphor has a quasi-rational dimension in that comparison lends itself to some degree of precision, which is often checked against the visual portion of the sensory realm. Despite this rational underpinning, however, faulty logic in metaphors results in pathetic improprieties—unintended bombast or burlesque. These faults are rooted in an effort on the part of the writer to express more than he feels; in so doing he also distorts the clear representation of the object of discourse.

Character, Epideictic, and Ethics (Lectures 7–11)

Having now closely examined the integrated nature of semantics, grammar, and emotive communication, Smith expands his theory of propriety in the seventh lecture by arguing that the sentiments expressed by a writer or speaker are bound to vary with his circumstances and general character, variables requiring different stylistic virtues. The variety is so great that even closely similar styles have significantly different implications (1.85). To illustrate, he compares the plain and the simple styles, though in a Theophrastian manner he makes little distinction between style and character:

> A Plain man is one who pays no regard to the common civilities and forms of good breeding. He gives his opinion bluntly and affirms without condescending to give any reason for his doing so; and if he mentions any sort of a reason it is only to shew how evident and plain a matter it was and expose the stupidity of the others in not perceiving it as well as he. . . . Compassion finds little room in his

breast; admiration does not at all suit his wisdom; contempt is more agreeable to
his selfsufficient imperious temper. (1.85–86)

And so on. The only explicitly stylistic attributes noted are that "[w]it would
ill-suit his gravity, Antitheses or Such like expressions" (1.87). This plain demeanor, Smith finds, is common in older people, inspiring respect and esteem
but not affection. The simple character, on the other hand, is more common
in the young and is the object of affection rather than esteem. The simple man
is generally modest, unassertive, and eager not to appear affected. While he is
not "studious to appear with all the outward marks of civility and breeding,"
the simple character is willing to use them "when they naturally express his
real sentiments" (1.88). Few passages make as clear as this one the degree to
which Smith considers style, habitual demeanor, and characteristic sentiments
to be an organic unity. The general rule is that "one should stick to his naturall character" and "regulate that character and manner" away from vicious
extremes (1.99).

Smith then argues that Swift's great mass appeal was precisely in such
consistency between his demeanor and style. Swift's more serious works are
generally regarded as "silly and trifling" because they do not suit his character (1.100). This is a more subtle point than it may at first appear. Later, Smith
does remark upon how Swift's personal life eventuated in his plain character
(1.118), but here he is not saying that Swift's appeal was in the perception
by his readers of some correlation between his "real" and his written character, for of course very few readers could have known Swift personally. The
appealing correlation can only be between the character suggested by the
opinions expressed and their stylistic mode of expression. In fact, this is precisely what Smith often means by the word *sentiment*: Although he sometimes uses the words *sentiment, passion,* and *emotion* together, he once
explicitly notes that by "sentiments" he means "morall observations" (1.144).
This is close to a meaning put forth by Kames in *Elements of Criticism*: a sentiment is a "thought prompted by emotion," rather than sheer affect or raw
passion (1:451). Sentiment in this sense has an intellectual element: a mixture
of emotion and critical judgment, a sentiment is a passion that extends itself
in the form of approbation or disapprobation. This implies that stylistic propriety is more than a superficial nicety or, as is often said of style in the
period, a managerial device whose role is simply to shape the form of communication once subject matter has been revealed by logic.[6] Instead, propriety must be understood as an integral part of successful communication, one
that works in concert with invention and arrangement. Smith's remark that

Swift has all three of the "perfections" of a good writer bears this out: (1) Swift has a complete knowledge of his subject; (2) he arranges the parts of his discourse in the proper order, a skill that follows naturally from his complete knowledge; and (3) he describes his ideas in the proper and expressive manner (1.105).

By implicating propriety in the communication of sentiments as moral judgments, Smith draws attention to the epideictic element inherent in all rhetorical discourse. The choice of Swift as subject here is significant, for it allows Smith to focus at length on ridicule. An epideictic genre that gets relatively little attention in most rhetorics, ridicule is naturally central to Smith, who regards fitting expression of approbation and disapprobation as essential to the formation of propriety in speech and moral character. In lecture 9 Smith asserts that ridicule is derived from combining aspects of admiration and contempt (1.121). The particular merit of ridicule as a subject of inquiry in a propriety-based rhetorical theory is that it is a mode of discourse in which the importance of the interrelationships between the rhetor's character and emotions, the subject and style are perhaps most obvious. Epideictic rhetoric is a likely area of inquiry for Smith, who so closely collocates rhetoric and ethics, because the epideictic rhetor's intention to do good or harm to another is always one with his or her practice. Epideictic is prone to be more overtly a form of moral action than is deliberative or judicial rhetoric, and the study of ridicule thus equally serves his students in rhetoric and moral philosophy. He remarks of Swift and Lucian, his two main exemplars of ridicule, that "both together form a System of morality from whence more sound and just rules of life for all the various characters of men may be drawn than from most set systems of Morality" (1.125).

Smith notes that ridicule is hurled at any subject that is "in most respects Grand or pretends to be or is expected to be so, [yet] has something mean or little in it or when we find something that is realy mean with some pretensions and marks of grandeur" (1.108). Ridicule teases the grand accident out of the mean subject and sarcastically represents it as a dominant property, or, conversely, it exposes the latent meanness in the grand or pretentiously grand subject (1.117). The effect is heightened through style that is appropriate, ironically, through incongruity with the subject matter (1.114). The resulting "burlesque" moves the listeners or readers to laughter and hence enables them to feel the passions and attitudes of the author, but also to sense something of the nature of the subject matter itself. Smith repeatedly points out that ridicule depends on the actual circumstances of the subject matter. "A sow wallowing in the mire is certainly a loathsome object, but no one would laugh at it, as it is agreeable to the nature of the beast. But if he saw the sow afterwards in a drawingroom, the case would be altered" (1.110).

Ridicule that issues not from the real defects of the subject but only from the accidental circumstances it happens to be in is "buffoonish" and "unworthy of a gentleman who has had a regular education." Ridicule is appropriate to gentlemanly character only when "Real foibles and blemishes in the Characters or behavior of men are exposed to our view. . . ." This, he adds, "is altogether consistent with the character of a Gentleman as it tends to the reformation of manners and the benefit of mankind" (1.116). Thus, ridicule is appropriate when it issues from an appropriate sentiment and communicates clearly the nature of the object that gave rise to that sentiment. For Smith, these two qualities are interlocked: the truthful expression of the sentiment displays the nature of the subject of the discourse. This is quite similar to Aristotle's contention that propriety and clarity are interlocked because propriety makes facts appear credible, although in Smith this effect is brought about through sympathy rather than through any acknowledged rational engagement. For Smith then, *pathos* does a good portion of the work that in classical rhetoric is more typically assigned to *logos*.

Smith pauses to summarize important points in lecture 11, once again emphasizing that good style answers to two interlocked rules: language must express the author's thought together with the sentiment thought produces. He remarks that this is "no more than common sense" and suggests even more explicitly that ethics and the art of effective communication are fundamentally intertwined: "But if you'll attend to it all the Rules of Criticism and morality, when traced to their foundation, turn out to be some principles of Common Sense which everyone assents to; all the business of those arts is to apply these rules to the different subjects, and shew what the conclusion is when they are so applied" (1.133). Moral conduct and effective communication are simply inseparable as matters of inquiry. There is essentially one rule, "equally applicable to conversation and behavior as writing": "For what is that [which] makes a man agreeable company, is it not, when his sentiments appear to be naturally expressed, when the passion or affection is properly conveyed and when their thoughts are so agreeable and naturall that we find ourselves inclined to assent to them" (1.135).

To this rule of moral and discursive conduct Smith adds a new corollary which further bridges his rhetorical and ethical theories. The wise man, like the perfect stylist, acts in a manner consistent with his prevailing temperament, but "he will only regulate his naturall temper, restrain within just bounds and lop all exhuberances and bring it to that pitch which will be agreeable to those about him" (1.135).This dictum, which is one of the few times Smith's theory of propriety explicitly points to the shaping influence of audience on discourse, is one of the central and original ideas in *TMS*: the most important move in moral development is the self-controlled regulation of passions such that they can be "entered into" by a spectator. The original-ity of this idea is owed in large part to its rhetorical assumptions, for this modulation of the expression of sentiments—which in turn teaches one to control the passions themselves—is made necessary when humans, as natu-rally sympathetic animals, confront the limitations of communicative reality. In other words, the formation of moral character, which aims at propriety of action, is shaped by rhetorical situatedness.[7]

Smith faults Shaftesbury's style for violating precisely these general rules. Instead of expressing naturally the disposition of his native character, Shaftes-bury concocted a highly artificial and idiosyncratic style that sought to "set off by the ornament of language what was deficient in matter" (1.144).The result is impropriety: his diction exceeds the dignity of his subject, his analy-ses rely on fatuous puns, and his emotional expressions tend to be "un-bounded, overstretched and unsupported by the appearance of Reason" (1.148). Smith suggests here that it is particularly the spoken as opposed to the written rhetorical situation that is the originary paradigm of both moral and rhetorical propriety, for he notes that since he wrote rather than orated, Shaftesbury "succeeded better in this attempt to form a stile than we could have expected and much better than any one could do in an attempt to form a plan of behavior." The written medium affords the writer slightly more control over the communicative situation than the speaker typically has over the live communicative situation; in particular Smith mentions here that "the writer may review and correct anything that is not suitable to the character he designs to maintain" whereas "in Common life, many accidents would occur which would be apt to cause him to loose his assumed character and if they are not immediately catched there is no remedy" (1.146).The matrix of time and exigency in live communication is likely to betray affectations such as Shaftesbury's; Smith notes Shaftesbury was undistinguished as an orator. By implication then, Smith's requirement that rhetors maintain a nat-ural uniformity of style and character is designed to give the live speaker a similar degree of control over the situation as the writer has. (This recalls Aristotle's notion of propriety as one way of guarding against the excesses and deceptions often associated with rhetorical practice.) The most impor-tant consequence of Shaftesbury's impropriety is not just the buffoonishness that redounds to him, but a distortion of the subjects about which he wrote:

Thus, "A Stranger who did not understand the language would imagine the most trivial subjects to be something very sublime . . ." (1.148).

Appropriate Description as Invention (Lectures 12-16)

Smith enters upon a new course in lecture 12, titled "Of Composition" by one of the student-scribes. Lecture 12 is the last lecture to be so titled, and the remaining lectures form a tighter unit than the first eleven. The subject was briefly foreshadowed in lecture 7 where Smith discusses how "circumstances"—mainly character types—of writers affect the communication of sentiments. Amid this is a brief preview of three types of writer—the didactic writer, the orator, and the historian—almost as if to suggest that mode of discourse were a character trait. The "didactic" writer is one who aims only to teach: he lays down his proposition and proves it. The historian simply and impartially narrates facts. The orator's duty is to "appear deeply concerned in the matter"; he uses "all his art" to prove his point and "insists on every particular, exposes it in every point of view, and sets of [*sic*] every argument in every shape it can bear" (1.82). The orator uses figures, whereas the didactic writer does so less often and the historian least of all. These distinctions, however, sometimes blur: the orator occasionally uses a didactic mode, especially when his audience is "of greater judgment and higher rank than himself." The didactic writer sometimes uses the oratorical mode, though this is improper (1.83–84).

When Smith reintroduces these "writers" in lecture 12, now calling them "species of composition," he says that for each he will treat five things: (1) the "facts" that concern each; (2) the "manner" of treating the facts, by which he means mainly how they are to be described; (3) their arrangement; (4) their style; and (5) exemplary models (1.151). (1) and (2) roughly correspond with the place typically taken by invention in the classical canons of rhetoric, and his statement a few paragraphs later that he will treat "how [facts] are to be expressed, in what order they are to be arranged, and in what expressions the idea of them will be best conveyed" (1.153) clearly shows that his intention is to parallel to the first three of the five traditional canons. Yet his scheme flattens invention and style into nearly the same matter, under the rubric of "expression." A standard view of Smith's rhetoric is that invention is absent—that, as Vincent Bevilacqua holds, he trusts invention to the prior application of Baconian experimental method (566). But this is inaccurate. Smith's only explicit statements on invention come late in lecture 25:

I might now . . . proceed to point out the proper method of choosing the arguments and the manner of arranging them as well as the Expression. But directions
of this sort can seldom be of any advantage. The arguments that are to be used
before a people cannot be very intricate; the Proposition generally requires no
proof at all and when it does the arguments are of themselves so evident as not to
require any elaborate explanation. . . . And in generall in every sort of eloquence
the choise of the arguments and the proper arrangement of them is the least difficult matter. The Expression and Stile is what requires most skill and is alone capable of any particular directions. (2.138)

Taking a misperceived cue from Cicero and Quintilian, he dismisses "topicks"
as "a very slight matter and of no great difficulty." (In lectures 28 and 29, he
apparently thinks better of this and provides a lucid, if brief, account of *stasis*
theory under his discussion of judicial rhetoric, updating it for contemporary
legal practice and even directing his students to Quintilian for more detail.)
But his close linking here of choosing with arranging, as well as his statement
about audiences suggest that he is addressing not discovery as a whole but the
narrower matter of selecting from content already discovered. In fact, Smith
does not wholly eradicate discovery from rhetoric nor, as the Ramists had
done, does he put it under the aegis of some other discipline.

Rather than enumerate anything like the classical heuristic theories of the
topoi or *stasis*, however, Smith is almost solely concerned with the way description presents objects, particularly those "internal" objects that are not
immediately present to the external senses, such as intentions or sentiments
of others. As the rather vague term *manner* may suggest in (2) above, this de-
scriptive invention is regulated by his theory of propriety. This may in part
explain why, when he finally gets to his full analysis of his three genres of
composition in lecture 18, Smith refers to them as "stiles" (2.37): he simply
does not make a sharp distinction between the discovery of subject matter
and its disclosure through appropriately styled speech. There is precedent for
this in the rhetorical tradition, wherein figures of speech have sometimes
been tasked with heuristic functions. (The *Rhetorica ad Herennium*, for example, lacking a system of topical invention, counts *definitio* as a figure). But as
we've seen, Smith is almost hostile to figuration, subordinating it entirely to
propriety, which for him performs heuristic work.

Smith presents two methods of description. First is the direct method, by
which one describes "severall parts that constitute the quality" one wishes to
express about an object; it is essentially enumerative and fits the commonplace
definition of description. The second method is something altogether original
with Smith, and is a direct entailment of his theory of propriety. In "indirect

description," the writer or speaker describes "the effects this quality has on those who behold it" (1.160). It should already be apparent that description here is treated in terms more traditionally associated with the discovery of arguments: the relation of parts to wholes (division), cause and effect, and testimony.[8] Smithian description, then, is inventive: A description of an object that is adapted through propriety to the multiple circumstances attending the situation is an argument about what is the case. It may be objected that description is not necessarily argument; but this depends on one's epistemological orientation. From the point of view of a social-construction theory of knowledge, every description is selective and hence an argument about reality. Even from a more realistic point of view, every description must deal with custom, convention, or empirical association in the same way that traditional rhetorical argument must be discovered out of reputable opinion, or *endoxa*, as Aristotle called it. Charles Griswold notes that one of Smith's central ideas in *TMS*— that moral conscience depends on the co-orientation of moral actors within a social realm—is reminiscent of Aristotle's concept of *endoxa* (1991, 219). In *LRBL*, Smith is interested in description as a way of communicating sentiments, which are not simply states of raw affect but are which are emotive, dispositional judgments about reality, and as such they abet the clear disclosure of that reality in communication.

There is a hint that Smith's own epistemological convictions tend toward the skeptical in that he has little to say about direct description, though perhaps this is evidence more of caution than thoroughgoing skepticism. In lecture 14, he treats direct description of natural objects, noting that there is little to help communicate an accurate image of such objects, as "no words can convey an accurate idea of the arrangement of objects unless they be accompanied by a Plan," that is, a visual diagram (1.177). The best one can do is describe their parts in the way that seems easiest, and let the reader "arrange them to himself in the manner that best suits his taste"; if the objects occur in succession, one should maintain the chronology (1.179). Curiously, man-made objects that are completely human contrivances are best described indirectly—"We form a much better idea of these works from the effects they have on the beholder than by any description of their several parts"—whereas man-made objects that imitate nature (such as paintings) are susceptible to direct description, which is capable of tracing the symmetry between the original and the imitation (1.180–81). If this is skepticism, it is a much milder form than that of a Gorgias or Hume.

As might be expected of a rhetorician who holds that communication of appropriate sentiments by sympathy is the mark of eloquence, Smith says that indirect description is "in most cases by far the best." This is especially the case, he will show in lecture 15, in addressing complex and abstract matters of human character and action. The only real exception is in representing violent emotional states, which are beyond all language; the best a writer can do is "barely relate the circumstances the persons were in, [or] the state of their mind before the misfortune and the causes of their passion" (2.7, see also 1.182). This comports with his view in *TMS* that painful emotions are difficult to sympathize with (6.3.14). The problem with direct description in most cases is that it is in a literal sense "uninteresting": it is not likely to present the subject matter as being related in any way to the interests of an audience: "[N]o action, however affecting in itself can be represented in such a manner as to be very interesting to those who had not been present at it, by a bare narration where it is described directly without taking notice of any of the effects it had on those who were either actors or spectators of the whole affair" (2.5). While either method can work for describing external, physical objects, the indirect method is the *only* way to describe "internall invisible objects" such as sentiments (1.182), because they are not immediately present to our senses, nor do they have distinguishable parts (1.162). Hence, they are also the more difficult to describe. Direct description of such objects is likely to be unintelligible (1.192).

Even "external objects"—Smith adopts Addison's trinity of the beautiful, the grand, and the new—are usually best presented through indirect description. Here Smith further details the method: in describing the effects of objects on the mind or body, one must first take care to know the character and disposition of the person who is the dative of those effects. Certain characters, that is, "fit one for that certain passion or affection of mind" (1.162). Thus, a beautiful object is best sensed by one with a serene and calm state of mind. By coordinating indirect description with a fitting spectator, the rhetor thus presents a more compelling, "interesting," persuasive view of the object, in effect summoning that spectator's character as testimony. The internal effects produced in the audience through this mimetic triangulation are admiration, desire, and/or hope toward the object. Whereas in classical rhetoric the rhetor chooses arguments appropriate to the situation, through Smith's indirect description the rhetor reconstitutes an appropriate spectator through whom to refract a presentation of the object of discourse.

Smith offers similar but more truncated explanations for the reaction to new and grand objects, but then gives up on this task, echoing Hermogenes' testimony to the daunting problem of specifying appropriateness in the face of so many rhetorical variables:

> [I]t would be both endless and useless to go thro' all these different affections and passions in this manner. It would be endless, because tho' the simple passions are of no great number, yet these are so compounded in different manners as to make a number of mixt ones almost infinite. It would be useless, for tho' we had gone thro all the different affections yet the difference of character and age and circumstances of the person would so vary the affects that our rules would not be at all applicable. (1.166)

In the face of such kairotic complexity, one must trust one's own natural judgment and knowledge of human character to create the appropriate description.

Smith appends to this discussion a few miscellaneous techniques for strengthening descriptions: make description "short and not taedious" (1.173), and use multiple objects "tending to the same point" (1.167), the technique known in classical theory as amplification. To amplify, he again insists on the value of indirect description as a bolster to direct description. But amplification too is subject to rules of propriety: the multiple elements must be "suitable" to the object, consistent with one another, focused on the most striking aspects of the object, and not too numerous. Faults in any of these may confuse, conflict or dilute the intended emotional impact of the description.

Digressio: Rhetorical Propriety and Sight

In lectures 12 through 16, Smith produces a rich and innovative theory of rhetorical description, or ekphrasis. One of the more striking elements of his discussion is the regularity with which he analogizes linguistic and visual representation. In lecture 13 for example, Smith turns equally to poets (Virgil, Milton, Thomson) and painters (Titian, Rosa, Poussin) to exemplify his theory of indirect description as refracted through a specatator.[9] In describing a waterfall, for instance, Virgil "strengthens the Picture by describing a traveller astonished and surprised on hearing it below him"; likewise, Titian made a rocky landscape more agreeable by adding a goat to the scene, but he made it more agreeable yet when he added "a shepherd lying along on the ground and diverting himself with beholding [the goat's] motions" (1.168). To amplify, one should synecdochally "choose out some minute circumstances which concur in the general emotion we would excite," just as a painting of flowers or fruit will "represent the down or the dew, which is not what is commonly observed altho to it the fruit and the flowers owe their Lustre." Again and again Smith deploys such visual analogy. Later in the lectures, even where description per se is not his subject, the visual remains a common point of reference, for example in lecture 21 where he draws on painting to clarify aspects of historical narrative (1.87), or in lecture 26, where he analogizes the etiology of splendor in Roman fashion to that of the Roman penchant for grand rhetorical style (2.162). Smith's purpose seems to have been to establish a close correlation between aspects of discursive propriety and visual perception, suggesting, albeit without philosophical rigor, that they have the same phenomenological deep structure. This idea merits closer treatment, for it is basic in Smith's rhetorical thought and key to understanding the interdisciplinarity of his work. My analysis of Smith's interest in the visual both extends and illuminates the ancient connection between visual perception and propriety in speech; it should deepen the prior section's discussion of the heuristic functions of appropriate description, and it will foreshadow a similar correlation Smith will make between sight and moral conscience in *TMS*.

In lecture 8 Smith refers to description as "the art of painting or imitation" (1.105), a metaphor likely borrowed from Dubos and extended in lecture 13. Painting was clearly an abiding interest with Smith, who, in an essay titled "Of the Nature of that Imitation which Takes Place in What are Called the Imitative Arts," discusses in detail the source of aesthetic pleasure derived from painting. By the nature of the medium, he writes, painting, like sculpture, produces not exact resemblances of objects but leaves some disparity between the object and the imitation, which in turn allows works of art to "carry, as it were, their own explication along with them, and demonstrate, even to the eye, the way and manner in which they are produced." (As we shall see, in *TMS*, the modification of sentiment required by moral propriety similarly supplies the kind of contextual information as to how the sentiment was "produced," which in turn allows spectators to sympathize.) Artistic production causes spectators to admire the ingenuity of the artist, but this is not merely admiration of raw skill. The skill includes a "manner"—that is, an ability to communicate sentiment. Even an untutored spectator, he says, will discern how the disparities between original and imitation enable artwork to "represent, with so much truth and vivacity, the actions, passions and behavior of men" (*EPS*, 185).[10]

Verbal description as a kind of "painting" or "picturing" is important to Smith's rhetorical theory because stylistic propriety calls for the accurate communication of emotion or sentiment; pictures, like emotions, are not linguistic constructs, nor do they admit of neat or easy (some would say *any*) linguistic representation. (Smith himself is skeptical: he notes in *TMS* (7.4.3) that in their descriptions of the virtues and passions, the ancients explained

the nature of those subjects "as far as language is capable of ascertaining.")
This commonality may in part explain why pictures provoke emotional response more readily than do words, and why words describing visible objects
do so more readily than do words about invisible, abstract things. But a picture that is agreeable to spectators and which wins admiration does not represent objects transparently, without disparity, as do mirrors. Smith similarly
argues in "Imitative Arts" that coloring statues makes them more realistic but
degrades their artistic and emotional power (*EPS,* 181); after their initial introduction, mirrors cease to be wonders altogether (*EPS,* 185–86). In a
painting there is still some "modification" which allows the imitation to
communicate "actions, passions, and behavior" (*EPS,* 185). By comparison,
language translates its objects into a wholly different medium, hence modi-
fying them all the more radically, which accounts for both the difficulty and
yet also the potential power of verbal description.

   If language is to do its work with propriety then, it will do well to ap-
proximate the work of picturing, which is a more primitive and immediate
capacity, one closer to directly perceived phenomena than is verbal representation, whether those phenomena are external (a building, the ocean) or internal (indignation, joy). This is why for Smith the most effective way of
communicating sentiment is not to use direct reports, which merely name
emotional states ("She is angry at Paul"): despite the name "direct" they are
already once removed from the object. Instead he recommends indirect description ("Her anger at Paul's rudeness took hold of everyone"), which first
takes account of the very capacity for having an emotion or a sentiment in a
particular way and in specific circumstances and also begins to contextualize
it for the audience.[11] In other words, Smith is saying, we have the best
chance of communicating a sentiment regarding some object to a hearer or
reader if we first implicitly bear witness to the capacity for emotional response in another spectator of the object. The communicated description is
"indirect," but it is of an experience that is in closer contact with the object
than a verbal account that merely names the sentiment. This co-spectator's
sentiments about the object mediate the hearer-reader's experience of the
object and help make it real to him or her. Through sympathy, the spectator
helps bring out the object's real "lustre."

   By insisting on the superiority of indirect description, Smith introduces
something like a stereoscopic effect which strengthens the audience's sense
of the object. This is demonstrated in the examples from Virgil and Titian
cited above: the key element common to both is the presence of a spectator.
Similarly, Smith observes that Shakespeare's descriptions had an advantage

over those of Spenser, because Shakespeare wrote in dialogue, and the resulting split perspective of multiple perceivers left it always in Shakespeare's
power to "make the persons of the Dialogue relate the effects any object had
upon them" (1.160). This process of indirect description functions as what
might be called "pathetic invention" in Smith's theory of communication. It
is a form of invention that trusts its work to stylistic propriety: The rhetor
must first have an appropriate sentiment toward an object (which presumes
having a certain "gentlemanly" *êthos* cultivated and educated in civilized society), then the rhetor must use the method of description suited to the
object and the aim of the discourse. The superior tactic is almost always the
indirect method, which refracts the sentiment through the sensibility of another spectator of the object. As will be shown in the next chapter, this basic
process is equally at work in Smith's moral theory, for precisely this mechanism—reference to a spectator—is the foundation of moral propriety in
TMS. It is so for much the same reason that indirect description is a key element of stylistic propriety: language has a limited ability to represent sentiments directly, and yet because of the way language implicates a complex
web of elements, it can, when used with propriety, overcome this limitation.

Perhaps the most striking thing about this aspect of Smith's thought is the
way it recalls *to prepon* in its most ancient sense, which denoted the conspicuous visual appearance of an object. Smith treated the science of vision in an
early essay, titled "Of the External Senses," and some of his remarks there reinforce the idea that his use of the visual sensory channel to discuss propriety
in verbal description is not just a convenient metaphor for him, but an inevitable comparison rooted in a process of conceptualization common to
both visual and linguistic media. His essay largely abstracts Bishop Berkeley's
Theory of Vision (1709). Following Berkeley, Smith believes that "[t]he objects
of Sight and those of Touch constitute two worlds, which, though they have
a most important correspondence and connection with one another, bear no
sort of resemblance to one another" (*EPS* 150). There is arbitrariness in visual
signification because the tangible world is three-dimensional, the visible
world only two-dimensional. Either through instinct, reason, or experience—
Smith admits he cannot say which—the imagination applies the rules of perspective to translate two-dimensional visual sensory data into apprehension of
the three-dimensional tangible world. Then Smith adds something not found
in Berkeley's theory: he notes that the "precision and accuracy" of this per-
spectival perception differ as they are "of more or less importance to us" (*EPS,*
151, 152). Things nearby tend to be of greater importance, and so we sense
their full dimensionality more accurately than we do that of things distant.

Different people may have different acuities in this as well, owing not only to different natural endowment in ocular structure, but also to the "different customs and habits" attributable to their occupations. Given these comments, "importance" in this passage is equivalent to "interesting" in his discussions of rhetorical propriety; it must be determined by a sentiment or subjective judgment. Just as the oldest known meaning of *to prepon* as "conspicuous appearance" was widened to encompass meanings having to do more with the representation of objects and persons through apt diction, character, emotion, and stylistic tone, here Smith has begun to widen visual appearance to encompass the variables of sentiment and habit.

The arbitrariness of visual signification suggests to Berkeley an explicit comparison to language which no doubt influenced Smith. Berkeley first makes the comparison in his treatise as a way of explaining the difference between primary and secondary objects of vision (respectively, sensory data, and mental apprehensions of the correspondence between these data and the objects of touch). Likewise, spoken language is an interaction between sensory data (physical sounds) and the mental apprehension of correlations between these data and the objects of language. So familiar are we with this operation of language, writes Berkeley, that we tend to overlook this fundamental binary structure; in fact, the ingrained habit of overlooking this in language is one of the causes of confusion between the primary and secondary objects of vision (1: 51).[12] This comparison resurfaces more forcefully later in the treatise, in a remark that all but erases its metaphorical quality, and Smith quotes it directly: "The objects of sight . . . constitute a language which the Author of Nature addresses to our eyes, and by which he informs us of many things, which it is of the utmost importance to know" (1:147; *EPS,* 156).[13] Smith repeats the reference to a visual language five more times over the next eight paragraphs.

Despite the underlying arbitrariness of this signification, however, Smith concurs with Berkeley that "certain visible objects are better fitted than others to represent certain tangible objects" (*EPS,* 156; cf. Berkeley 142, 152). Then again, Smith notes with Berkeley that language *does* attain this "fitness" on a higher level: "When custom, indeed, has perfectly ascertained the powers of each letter; when it has ascertained, for example, that the first letter shall always represent such and such a sound, and the second letter such another sound; each word then comes to be more properly represented by one certain combination of letters of characters, then it could be by any other combination." (*EPS,* 157)

Smith is not mainly analyzing language here but using it with Berkeley as an explanatory comparison to sensory processes; had he been discussing language, he might have further extrapolated Berkeley's insight from the phonological to the semantic level to arrive at something like Ferdinand de Saussure's concept of semiotic motivation (cf. Saussure, 132). Yet another step would have taken him to grammar, which (from Smith's point of view) attempts to describe or formalize the customs of syntax into rules of fitting expression. Lastly, he might have extrapolated further to composition, which, though allowing far greater flexibility in what constitutes proper expression (due to the larger number of syntagmatic elements and all the variables of situation), still aims to transmit accurately the sensed nature of an object to an audience.

Thus, the language of vision is related to the rules of propriety in composition as an ideal. This is all the more true in that the objects of sight are not merely sensory data but also secondary mental effects that come to be connected to tangible objects through the association of ideas (*EPS*, 163). In a parallel way, language is tasked with reflecting not only visible objects but also the effects of "invisible, internall" ones through indirect description. To some degree, composition compensates for language's imprecision by being able to communicate not only directly about objects, but also indirectly about the sentimental effects of objects, whether visible or invisible. Such indirect communication supplies a context for interpretation from which, in turn, hearers or readers gain a sense of the reality and/or truth of the object(s) about which a writer or speaker communicates. Berkeley has this parallel in mind when he remarks that we see distance and magnitude "in the same way that we see shame or anger in the looks of a man"—that is, through empirical association (1:65). He repeats this point in regard to faintness, explaining analogously that "a word pronounced with certain circumstances, or in a certain context with other words, has not always the same import and signification that it has when pronounced with some other circumstances, or different context of words" (1:73). Smith is most interested in character as a contextual cause of such effects, and in emotions and sentiments, which are the effects themselves. Whereas cause and effect is traditionally seen as a *topos* of invention, in Smith's theory, stylistic propriety regulates the use of cause and effect as a mode of presenting the objects of discourse.

There is even a sense in which discursive propriety is assumed in "visual language" as Smith and Berkeley understand it: the "speaker" of visual language is the "Author of Nature," who "speaks" in a language fit to him. This language "is not liable to that misinterpretation and ambiguity that languages of human contrivance are unavoidably subject to" (1:152; *EPS*, 158). The Author of Nature furthermore "informs" the audience—human beings—

about a subject that is "of the utmost importance to us to know" in a perspicuous "language" suited to His didactic purpose. Through the "universal language" of the Author of Nature, writes Berkeley, we are "instructed how to regulate our actions in order to attain those things that are necessary to the preservation and well being of our bodies as also to avoid whatever may be helpful or hurtful and destructive of them" (1:147; *EPS*, 168). Although Smith's theory of propriety has less to say about the way audience affects style than about the way subject, character, and emotion affect it, Smith notes that this concern for what is "important" and "interesting" (in a literal sense) always implicitly governs the appropriateness of description: "It is only the more important objects that are ever described; others less interesting are so far from being thought worthy of description that they are not reckon'd to deserve much of our attention" (*LRBL*, 2.1).

Visual propriety was for Berkeley a proof of the existence of God.[14] "I have found that nothing so much convinces me of the existence of another person as his speaking to me," says Berkeley's Alciphron, in the dialogue of the same name (1:6). Likewise, the mastery of so many variables of visual situation—"[t]he instantaneous production and reproduction of so many signs, combined, dissolved, transposed, diversified, and adapted to such an endless variety of purposes, ever shifting with the occasions suited to them"—testifies to the existence of "one wise, good, and provident Spirit" (1:14). Though Smith is silent on this particular matter, he is adamant in his rhetoric lectures that propriety of style testifies to the reality of the rhetor's sentiments, which in turn have probative value as to the object(s) of the rhetor's discourse.

Propriety in the Styles of Composition (Lectures 17–30)

The second half of the rhetoric lectures (17 through 30), takes up the "stiles of composition" previewed in lecture 7. Smith's tripartite typology of historical (or narrative), didactic, and oratorical discourse has often been seen as the central contribution of *LRBL*, for it widened the rubric of "rhetoric" to include traditionally nonrhetorical modes of discourse and set a pattern for approaching the study of discourse through such modes. With some variation, they continued to be followed by such influential figures as Hugh Blair and George Campbell, eventuating in the "current-traditional" approach that dominated composition into the twentieth century (Howell 1971, 405; Carter, 7). This aspect of *LRBL* is no doubt of significance, but it should not be allowed to eclipse the conceptual centrality of propriety in the first half of the lectures. Though not an explicit focus of the latter lectures, propriety continues to be a strong undercurrent, guiding Smith's discussion of the adaptations writers should and do make within each of the styles of composition. Smith's point in artificially designating these types of discourse was not to make them rigid templates for the production of discourse (in fact, he does not always keep them straight, more often than not discussing principles that apply severally in them, and indicating that they can and do overlap in practice), but to illustrate the relevance of propriety throughout all discourse (including poetry). The aims of discourse—to narrate facts (historical style), prove propositions (didactic), and persuade audiences (oratorical)—typically involve matrices of circumstance (in particular the cultural setting and the character of the rhetor) that require "suitable" content, arrangement, and form of expression. Smith's focus is always the appropriate adaptation to circumstance (an oft-repeated term), as he clearly asserts even before his first mention of the three styles in lecture seven: [T]he various styles in stead of being condemned for the want of beauties perhaps incompatible with those they possess may be considered as good in their kind and suited to the circumstances of the author" (1.79). In the latter lectures, Smith is most intent on providing examples that demonstrate this rule. He clearly intends his theory of propriety to carry forward, and he regularly refers back to the earlier lectures, especially to his theory of ekphrasis. His concern with writing and speaking as means of communicating "sentiment" is consistent throughout and applies even to traditionally nonrhetorical discourse: "[T]he same sentiment may often be naturally and agreeably expressed and yet the manner be very different according to the circumstances of the author. The same story may be considered either as plain matter of fact without design to excite our compassion, or in a moving way, or lastly in a jocose manner, according to the point in which it is connected with the author" (1.76–77). Throughout this section, I will adopt Smith's terminology of referring to these types as "styles," but it should be kept in mind that the term has a far wider application than usual, encompassing typical subject matter; the rhetor's character, emotions, and intentions; arrangement; modes of description; and use of stylistic devices. Smith reflects this in his use of various terms to designate these "styles," referring to types of "writer" (1.79ff), "stiles" of composition (2.13ff), "species of writing" (1.116), or "methods of writing" (2.97).

Smith begins with the historical or narrative style, not only because it is used, he says, in the other two styles, but clearly because it interests him most: he takes up the subject for six full lectures (17 through 21, and 27), and he mentions it frequently throughout, as if narrative were essentially paradigmatic and normative. He has the least to say about didactic, claiming that the rules of history writing can suffice for it as well, "with a few alterations" (2.74) having to do mostly with arrangement; otherwise, rules for didactic are "very obvious" (2.97). Even his treatment of oratorical composition, which ranges over methods applicable to the three Aristotelian fields of practice—demonstrative (epideictic), deliberative, and judicial—refers to the standard of history writing, as in lecture 27 where he takes up the unusual subject of speeches within histories mainly to show that they typically have none of the adaptive features of the actually situated oratory he describes in his immediately preceding discussions of deliberative rhetoric.

Yet through and through, Smith's historiography is itself governed by propriety and situatedness. Perhaps this will appear less surprising when we consider that for Smith history writing is a species of *rhetorica docens*: its aim is "not merely to entertain" but "it has in view the instruction of the reader" (2.16). As such its mission is not so different from the appropriate communication of sentiments (moral judgments) described in the first half of the lectures: "It sets before us the more interesting and important events of human life, points out the causes by which these events were brought about and by this means points out to us by what manner and method we may produce similar good effects or avoid Similar bad ones" (2.17). Those causes are either external events or internal motives of historical actors (terms probably derived from Addison); the appropriate method depends on the situation—that is, the temperament of the historian, and whether or not the writer was a participant in the action (2.v.20, 26). Situation further governs the use of direct or indirect description to this end, and once again it is the indirect method that is "preferable" and "proper" (2.28), for it allows us to "enter into the concerns of the parties" (2.95). Indirect description yields the added benefit that, thus sympathetically engaged, the reader can "with patience attend to the less important intervening accidents," which otherwise would be an inappropriate digression from the narrative chain (2.29). Whereas the indirect method was inapt for the description of violent emotion, it is well suited to actions whose effects are "strong," because those actions are "interesting." Historical facts, then, do not speak for themselves. The historian is charged not just with revealing them, but with "setting them in as interesting a view as he possible can" (2.38), raising "sympaticall affections" in the audience (2.16). The historian can even inspire sentiments and include observations and reflections "not so properly made in the person of the writer" (2.43) by inserting them into speeches made by actors within the narration. To be an "impartiall narrator" (1.83)—the phrase obviously resonates with the *TMS*'s "impartial spectator"—the narrative writer is not to be affectless or numb to human sentiment, for then the historian would have no sense of the "interesting" and no ability to convey the nature of historical reality.

Smith offers in lectures 19 and 20 what he calls a "history of historians," which in part affords an entertaining digression, but also leads him to reflections on the relationship between situation and narrative invention. The first historians were poets centrally concerned with the "marvellous" who therefore wrote in "the language of wonder" (2.45). As audiences became more sophisticated, however, historians moved to the different subject matter of "affecting and interesting passions and actions"—first in poetic tragedy, but later in prose, as societies (such as the Roman Republic) developed commerce, achieved greater security, and cultivated a refined taste in manners and the arts (2.63). Historians (here, Tacitus) simply adapted to the changed situation, doing what was "suitable" for their times and the characters they themselves developed partly in response to those changes. Smith then asks (lecture 21) if there are essential differences between historical poetry and prose. Verse is simply more entertaining, and appropriate where that is the author's aim. He then shows how the well-known trinity of aesthetic criteria—unity of interest, time, and place—are all subject to this more general criterion of fitness. So long as this rule is adhered to, the unities may be violated: The orator, for example, may use much repetition; a different medium of communication (Smith again references painting) may impose spatio-temporal limits. Throughout, "propriety of character" is essential (2.90), as is keeping the length of discourse coordinate with emotions "we can best enter into" (strong emotions are not aroused in a short span of time). Here Smith describes unity of interest (for him both subject matter and discursive aim) as cognate with "propriety," "decency," and "decorum" (2.94).

Smith begins his treatment of the oratorical style with demonstrative (or epideictic), for its rules extend to the other two types of oratory. It has two methods that parallel the external and internal aspects of history: description of a subject's actions, and praise for a subject's character. As before, Smith refers us back to his theory of description. He then offers what might be called special topics apt to produce admiration and wonder (*viz.*, description of the respectable virtues) and esteem and love (*viz.*, description of the amiable virtues). With the acuity and realism characteristic of his moral analyses in *TMS* he notes an external, situational qualification, however: good fortune conduces to admiration, the more so when it is met with hardships that are overcome. Generally, demonstrative discourse calls for arrangement based on life chronology, yet even this is subject to requirements of "circumstance" which may allow a different method (2.106–109). In manner, the panegyrist generally uses ornament; arousing admiration and esteem requires correspondingly appropriate manners of expression: amplicatives and superlatives suit the former, diminutives the latter (2.104).

Were there any doubt that rhetoric is Smith's rubric for all communication, he interrupts his treatment of the oratorical style to take up didactic, presumably because like the remaining two species of oratory (deliberative and judicial) didactic involves laying down a proposition and proving it, but also because the two methods of didactic arrangement he introduces roughly parallel two methods used in deliberative rhetoric. In didactic, one may either "lay down one or a very few principles" (2.132), which then account for multiple phenomena (in effect a deductive arrangement); or one may treat the phenomena first, arriving secondarily at a single, or more typically multiple principles that account for them (essentially an inductive arrangement). The first method, used by Newton, is "the most philosophical one"; it is "vastly more ingenious and for that reason more engaging than the other" (2.133). For this reason, it may seem that Smith holds this method to be without qualification superior (which is peculiar given that neither of Smith's major published works, *TMS* and *WN*, follow such a method). But appropriate use of didactic arrangement depends on circumstances. When it was first implemented by Descartes, it won adherence simply because of its novelty, even though his work "does not perhaps contain a word of truth" (2.134). In this sense, the first method resembles narration used in deliberative and judicial rhetoric, wherein fluid and "agreeable" connections between parts of the narration distract from the weakness of the content, so that "when the adversary tries to contradict any of these particulars it is pulling down a fabric with which we are greatly pleased and are very unwilling to give up" (2.197). He notes that such narrations are not used in modern English practice partly because of this (2.206). Though Smith does not say so, clearly application of the two didactic methods depends on subject matter, circumstances, and aim of discourse. Circumstantial constraints likewise govern the use of two methods of deliberative arrangement, which he treats immediately after the didactic methods, suggesting a parallel between the two. First is the Socratic method, whereby the rhetor inductively leads the audience by gradual steps toward a conclusion, second is the Aristotelian method, where the rhetor deductively begins with a proposition, then follows with particular entailments. The former is the "smoothest" and "most engaging" and therefore is suited to hostile audiences; the latter is best adapted to favorable audiences.

Lectures 25 and 26 are ostensibly devoted to Demosthenes' and Cicero's styles, but in keeping with his extension of "style," Smith addresses not so much how their individual characters relate to their practices, but extends a theme he has already alluded to in his discussion of prose and commerce: how wider social and political circumstances shaped their oratory. In his Philippics, for example, Demosthenes was charged with rousing the Athenians, who had been made idle and inactive by "commerce and luxury" and had come to prefer private pleasure to civic duty. When Smith speaks of Demosthenes' "manner," he addresses not style, but the orator's argumentative strategy of "expostulate[ing] with them on the folly of their conduct, and shew[ing] them the practicality and advantage" of going to war. Cicero, on the other hand, adapted his practice to suit the social changes of his times—the displacement of social factions based on heredity (patricians and plebeians) with those based on affluence (optimates and populares). The new sociopolitical milieu was both conducive and responsive to Cicero's "gravity and affectation of dignity," as well as his often fashionably (though unnecessarily) extensive argumentation. For both orators, their situations and the adaptations appropriate to them had heuristic consequences: Demosthenes was led to "low and ludicrous" comparisons and examples, whereas Cicero was apt to use inflated ones (2.167–68).

Conclusions

So what had Smith's rhetoric lectures accomplished? This reading of *LRBL* has sought to show that the central and unifying concept in his theory of communication is propriety, which is understood largely in classical terms: propriety requires the adaptation of speech to the circumstances of the speech situation—principally the subject matter, the communicator's character and emotional disposition, the intended discourse aim, and the audience's ability to sympathize with the emotions and judgments of the speaker. Propriety and perspicuity are interlocked, as they had been for Aristotle, and there is a strong association in Smith's thought, as there had been in early Greek rhetoric, between propriety and sight. But what is essentially latent in the classical relation between these elements takes on a new and striking realization in Smith's theory: for Smith, perspicuity is imperfect unless the speaker or writer conveys the sentiment he intends "by sympathy" to the audience. Thus, Smith makes propriety functionally more extensive than classical rhetoricians had. By showing how propriety communicates sentiments—emotions that issue as judgments about subject matter—Smith assigns propriety both heuristic and probative roles in addition to its usual stylistic one of abetting clarity. Nowhere is this more evident than in Smith's theory of indirect description, an original contribution to rhetorical theory. Past studies of Smith's rhetoric have emphasized the importance of his ground-breaking expansion of rhetoric's domain to include virtually all forms of linguistic communication; my interpretation has sought to demonstrate that it is his innovative approach to propriety that licenses the expansion.

As we have seen, for Smith propriety is particularly implicated in the communication of moral approbation and disapprobation, suggesting that the "rules of criticism" and the "rules of morality" are fundamentally related. This is most evident in his view that indirect description is necessary to effectively convey "internal invisible objects" such as sentiments. My analysis has shown that this is because sympathy is achieved only if sentiments are accompanied by a sufficient etiological account of their unfolding in response to a set of original circumstances. In the next chapter, these characteristics of Smith's theory will ground an interpretation of *TMS* as being architectonically informed by his understanding of rhetorical propriety. As we shall see, the basic requirement for rhetorical propriety—that is, the self-regulation of sentiments according to the communicative situation so they may be "entered into" by a spectator—plays a key role in the development of moral conscience.

CHAPTER 5

Propriety in The Theory of Moral Sentiments

“The desire of being believed, the desire of persuading, of leading and directing other people, seems to be one of the strongest of all our natural desires. It is perhaps, the instinct upon which is founded the faculty of speech, the characteristical faculty of human nature.” This statement by Adam Smith appears not in his rhetoric lectures but near the end of his treatise on moral philosophy (7.4.25). Smith published *The Theory of Moral Sentiments* in 1759, while he held the Chair of Moral Philosophy at the University of Glasgow. During that period (1752–1763), he continued to deliver his lectures on rhetoric and belles lettres, and clearly there was much fruitful interaction in Smith's mind between his theorizing on both subjects. This chapter will explore in greater detail a point alluded to several times in the last chapter: namely, the centrality of Smith's concept of rhetorical propriety to his ethical theory. Its aim is to show that for Smith, the nature of rhetorical action as he describes it in *LRBL*—its epistemological conditions, its situatedness in particularity and contingency, and its expression in a manner appropriately adapted to these conditions—made it the originary site of moral thinking, the medium through which humans first take cognizance of moral being.

Charles L. Griswold has recently made a compatible argument about rhetoric and ethics in Smith's thought, but it should clearly distinguished from the aim of this chapter. Griswold convincingly demonstrates how rhetorical surface features of *TMS* (he points to Smith's use of a protreptic "we," his hypothetical, literary, and dramatic examples, and the organization of the text) enact, reinforce, and harmonize with Smith's method of moral inquiry (1999, 48–75). Smith's rhetorical practice, that is, constitutes his ethical metatheory.

Griswold claims his purpose is not to use the categories of discourse in *LRBL* to taxonomize or otherwise analyze *TMS* (1991, 215). While my central argument is compatible with Griswold's conclusions, my focus and approach are significantly different. Instead of drawing insight from the rhetorical features of *TMS* into Smith's theory of ethical inquiry, this chapter does use the rhetorical theory of *LRBL*—not Smith's categories of discourse, but his theory of rhetorical propriety—to gain insight not so much into Smith's theory of ethical inquiry (though my reading will support Griswold's) as into Smith's theory of moral conscience itself. Indeed, a further aim of this chapter will be to take the consequences of this reading of Smith's moral philosophy as grounds for seeing *TMS* as having made a significant contribution to rhetoric. Whereas Griswold is concerned with how rhetorical practice informs Smith's view of the proper method to be taken by moral philosophers, I will be primarily concerned with the way Smith implied and applied his own stated conception of rhetorical propriety in his account of the development of conscience in moral agents.

To be sure, in Smith's view there is an inevitable parallel between what moral philosophers should do as rhetoricians and how moral agents in fact rhetorically interact with one another. Thus, in a passage (already quoted in the previous chapter) that is key to understanding Smith's rationale for approaching ethical theory (and metatheory) through rhetoric, Smith compares the rule of justice to the rules of grammar; the rules of the other virtues he likens to the rules of composition. The former are "precise, accurate, and indispensable"; the latter are "loose, vague and indeterminate" and present a goal to be reached for more than a certain means of attaining it. One can learn to write grammatically by observing rules, but this will not lead to "elegance or sublimity" of writing. Thus, ethics and rhetoric share a fundamentally situational problem: the rules of action beyond what justice requires, like the rules of composition beyond grammar, help us not by telling us what to do in all circumstances, but by enabling us "to correct and ascertain, in several respects, the imperfect ideas which we might otherwise have entertained of those virtues" (3.6.11). Ultimately, however, mere rules, as Smith had also indicated in *LRBL*, will not accommodate us "to all the different shades and gradations of circumstance, character, and situation, to differences and distinctions which, though not imperceptible, are, by their nicety and delicacy, often altogether undefinable" (6.2.1.22). Only through the mechanism of the impartial spectator—which, I shall argue, is parallel to the operation of propriety in rhetoric—can we reliably take account of these.

The Theory of Moral Sentiments is an eclectic, unusual book which, though briefly popular during Smith's lifetime, has never been accorded high status in the read canon of ethics treatises. Presumably this is because it has been seen as merely derivative of Shaftesbury, Hutcheson, and Hume (though this is hardly accurate) and also no doubt because it has been eclipsed by attention to *WN*. One of the peculiarities of *TMS* is that it contains no distinct statement of epistemological or metaphysical premises: there is nothing comparable to Locke's *Essay*, nothing like book one of Hume's *Treatise*, nothing even so sketchy as the first chapter of Hutcheson's *Inquiry* undergirding Smith's moral philosophizing (Morrow, 69). But did Smith mean to wholly ban such concerns from ethics? A letter of 1786, in which he comments on John Bruce's just-published *Elements of the Science of Ethics on the Principles of Natural Philosophy* hints as to his attitude: "It is as free of Metaphysics as is possible for any work on that subject to be. Its fault, in my opinion, is that it is too free of them" (*Corr.*, 261). In the last book of *TMS*, Smith says that ethics asks two questions—one practical: What constitutes excellent and praiseworthy character? and the other of purely speculative interest: By what power of the mind do we come to know and prefer this character (7.1.2)? Smith's answer in *TMS* to the latter, epistemological question is the "immediate sense and feeling" of sympathy, which he distinguishes from self-interest, reason, and an autonomous moral sense. But sympathy is laid down in *TMS* as something of a psychological absolute, a natural instinct—the only sensible alternative to these other systems—whose inner workings are either too obvious or, perhaps conversely, too obscure to be amenable to further analysis. Yet John Millar's testimony (quoted in chapter 1) that Smith thought the study of human communication to be the "best method of explaining the various powers of the human mind, the most useful part of metaphysics," suggests that Smith's theory of rhetorical propriety given in *LRBL* supplies the missing propaedeutic material.

It might be objected at the outset that this analysis is based on an equivocation—that Smith used propriety in two distinct and unrelated senses, one for propriety of moral action, one for propriety of speech. As evidenced by Smith's review of Johnson's dictionary, he was quite sensitive to the confusion that can be caused by ambiguity of reference, and he does occasionally refer separately to both "propriety of action" and "propriety of speech" in *TMS*.[1] At the same time, however, he was clearly aware that speech is a kind of action, and that propriety of speech plays an indispensable role in the mind's ability to grasp the very idea of moral action. Given that other terms were available to him, his use of "propriety" in both settings can only mean that he thought it was a concept common to both fields of inquiry.[2] This is evident from the very first lines of his ethics treatise.

A Theory of Persuasible Sentiments

TMS opens with a salvo aimed at the philosophers of self-interest, Thomas Hobbes and Bernard Mandeville. The title of part one, "Of the Propriety of Action," clearly positions his attack: instead of beginning with a contradiction of their view by asserting benevolence as the fundamental human motive (as Hutcheson had done), Smith asserts that howsoever humans are inclined to act out of selfishness, they are also naturally disposed to sympathize with others. In terms that recall the close connections made in *LRBL* between clarity, appropriateness, and vision, Smith asserts that sympathy is based on the pleasure derived either from "seeing" the condition of another or from having been "made to conceive it in a very lively manner" (1.1.1.1).[3] A fundamental reality of the human condition is that we have no capacity to feel directly what others feel—we exist in a state of "division," as Kenneth Burke puts it—but, according to Smith, we sympathize with others because the imagination allows us to conceive for ourselves something of what others experience: "By the imagination we place ourselves in his situation, we conceive ourselves enduring all the same torments, we enter as it were into his body, and become in some measure the same person with him, and thence form some idea of his sensations, and even feel something which, though weaker in degree, is not altogether unlike them" (1.1.1.2). But imagination is not wholly autonomous in this function: It is moved to sympathy only "in proportion to the vivacity or dulness of the conception" it receives of the witnessed condition (1.1.1.2), and sympathy often does not arise at all without full knowledge of the causes of such a condition (1.1.1.7). As an example, Smith points out that we are unlikely to sympathize with another's anger unless we know what motivates it; in fact, lacking knowledge of the cause of another's anger, we tend to sympathize with the person who is the object of the anger, for the cause of that person's fear or resentment at being the object of the anger is readily evident as the anger itself.

So how does the imagination acquire a perspicuous and causally informed conception of sentiments? In the case of some of the passions (Smith names joy and grief—the sorts of violent emotion that, as he had pointed out in the *LRBL*, resist expression in language), we can gain contextual knowledge through direct observation—by "seeing it," as he says in his very first sentence. A moment's reflection, however, will easily suggest how liable to error this is.[4] As the Ramist Bernard Lamy had written in the opening of his *Art of Speaking:* "We may speak with our Eyes, and our Fingers, and make use of those parts to express the Idea's [*sic*] which are present to our minds, and the Affections of our Wills: But this way of Speaking is not only imperfect, but troublesome" (Hobbes and Lamy, 180). Furthermore, Smith points out, the effects of emotions such as joy and grief, for example, ordinarily "terminate" in the person who feels them in a way that directed, transactive sentiments such as resentment do not so end. Smith implies that these latter emotions are more important as moral sentiments (as opposed to raw, spontaneous, "terminal" emotions) because they involve goods and evils not simply as happenings, like the weather—not simply as fortunate or unfortunate events over which we have no control—but as transactions between individuals. The emotions that most readily beg for approval or disapproval are also the ones that get the bulk of Smith's attention. When Smith does take up "terminal" emotions such as joy and grief, he analyzes them in terms of the way they engender sympathy as a moral transaction rather as states of self-contained, individual affect. Though he recognizes that certain emotional states may cause others to register an understanding of the emotion intuitively and immediately, he shows almost no interest in such cases as the subject of moral philosophy.

The transactive emotions are what Smith means by the term *moral sentiments*. As we have already seen, sentiments have a special ontological status for Smith: They are in some measure not merely emotions but also judgments that involve human agents in the coidentification of good and bad. They do not simply terminate; they communicate. But if these sentiments are to excite sympathy, they must communicate a kind of contextual information about the causes of emotion that is not directly or reliably accessible to the eye or to any other physical sense. Even the intuitively apprehendable emotions of joy and grief, insofar as they can be considered as moral transactions and not simply as spontaneous affect, must be accompanied by more complex contextual information than the physical senses can perceive on their own if these emotions are to engender sympathy. "Even our sympathy with the grief and joy of another, before we are informed of the cause of either," Smith admits, "is always extremely imperfect" (1.1.1.9). As we have already seen, causal, contextual explanation of sentiments was a key function of indirect description.

What, then, perfects sympathy? Smith hints at an answer in the next chapter, where he remarks that "we are always more anxious to communicate to our friends our disagreeable than our agreeable passions . . ." (1.1.2.3). The disagreeable sentiment he is discussing here is resentment. Passions such as resentment prompt us to communicate, that is, to seek sympathy, because the assent of others to our state of mind removes the pain of the emotion (1.1.2.2). This remark in itself already implicates a theory of communication in his moral theory. But, Smith's rhetoric students could add, it is not simply any sort of communication that brings about such assent. There can be only one kind of communication that perfects sympathy: perspicuous and appropriate rhetorical language. Only perspicuous language can communicate the often abstract complexities of contextuality with any precision, and only appropriate language—speech rhetorically adapted to the nature of the speaker, subject, audience, and moment—discloses sentiment not as mere psychological fact or raw affect, but as a particular kind of moral state itself emanating from the causal web of emotion, character, social context, and circumstance. Any kind of emotional display, whether linguistic or physical, can convey the mere fact that a person is simply having an emotion. But only appropriately made speech reliably discloses what otherwise might appear to be merely reflexive behavior as a kind of moral action. When such communication is not rhetorically shaped in response to the constraints of situation, speaker, subject, and audience, it is often a sign of conditions, such as compulsion or ignorance, that generally exempt one from moral judgment. Or impropriety might be a sign of poorly formed moral character.

For Smith, then, to be moral is to have emotions in a certain way with regard to the factors that cause them, the situational contexts in which they arise, and others in society. Moral sentiments must be communicable sentiments, and to be communicated in a way that will reliably achieve sympathy, they must be shaped by the requirements of rhetorical propriety. Sympathy is essentially the "correspondence" of sentiments (1.1.3.2), a rhetorical consensus between moral agents, one of whom is the principal or dative of sentiment, the other of whom is a spectator.[5] If Smith's treatise argues for "virtue by consensus," as V. M. Hope has phrased it, then we should not be surpised that a theory of rhetoric, which works within consensual limits in order to modify and recreate consensus, is implicated by his moral theory (Hope, 2).

It might be argued against this view that for Smith, sympathy is a natural component of human psychology, which has no need for an artificial art such as rhetoric. But although sympathy is in fact a natural capacity according to Smith, it is also an achievement—"the endpoint of that very process of interpersonal negotiation" as John Dwyer has put it—and like many natural capacities it is "imperfect" as an achievement unless practice is guided in some manner by theory (Dwyer, 53). In this case, the theory is rhetoric, and specifically the propriety-centered rhetorical theory of *LRBL*. That persuasion is at the theoretical core of sympathy is left indisputable by Smith in chapter 3: "To approve of another man's opinions is to adopt those opinions, and to adopt them is to approve of them. If the same arguments which convince you convince me likewise, I necessarily approve of your conviction; and if they do not, I necessarily disapprove of it. . . . But this is equally the case with regard to our approbation or disapprobation of the sentiments or passions of others" (1.1.3.2).

It may appear at this point that Smith is saying that moral being is merely a rhetorical construct. He is very nearly saying this, but it must be kept in mind that the origin of sympathy is natural, and that propriety of action is based on approval or disapproval of the passions of another insofar as they are proportionate to a real and knowable cause. As my analysis of *LRBL* has shown, Smith presents rhetorical propriety as an epistemologically valid means of coming to know the causes of sentiments. These causes are not constructs of language; on the contrary, appropriate language for Smith is in a sense a construct of and an adaptive response to the causes of emotion. Furthermore, the rhetorical propriety that governs the social appearance of moral action implicit in the use of language does involve perspicuity, or suitability of discourse to object. Thus, for Smith, who believes that appropriate language is a device for presenting sentiments as they really are, morality is undergirded with a degree of realism not common to modern social-construction theories of knowledge.

The Rhetorical–Aesthetic Basis of Sympathy

If morality is so enacted by its appropriate rhetorical representation in discourse, it may likewise seem that moral truth is merely a matter of aesthetic taste, the danger implicit in Hutcheson's philosophy. To avoid this imputation Smith delineates in chapter 4 of part one two different but closely related types of judgment of propriety. Both kinds involve rhetorical propriety, but in different degrees, and the nature of the rhetorical adaptations required by each differs as the nature of the object (or cause) of each judgment differs. First, some judgments of propriety are made when the objects that give rise to emotion are "without any particular relation" to either the spectator or principal. These are judgments of the "general subjects of science and taste": they concern matters such as the beauty or grandeur of nature, the execution and ornamentation of works of art, the composition of a discourse, and so on. Such judgments inspire admiration (defined as "approbation heightened by wonder and surprise") when they are "precisely suited" to the object (1.1.4.3). Difference of opinion in these matters is inevitable due to different habits of attention and different degrees of "natural acuteness," but disagreement in matters of taste is of relatively little consequence, because the objects of taste do not "interest" those concerned (i.e., they have no direct effect on their well-being).

On the other hand are judgments of propriety where individuals *are* directly interested—where the well-being of either party is at stake. In such cases the agreement of sentiments is of great consequence: absence of sympathy in such matters breeds indignation, intolerance, and animosity, with the result that "we can no longer converse upon these subjects." This consequence must be seen as fateful for morality, because successful communication is the best hope for achieving sympathy. To avoid such an outcome, the spectator must strive to comprehend the situation of the principal in its full situational complexity: the spectator must "adopt the whole case of his companion with all its minutest incidents; and strive to render as perfect as possible, that imaginary change of situation upon which his sympathy is founded" (1.1.4.6). But all the efforts of the spectator's imagination are bound to be inadequate to this task unless the principal communicates his sentiment in such a way as to articulate that situation fully. The principal, who desires sympathy but must not alienate the spectator with the intensity of raw emotion, must then regulate the appearance of the emotion, lowering it "to that pitch in which the spectators are capable of going along with him." He must "flatten . . . the sharpness of its natural tone, in order to reduce it to harmony and concord with the emotions of those about him." (Recall that identical instructions are given to the rhetorician in rhetoric lecture 11, 1.135.) The resulting correspondence, though not exact, is "sufficient for the harmony of society" (1.1.4.7). Although it is possible that this process could occur without verbal communication, verbal communication would often if not almost always be involved. Smith makes this clear at the conclusion of the chapter, where he remarks that "Society and conversation, therefore, are the most powerful remedies for restoring the mind to its tranquillity, if, at any time, it has unfortunately lost it" (1.1.4.10).[6]

The modulation of sentiment here should be understood as rhetorical to the extent that rhetoric involves adapting communication to an audience. The principal must engage in an act of rhetorical invention, shaping the way emotions are expressed so that they achieve sympathetic assent. This anticipation of the need to persuade others effects not only the public appearance of sentiments but also reciprocally shapes the character and conscience of the principal: "[A]s the reflected passion, which [the principal] thus conceives, is much weaker than the original one, it necessarily abates the violence of what he felt before he came into their presence, before he began to recollect in what manner they would be affected by it, and to view his situation in this candid and impartial light" (1.1.4.8). Hence, propriety is not simply the self-interested achievement of humans desiring the pleasure of sympathy. By seeking sympathy through propriety, they actively transcend self-interest. It is for this reason that the virtues themselves, Smith points out in the next chapter, can be founded on this transaction between a principal moral agent and a spectator: The spectator's effort to empathize with the principal is the foundation of the "the soft, the gentle, the amiable virtues . . . of candid condescension and indulgent humanity"; the effort of the principal to modulate his passions with respect to the spectator is the source of "the great, the awful, the respectable virtues of self denial, of self government" (1.1.5.1). Smith's *TMS* thus makes explicit something implicit in *LRBL* (and much debated throughout the history of rhetoric), namely, how rhetorical theory and practice can be and are ethically formative.

It is not until this point in his treatise, *after* he has set down the idea that knowledge of the moral evolves in the thick of communicative action, that Smith uses the term *impartial spectator* (1.1.5.4). The impartial spectator, rather than being any particular spectator of a particular action by a particular agent, is a kind of internalized idealization of "every indifferent person." Over time, this projection of the social other may lessen the need for verbal communication about the context and causes of passion in particular incidences of interaction, but the essentially rhetorical quality of the modulation of sentiment remains. In his seminal essay, "The Rhetorical Situation," Lloyd Bitzer has pointed out that the essentially rhetorical nature of situations having a persuasive exigency is not lost just because the occasion to speak is not acted upon: "Rhetoric always requires an audience, even in those cases when a person engages himself or ideal mind as an audience" (7–8). In one respect, the nature of moral transactions becomes more fully rhetorical at this stage of moral development in that the communication that occurs is bound to be enthymematically premised on shared cultural knowledge—what Aristotle called *endoxa*, or "reputable opinion."

Curiously, though Smith had previously been careful to distinguish the faculty of aesthetic taste from moral judgment, he next analogizes the two: Just as acuteness of taste is not common, he writes, neither is virtue. The amiable virtues cause surprise; the respectable virtues astonishment and amazement—all reactions Smith had previously associated with aesthetic admiration (1.1.5.6). After observing that we praise and/or blame an action or passion either against the ideal standard of perfect propriety, which is never attainable, or according to how far the action exceeds what is common and therefore approaches virtue, Smith again draws the analogy to aesthetic judgment. He notes that this latter standard of judgment is "in the same manner that we judge of the productions of all the arts which address themselves to the imagination" (1.1.5.10). Why this sudden reversion to models of aesthetic judgment? It would seem that once the impartial spectator is internalized, judgment need no longer make an immediate reference to those around; judgments of moral propriety become more like judgments of taste in that one can maintain one's tastes even in the presence of those of differing tastes. It could also be that the impartial spectator is a kind of social average: the result of the sum of moral-rhetorical experience, and thus is empirically and socially shaped.

In his next chapter on propriety, Smith notes in an Aristotelian vein that propriety consists in a mean. For Aristotle virtue is a habituated mean with respect to an excess or defect of passion, and Smith likewise takes this view. Smith even points out, as does Aristotle, that the mean varies, either closer to the excess or to the defect, from passion to passion. But for Smith there is this key emphasis: propriety consists in a "mediocrity" of passion so that others may come into sympathy with one's sentiments. Whereas for Aristotle virtue was action in accord with a natural, internal *telos*, for Smith, passions "are regarded as decent, or indecent, just in proportion as mankind are more or less disposed to sympathize with them" (1.2.intro.2). Smith thus brings out the rhetorical quality of mean-based virtue. This view seems to lie somewhere between Aristotle's entelechial view and a more radical social-constructionist view of morality: The source of decency is still natural—the disposition to sympathize is instinctual even to "the greatest ruffian, the most hardened violator of the laws of society"—but knowledge of and access to this decency is mediated through a fundamentally rhetorical form of social interaction. Whereas for Aristotle the highest virtue is intellectual because of its self-sufficiency, for Smith virtue is unattainable without the help of an audience.

The Indirect Style of Moral Sentiments

As if to emphasize the discursive quality of moral sentiments, Smith occasionally refers to propriety in *TMS* as a "style." He notes, for example, that highly idiosyncratic, personal sentiments, such as love for a particular person, cannot be expected to occasion sympathy directly, and are thus literally "ridiculous"—that is, since others cannot be expected to enter into them, "all serious and strong expressions of it appear ridiculous to a third person." The person who feels such idiosyncratic sentiment "is sensible of this, and as long as he continues in his sober senses, endeavors to treat his own passion with raillery and ridicule. It is the only style in which we care to hear of it; because it is the only style in which we ourselves are disposed to talk of it" (2.2.2.1).

Those acquainted with Smith's rhetoric lectures could add that such ridicule is a kind of indirect description. The idiosyncratic sentiment is made appropriate and rhetorically effective not through direct representation of the sentiment, but by being refracted through a secondary sentiment, one that stands in for the judgment of a spectating audience. This makes sense, for if a third person is to sympathize at all with such idiosyncratic sentiments, it will not be with the principal's primary sentiment (of love, in this case), but with parallel, ancillary sentiments, such as hope for future happiness, or dread of disappointment. These sentiments directly interest us, whereas the principal's love for another person does not: "It interests us not as a passion, but as a situation that gives occasion to other passions which interest us." That Smith has in mind here his theory of description is suggested further in his next comment, which likens this case to "a description of a sea voyage": "[I]t is not the hunger which interests us, but the distress which that hunger occasions." Likewise, soothing descriptions generally "interest us most, when they are painted rather as what is hoped, than as what is enjoyed" (1.2.2.2). Smith gives a similar treatment to the representation of bodily passions: "[A]ttempts to excite compassion by the [direct] representation of bodily pain, may be regarded as among the greatest breaches of decorum . . . " (1.2.1.11). Direct representation in such cases, such as groans of pain, only calls attention to our "insensibility"—that is, our inability to feel directly and sympathize with what another is feeling. Patience and endurance of bodily pain, on the other hand, take cognizance of our social relatedness and enable the one in pain to "keep time with our indifference and insensibility." This evokes the onlooker's approval, admiration, wonder, and surprise (1.2.1.12).

Similarly, "unsocial" passions such as hatred and resentment are only made agreeable through the refractive interaction of propriety: "We should resent more from a sense of the propriety of resentment, from a sense that mankind expect and require it of us, than because we feel in ourselves the furies of that disagreeable passion." In other words, our passions are made ethical through the mediation of a set of constraints which are properly understood as rhetorical: Who is our audience? How well do they understand the context of this emotion? How well do they know us? How easily can they be expected to enter into our frame of mind? This sense of propriety, of a "cool and impartial spectator" looking on, is natural, but the motive to use it is socially organized: we wish to appear magnanimous, which is a "regard to maintain our own rank and dignity in society." Here Smith again uses the word *style* to refer to rhetorically modified passion, this time in terms that identify moral sentiments with the natural and unaffected style he advocates in *LRBL*: "This motive must characterize our whole stile and deportment. These must be plain, open and direct. . . . It must appear . . . from our whole manner, without our labouring affectedly to express it, that passion has not extinguished our humanity" (1.2.3.8). Smith is saying that we should mediate our emotions through our knowledge of how they are communicable and how their appearance in communication will in turn affect us by causing or failing to cause the sympathy we naturally desire from others. To put it another way, we shape and modulate them because of knowledge that they will be mediated through social channels, and this mediation is principally affected by our natural sense of propriety.

It may seem that this modification in the passions is a kind of *sprezzatura*: a studiously affected unaffectedness that, to use a more contemporary term, represses natural passion. But it must recalled that, as noted above, the rhetorical shaping of passion actually changes the passion itself by changing the way one is dispositionally prone to have passions in the first place. We are then morally related to our own sentiments through knowledge of their rhetorical efficacy: while our direct relation to raw emotion is pre-ethical, it becomes ethical when it is shaped because of our nature as socially communicating animals.

Ethical Invention

Just as Smith had presented rhetorical propriety in *LRBL* in such as way as to have style suffice for the heuristic part of rhetoric he otherwise felt little need to deal with, propriety as the congruity of feeling between a moral agent and a spectator can be seen as a kind of moral invention. The discovery that takes place is not of arguments per se, as in classical topical invention, but, again, of a persuasible "style," which in the process of perfecting sympathy discloses the moral nature of human action.

This point is made most evident in a footnote added to the second edition of *TMS* in which Smith responds to an objection Hume raised after the book's initial publication. Hume questioned Smith's characterization of sympathy as being always an agreeable sensation; Hume found that there were kinds of disagreeable sympathy: "[A]s the Sympathetic Passion is a reflex image of the principal, it must partake of its Qualities, and be painful where that is so . . ." (46n2). Smith handles this problem by explicitly bifurcating sympathy into a direct and an indirect response (as he had already done implicitly in his treatment of ridicule, bodily pain, and the unsocial passions):

> [I]n the sentiment of approbation there are two things to be taken notice of; first, the sympathetic passion of the spectator; and secondly, the emotion which arises from his observing the perfect coincidence between this sympathetic passion in himself, and the original passion in the person principally concerned. This last emotion, in which the sentiment of approbation properly consists, is always agreeable and delightful. The other may be agreeable or disagreeable, according to the nature of the original passion, whose features it must always, in some measure retain. (1.3.1.9n)

This bifurcation may have been suggested by its close resemblance to Berkeley's primary and secondary objects of vision, which in turn (as described in the previous chapter) are analogous to spoken language as sensory data and the mental apprehension of congruity between these data and the objects of language. One can sense here the action of a dialectical/rhetorical *topos*: The topic of similarity underlies the moral approbation of the spectator. That is, approbation is rooted in the discovery of a fundamental similarity between the emotion of the principal and that of the spectator. Moral sentiments are then quite literally "theoretical": they arise from observation of and discovery of similarities between humans and their actions.

This bifurcated response does not exist solely in the reaction of the spectator, however. For it to come about in a way that issues in sympathy, the principal must have already anticipated it in his or her "invention" of persuasibly styled sentiment. In *LRBL*, indirect description is deemed appropriate for the representation of "internall invisible objects" such as emotions because it discloses the reality and nature of such objects by first acknowledging the capacity to be humanly affected by them in a given way. Similarly, here in *TMS* the shaping of moral sentiments requires a prior consideration and acknowledgement on the part of the principal of the way in which his or her emotions will affect others. Rhetorically shaped sentiments are then a kind of recognition of the human and cultural context shared by the principal and the spectator. They stand as a probable sign of common interests, discovered, as it were, through similarity.

Propriety and Social Appearance

As suggested by Smith's remark quoted above that propriety is motivated out of a desire to appear magnanimous, his presentation of propriety agrees with the ancient Greek formulation of *to prepon*, according to which fitness or suitability, far from effecting social disappearance, conferred conspicuous regard onto speech and action. Smith's remarks further illuminate the connection he often makes between propriety and vision. In a chapter titled "On the Origin of Ambition and of the distinction of Ranks" (1.3.2), he observes that the desire for social distinction—"the pursuit of wealth, power, and preheminence"—arises out of the consciousness of "being the object of attention and approbation" before an onlooking public:

> The man of rank and distinction . . . is observed by all the world. Every body is eager to look at him, and to conceive, at least by sympathy, that joy and exultation with which his circumstances naturally inspire him. His actions are the objects of the public care. (1.3.2.1)

Contrarily, those in poverty have little hope of achieving such sympathy; their "shame" is really a fear of being "out of the sight of mankind" or of not being the object of "fellow-feeling" due to the "extremity of their distress." The propensity of mankind to sympathize with the condition of superiors, which "arises from our admiration for the advantages of their situation," is the foundation of social hierarchy and social order (1.3.2.3).

Although it is not truly the case, Smith writes, inferiors tend to imagine that their superiors live in "a perfect and happy state" (1.3.2.1). This introduces something of a political problem for the great, who must render themselves worthy of their superiority over their fellow-citizens. This is not accomplished by knowledge, industry, patience, self-denial, or any other virtue, but by speech and action exactingly adjusted to the variables of the situation: "As all his words, as all his motions are attended to, [the man of distinction] learns an habitual regard to every circumstance of ordinary behavior, and studies to perform all those small duties with the most exact propriety." This art of propriety enables him to "make mankind more easily submit to his authority" and is "sufficient to govern the world" (1.3.2.4).

It is no simple matter to appropriate such propriety, however. The "coxcomb" who merely imitates the manner of the great and "affects to be eminent" is regarded with contempt. Propriety for the inferior consists in waiting for the right opportunity; Smith advises him to "be forward to engage in all those situations, in which it requires the greatest talents and virtues to act with propriety." Times of war or "civil dissention" are the most propitious, because the confusion offers moments in which the ordinary person can "draw upon himself the attention and admiration of mankind"; a man of rank, on the other hand, avoids all such "public confusions . . . from a consciousness that he possesses none of the virtues which are required in such situations, and that the public attention will certainly be drawn away from him by others" (1.3.2.5).

Smith is no aristocratic utopian. He points out in the last chapter of part one that the tendency to admire, "almost to worship," the rich and powerful at the expense of attention to the poor and miserable is "the great and most universal cause of the corruption of our moral sentiments" (1.3.2.1). Such admiration diverts our attention and our interests from their proper objects of wisdom and virtue. The situation is lamentable, Smith finds, and even "extraordinary" given that such admiration is "disinterested," but it is so widely the case that it must be regarded "in some respects" as natural (1.3.3.4). The danger of this proclivity is that it can drive a wedge between what is praised and what is truly praiseworthy. The only way to reestablish congruity between praise and praiseworthiness is through a consideration of the merit and propriety derived from the suitableness of manners to the conditions in which they arise. Fortunately, he finds, the conditions of the majority—"the middling and inferior stations"—are such that the paths to fortune and virtue are the same: "Real and solid professional abilities, joined to prudent, just, temperate and fair conduct, can very seldom fail of success" (1.3.3.5).

The Rhetoric of Utility

To act justly, according to Smith, we must in a sense act rhetorically, imagining ourselves in a rhetorical situation wherein our aim is to persuade others of the propriety of our sentiments and actions with regard to all of the circumstances that attend them. This involves not merely postulating and internalizing an audience, but actively viewing ourselves as a spectator would: we must "view ourselves not so much according to that light in which we may naturally appear to ourselves, as according to that in which we naturally appear to others" (2.2.2.2). Only then are we inclined to bring our passions to a level that others can go along with. If we fail in this, we inevitably incur the "justly provoked resentment of all rational creatures" and isolation from the community (2.2.2.3).

This state of affairs, Smith notes, is socially and politically useful. Justice, enforced by our "consciousness of ill-desert" working through myriad small rhetorical transactions aimed at achieving propriety, is the cornerstone of society (2.2.3.4). But Smith is careful to distinguish between the final and efficient causes of justice. Social utility is the terminal outcome of justice; an "orderly and flourishing state of society" even has an aesthetic appeal which we take delight in contemplating (2.2.3.6). But we are not really motivated to do justice by the appeal of its usefulness; it is simply the "intrinsic hatefulness and detestableness" of injustice that initially moves us against it. One of the curious aspects of this point, Smith notes, is that it is rhetorically ineffective. In fact, the argument cannot really be advanced before an audience that thinks otherwise:

> [W]hen we are asked why we should not act in such or such a manner, the very question seems to suppose that, to those who ask it, this manner of acting does not appear to be for its own sake the natural and proper object of those sentiments. We must show them, therefore, that it ought to be so for the sake of something else. Upon this account we generally cast about for other arguments, and the consideration which first occurs to us, is the disorder and confusion of society which would result from the universal prevalence of such practices. We seldom fail, therefore, to insist upon this topic. (2.2.3.8)

But despite the efficacy of consequentialist rhetoric, the motive to do justice is not founded in a desire to preserve society: "We are no more concerned for the destruction or loss of a single man, because this man is a member or a part of society, and because we should be concerned with the destruction of society, than we are concerned for the loss of a single guinea, because this guinea is a part of a thousand guineas, and because we should be concerned for the loss of the whole sum." On the contrary, our regard for society generally is "compounded and made up of the particular regards which we feel for the different individuals of which it is composed" (2.2.3.10).

Later in the treatise, Smith devotes all of part four to an extended critique of utility, reinforcing the importance of the sum of "particular regards" to the development of moral conscience. He argues again that philosophers are mistakenly drawn to utility as an explanation of human kindness and cruelty by its rhetorical effectiveness. As a species of beauty—that is, as a measure of the "fitness of any system or machine to produce the end for which it was intended" (4.1.1)—utility is intrinsically appealing. It is useless to talk about just political ends as a means of inspiring public virtue in audiences little inclined to feel it; instead, one will be "more likely to persuade" by focusing on "the great system of public police" that confers public advantages (4.1.11). Furthermore, as a kind of philosophical explanation, utility derives great appeal from the way it elegantly generalizes to fit many particular cases. "But," Smith argues, "it is in particular instances only that the propriety and impropriety, the merit or demerit of actions is very obvious and discernible." While utility may "enliven" and "enhance" moral sentiments, "[i]t is only when particular examples are given that we perceive distinctly either the concord or disagreement between our own affections and those of the agent. . . ." Virtue, then, must not be studied in "an abstract and general manner," removed from the plane of actual moral transactions (4.2.2). The very notion of moral conscience presupposes "communication with society" and "the idea of some other being, who is the natural judge of the person that feels them" (4.2.12). This is identical to Aristotle's conception in the *Rhetoric* of audience as both spectator and judge.

Moral Propriety and Rhetorical Situation

The origin of our sense of justice is, then, in the particularity of "fellow-feeling" (2.2.3.10). Smith's focus on the particularity of multiple "regards" suggests that the situated, kairotic quality endemic to rhetorical action is why he puts the sense of propriety at the core of moral conscience, just as he had put it at the center of his theory of communication. Rhetoric is always concerned with the here and now, with particular actions presented for judgment in particular contexts: This woman is praiseworthy; this man is guilty; this course of action in this situation is expedient or just. The special relevance of Smith's use of propriety as a gauge of the fitness of sentiments to such particular contexts is that propriety—particularly as it is revealed in speech—seems uniquely capable of conveying a sense of human commonality and shared grounds of interest.

Nowhere is this made more evident in *TMS* than in the last section on merit and demerit (2.3), which deals with the impact of fortune on moral relevance. There Smith is concerned with addressing what he finds to be an "irregularity of sentiment" (2.3.intro.6). Whereas praise and blame bestowed on actions ideally should be and justly are accorded only on the basis of the "intention or affection of the heart . . . the propriety or impropriety . . . of the design" from which actions spring—and not on the basis of either the bodily movements involved ("the event of the action") or the good or bad consequences that follow from actions—in practice this is not the case. (Recall here Smith's discussion in *LRBL* on the impact of good fortune on admiration.) It seems obvious to Smith that the actual motions involved are not worthy of moral attention: "He who shoots a bird and he who shoots a man . . . perform the same external movement," yet the moral status of the action is greatly different in each case. Consequences also should not be morally relevant, for they depend on fortune, over which no agent has control. And yet, Smith admits, in practice outcomes do have an effect on moral sentiments. That Smith takes notice of this "irregularity" can be credited in part to his characteristic determination neither to look away from nor to discard the realm of appearances—that is, the realm in and with which rhetoric characteristically must operate. While the aim of his treatise is to discover and analyze the praiseworthy and blameworthy, he does not look askance from the way humans typically and actually practice praise and blame. Nor does he merely recognize this inconsistency to dismiss it as some kind of human ineptitude. Furthermore, the ingeniousness of Smith's response to this would-be challenge to his system is in some measure owed to his having used rhetorical propriety as a paradigm of moral propriety.

Smith's first step in dealing with this problem is to articulate with more precision than he has yet done the nature of the sympathetic identification that occurs between principal agents and spectators of moral action. Here his focus is on gratitude and resentment, which are the principal expressions of merit and demerit. Gratitude and resentment, he finds, are properly bestowed only on animate objects capable of sensing for themselves the pleasure or pain of the gratitude or resentment that are returned for good or harm done. Furthermore—and this is the critical distinction—the objects of gratitude and resentment must be capable of recognizing the way those sentiments work to reveal the agent of good or harm as a discrete individual:

> What gratitude chiefly desires, is not only to make the benefactor feel pleasure in his turn, but to make him conscious that he meets with this reward on account of his past conduct, to make him pleased with that conduct, and to satisfy him that the person upon whom he bestowed his good offices was not unworthy of them. What most of all charms us in our benefactor, is the concord between his sentiments and our own, with regard to what interests us so nearly as the worth of our own character, and the esteem that is due to us. We are delighted to find a person who values us as we value ourselves, and distinguishes us from the rest of mankind with an attention not unlike that with which we distinguish ourselves. (2.2.1.4)

Conversely, injury prompts resentment against the injurer because of the "little account which he seems to make of us, the unreasonable preference which he gives to himself above us, and that absurd self love, by which he seems to imagine, that other people may be sacrificed at anytime, to his conveniency or his humour" (2.3.1.5).

Hence, the propriety of gratitude and resentment are connected to one of the most ancient characteristics of rhetorical propriety: far from achieving social disappearance by simply hewing to culturally constructed protocols of speech and/or action, appropriate gratitude and resentment acknowledge and articulate a shared sense of human individuality and uniqueness. Gratitude given to a benefactor communicates to him—"make[s] him conscious" of—the fact that the intention and affection of his past conduct has been a good thing for the beneficiary in particular. What this kind of moral propriety has in common with rhetorical propriety is rather broad but still evident here: in rhetorical situations, the appropriate adaptations of language to circumstances is the rhetor's central way of acknowledging the particularity of the situation, and of displaying his or her good will with respect to the audience in that set of circumstances.

Having thus accentuated the rhetorical dimensions of gratitude and resentment, Smith has little difficulty explaining the "irregularity of sentiment" whereby humans to some extent inevitably thank, resent, praise, and blame not solely on the basis of intentions, as "cool reason" would have it, but also with respect to consequences of actions. The cause of this behavior, he explains, is the same simple fact of the human condition that lies behind sympathy: humans have no ability to know directly the internal motivating sentiments and intentions of others. "[T]he great Judge of hearts" has placed such knowledge "beyond the limits of every human jurisdiction." Thus, the "shadow merit" that causes us to praise the good intention that actually comes to fruition more highly than the one that fails or remains latent is "salutary and useful" (2.3.3.2) in a rhetorical way. It tends to promote in others the exertion to follow through on intentions, and it discourages the conviction that nice thoughts suffice for good deeds (2.3.3.3).

Rhetorical Vision and Moral Self-Knowledge

In part three of his treatise, Smith extends his analysis of the way experience of particular moral transactions develops into a sense of duty or moral conscience. The nature of communication, especially communication that praises and blames, is absolutely central to this: "[W]ithout any communication, with his own species, [a human creature] could no more think of his own character, of the propriety of demerit of his own sentiments and conduct, of the beauty or deformity of his own mind, than of the beauty or deformity of his own face" (3.1.3). If society is the "mirror" or "looking-glass" with which one views one's moral self, then communication is the light. We gain awareness of the morality of our own sentiments and actions after we perform our first "moral criticisms" on others; when we realize that others are doing the same thing with us, we likewise try to understand ourselves morally, so that we might make ourselves "agreeable" to others. We achieve this when we internalize the rhetorical situation: each moral agent divides him or herself into "two persons"—one of whom is spectator and judge, the other of whom is principal agent and object of judgment.

But in winning the agreement of others with our moral state or action, it is not enough, writes Smith, to seek mere praise. To do so is vanity. We seek not just to win praise but achieve real praiseworthiness, not to avoid blame so much as to avoid blameworthiness. But how do we learn to distinguish these? The internal division of self into spectator and agent, judge and person judged, audience and rhetor, provides us with the means to make this crucial distinction. Only when we move to view ourselves through the eyes of others, secondarily and indirectly, can we actually see ourselves as we are. There is thus no distinction in Smith's moral ontology between human being and social being. In order to distinguish what is praiseworthy from what is praised,

> [W]e must endeavor to view [our character and conduct] with the eyes of other people, or as other people are likely to view them. When seen in this light, if they appear to us as we wish, we are happy and contented. But it greatly confirms this happiness and contentment when we find that other people, viewing them with those very eyes with which we, in imagination only, were endeavouring to view them, see them precisely in the same light in which we ourselves had seen them. Their approbation necessarily confirms our own self-approbation. (3.2.3)

This mechanism has much in common with the theory of indirect description presented in *LRBL*: just as we better discover the nature of certain objects by considering the sentiments they occasion than by directly observing their immediately sensible qualities or parts, we discover who we are and the moral status of our actions by imaginatively putting ourselves in the reactive position of observers. Not only does this distance us from the potentially corrupting effect of our own sentiments upon the judgments we may have of them (e.g., selfishness does not appear selfish from a selfish point of view), but it allows us to compare our self-judgments to the judgments others make of us, the agreement of which strengthens our sense of the praiseworthy. It is as if we gain by this internal division of self a stereoscopic view of sentiments that reveals them in their full dimensionality, as they actually are, not simply as affect but as a kind of transaction that affects others. In other words, we begin to distinguish moral action from mere behavior. From this point of view, the love of praiseworthiness is not derived from the love of praise; to the contrary, the love of praise is derived from the love of praiseworthiness (3.2.2.3).

The need to undergo this process derives from the same set of conditions that gives rise to rhetorical practice generally and to the need for propriety in expression specifically. Lacking moral experience, we are uncertain about the propriety and merit of our sentiments, and hence we are anxious to communicate with others, learning their opinions (3.2.24). The importance of securing the agreement or avoiding the disagreement of others with our own sentiments is inversely proportional to our certainty in their propriety and the accuracy of our judgments (3.2.16). Thus, paradoxically, while it is through the practice of persuading others to agree with our moral sentiments that we become more adept at distinguishing the merely praised from the actually praiseworthy, over time we become less dependent on—though never completely free from—the judgment of others in forming moral judgments. As Smith notes elsewhere in an Aristotelian vein, the virtuous agent internalizes the judgment of the impartial spectator by habit, not just in order to make his sentiments outwardly appear in a certain way, but so that his sentiments actually become a certain way: "He does not merely affect the sentiments of the impartial spectator. He really adopts them" (3.3.25). Yet virtuous habits cannot be learned abstractly: even agents with the highest natural disposition toward goodness require opportunities and situations that demand the exercise of the impartial spectator. At least some of the time, moreover, there is a need for "the presence of the real spectator" (3.3.36–37).

This irony is given further treatment in a section Smith included in the second through fifth editions of his work. It is noteworthy here because this passage again links metaphors of vision with the internalized, rhetorical interaction of moral agent and impartial spectator, and it further explains the relationship between moral conscience and the kind of opinion that operates in rhetorical action. Our vision of the divine or natural law that would ideally guide our conduct, Smith writes, is always "faint and feeble": "the great judge of the world" has set a "degree of obscurity and darkness" between the "weak eye of human reason" and "eternal justice." This is for good reason: if we knew his plan perfectly, "it is absolutely impossible that the business of society could have been carried on." Hence, humans answer not directly to God but to the "inferior tribunal" of human judgment, "which is continually before their eyes." But human judgment is often inaccurate and occasions disagreement, so there must be a "superior tribunal" to which appeal can be made and which can reverse the judgments of mankind. This tribunal (Smith's repeated use of this term suggests he had a rhetorical venue in mind) is the one "established in their own breasts": the internalized impartial spectator or conscience. The paradox is that the authority of the impartial spectator "is in great measure derived from that very tribunal, whose decisions it so often and so justly reverses" (3.2.30n).

Smith explains this as follows: Early in life, we attempt to win universal approval from everyone; later we learn that this is impossible—opinions and interests are too diverse, and inevitably others fail to see the way that our conduct is "perfectly suitable to our situation." This is what prompts us to set up the impartial spectator as an internal audience that judges our conduct. It allows us to transcend in some measure the vicissitudes of local, fallible, human judgments, and yet it only arises in the first place from the discovery of our own particularity and the way our particular actions may issue from and be adapted to particular circumstances and causes others cannot see. Just as "the eye of the body" discerns objects "according to their real dimensions, as according to the nearness or distance of their situation," it is only through the mediation of the impartial spectator, the "natural eye of the mind," that "we can ever see what relates to ourselves in its proper shape and dimensions; or . . . ever make any proper comparison between our own interests and those of other people" (3.2.1). In other words, the impartial spectator helps disclose what is really "interesting." It has been the purpose of this chapter to argue that this kind of moral vision—the ability to see just how our interests are interrelated with the interests of others, which is so crucial to successful and, indeed, to virtuous rhetorical practice—is made possible for Smith through an element of rhetorical practice itself: the need to adapt discourse appropriately to an audience. This is perhaps Adam Smith's most significant contribution to rhetorical theory, and its implications for both contemporary rhetorical practice and ethics will be examined in the next chapter.

CHAPTER 6

Conclusions, Provocations

The purpose of this study has been twofold. First, I have attempted to explain the basic problem of propriety and delineate some of the main ways it has been articulated and dealt with in rhetorical theory up to the time of Adam Smith. Second, against this backdrop, I have described Smith's own treatment of rhetorical propriety, argued that while it shares much with classical sources, his treatment of it is insightful and new, and shown that it serves as a key bridge between his ideas on communication and ethics. While it is possible to view the ideas in *LRBL* as informed by those of *TMS*, I have argued that there is a good case for doing the reverse, and that this is a potentially revealing approach to Smith's thought and to our knowledge of rhetorical propriety. In this chapter I shall consider some further implications of my reading of Smith. First, what does this reading of the role of rhetorical propriety in Smith's moral philosophy mean for our understanding of his most famous work, *The Wealth of Nations*? Second, what implications does this reading have for assessing the validity of his ethics? And lastly, what value might his theory have for contemporary rhetorical practice and pedagogy?

Commerce, Civil Society, and Rhetorical Education

A commonplace about *The Wealth of a Nations* is that it is more often quoted than read. At least one reason for this is the striking and memorable nature of many passages in Smith's writing; he was indeed sharply attuned to the way his own rhetorical choices would affect the reception of his ideas. A good example is probably the most famous line in *WN*, in which Smith vividly, succinctly, and alliteratively rejects natural benevolence as a fundamental motive among humans, particularly in their commercial relations. "It is not from the benevolence of the butcher the brewer or the baker that we expect our dinner, but from their regard to their own interest." Less often cited is the context for this famous sentence.

Immediately before and after his remark, Smith is not on the subject of benevolence per se, but is discussing the centrality of persuasion as a means of achieving the cooperation necessary in a civil society. Humans sometimes fall back on a primitive, animal-like means of persuasion—a "servile and fawning attention" that appeals to the benevolence of others—to achieve their interests, but in civilized society, this is inefficient. There is simply no time for it. Furthermore, such appeals are only effective where close friendships exist, and these are relatively few within the life of any individual, whereas the needs of the individual in society are many and constant, extending to many other individuals, and requiring the "cooperation and assistance of great multitudes." Instead, "he will be more likely to prevail, if he can interest their self-love in his favor, and show them that it is for their own advantage to do for him what he requires of them."

This discussion comes in a chapter titled "Of the Principle which gives occasion to the Division of Labour" (*WN*, 1.2). The division of labor does not originate in applied reason, Smith argues, but emanates from "a certain propensity in human nature . . . the propensity to truck, barter, and exchange one thing for another." Curiously, scholars who cite this point as a cornerstone of Smith's economics rarely attend to his further suggestion that this "trucking disposition" might be simply spontaneous in human nature, or it might be "the necessary consequence of the faculties of reason and speech." Though he demurs from further speculation in *WN*, in both versions of his earlier *Lectures on Jurisprudence* (*LJ*), Smith put a finer point on this observation. He notes in the first version, dated 1762–1763 (the same year as the extant *LRBL*), that mankind's commercial disposition is founded on "the naturall inclination every one has to persuade." Smith saw humans as being in a constant state of persuasion, perpetually trying to alleviate the discomfort of disagreement through the endless making and remaking of social consensus. "And in this manner," wrote Smith, "every one is practising oratory on others thro the whole of his life" (*LJ*(A), 352). The *Lectures on Jurisprudence* dated 1766 (*LJ*(B)) concur:

> The real foundation of [the division of labor] is that principle to perswade which so much prevails in human nature. When any arguments are offered to perswade, it is always expected that they should have their proper effect. If a person asserts any thing about the moon, tho' it should not be true, he will feel a kind of uneasiness

in being contradicted, and would be very glad that the person he is endeavoring to perswade should be of the same way of thinking with himself. We ought then mainly to cultivate the power of perswasion, and indeed we do so without intending it. Since a whole life is spent in the exercise of it, a ready method of bargaining with each other must undoubtedly be attained. (*LJ*(B), 493–94)

In neither *WN* nor *LJ* did Smith develop these ideas further, and he did not explicitly bring his rhetorical theory to bear on how persuasion issues in our commercial propensities other than to note that prose is the "natural language of commerce." And yet it takes little effort to see that though we cultivate persuasion without intending it, the intentional study and informed practice of persuasion would only improve the performance of persuasion so basic to commercial society. Of course, critics of liberalism and capitalism would lament any practice that abetted the "success" of such a society, arguing that it would always come at the price of injustice to significant portions of the population. If, as I have argued Smith's system shows, the study and practice of rhetorical propriety is conducive to the development of virtuous character, then at least it can be said in defense of Smith that such character may play as a check against the rapaciousness of individuals and groups who seek to exploit others.

In *TMS*, as we saw, Smith similarly held that "[t]he desire of being believed, the desire of persuading, of leading and directing other people, seems to be one of the strongest of all our natural desires" (7.4.25). And in *TMS* Smith does make use of his theory of rhetorical propriety in describing the way humans "bargain," *mutatis mutandis*, not in material goods, but in emotions, interests, and moral judgments, the successful communication of which, it is reasonable to speculate, would only benefit a commercial society. As he presents it, moral virtue is potentially the unintended consequence of the exercise of rhetorical propriety. Given that Smith held persuasion to be at the core of the economic, political, and moral nature of human beings, this study's analysis of rhetorical propriety in his ethical thought may further point to the underlying unity of Smith's "civilizing project," to borrow an apt phrase from Jerry Z. Muller.

Smith scholars have long come to appreciate the essential coherence between *TMS* and *WN*—that Smith had not imagined two separate worlds, one governed by sympathy, the other driven by self-interest. "The Adam Smith Problem" that once found conflict between the works has been largely dismissed as the product of uncareful reading and a failure to grasp Smith's own rhetorical strategies adapted to addressing different audiences in different ways for different purposes. The mere fact of Smith's early interest in rhetoric has played some role in scholars paying more attention to these discursive methods, serving as a general impetus for examining rhetorical elements of the works that perhaps made the consistency of vision between *TMS* and *WN* less than immediately obvious. However, scholars generally have not reverted to the content of the lectures themselves to ask what bearing those ideas had on his other work (but for a few who have taken sides over whether Smith did or did not practice himself the "Newtonian" method of arrangement).[1] This study then provides one more site of connection between *TMS* and *WN*: Persuasion is fundamental to commercial society; prose is the medium of commercial rhetoric; propriety is fundamental to effective prose communication. The most effective mode of communication will also be conducive to the development of virtues that may counteract exploitative tendencies of individuals.

The society Smith intended to promote in both his works was no libertarian utopia wherein a free-market "invisible hand" takes care of all. As Muller reminds us, for Smith central government is indeed necessary, but "only desirable when coupled with a panoply of social institutions which fostered self-control" (Muller, 2). My examination of the connection between rhetoric and ethics in Smith's thought suggests that rhetorical education closely attentive to the efficacy of propriety as a means of communicating sentiments ("moral observations") and shaping character is one such critically important institution, without which the liberty accruing to any society of advanced commercial prosperity will always be threatened. To say this is only to state in more particular terms what Smith himself argues in *WN*. In book five, Smith describes with unblinking clarity the deplorable state of many workers if the extreme division of labor common in advanced commercial societies is not offset by some form of education. "The torpor of [the worker's] mind renders him, not only incapable of relishing or bearing a part of any rational conversation, but of conceiving any tender sentiment, and consequently of forming any just judgment concerning many even of the ordinary duties of private life." He will be even more incapable of judging of "the great and extensive interests of his country," and useless in its defense (5.1.f.50). Clearly Smith conceives these capacities—for civil conversation, for conceiving apt sentiments, for judging the duties of private life, and for judging civic matters—as related in a causal chain. Those who have benefited from education will be not only less prone to "the delusions of enthusiasm and superstition" but:

> They feel themselves, each individually, more respectable, and more likely to obtain the respect of their lawful superiors, and they are therefore more disposed

to respect those superiors. They are more disposed to examine, and more capable of seeing through, the interested complaints of faction and sedition. . . . In free countries, where the safety of government depends very much upon the favourable judgment which the people may form of its conduct, it must surely be of the highest importance that they should not be disposed to judge rashly or capriciously concerning it.

This sort of practical wisdom that Smith approves for bettering the lives of such people as well as the safety of the states in which they live would be abetted by the kind of study and practice of rhetorical propriety described in *LRBL* and implicit in *TMS*. This perspective may thus temper claims that Smith produced a thoroughly depoliticized and essentially hegemonic rhetoric. Such is the position, for example, of Thomas Miller (202), though perhaps tellingly he bases his argument mainly on a reading of *TMS* as Smith's essential work of rhetorical theory, without any substantial consideration of either *LRBL* on its own terms or as providing a discursive basis for Smith's ethics. While it is undeniably true that Smith's rhetoric and ethics were written in the context of a society experiencing economic expansion, political assimilation, and in broad terms a transition from structures characterized in terms of civic humanism to civil liberalism, my interpretation suggests that his reidentification of civic virtue and practical reason in terms of appropriate communication does more to politicize the social sphere (albeit perhaps subtly) than to isolate or contain it so that a cartoonish "invisible hand" of the marketplace would be left undisturbed in mediating all conflicts between self-interest and public good (T. Miller, 186).

Rhetorical Propriety and Ethics

In turning to evaluate whether my discernment of a rhetorical infrastructure in Smith's ethics has any import for our understanding of his account of moral conscience, it may first be useful to reprise some of the key themes discussed in chapters 2 and 3, the better to take stock of Smith's contribution to the theory of propriety. Smith's theory of rhetorical propriety shares several characteristics with its predecessors in the rhetorical tradition. In particular, his similarity with Aristotle is noteworthy. With Aristotle, Smith makes stylistic propriety inseparable from perspicuity, and he sees moral propriety as involving a mean. Aristotle and Smith share the idea that stylistic adaptations help make discourse intelligible. Both considered the way this is true for subject matter and character; Smith provides special insight into the way it is true for sentiments as both a special kind of subject matter and a dynamic operating within rhetorical situations. Like Cicero, Smith sees mankind as having a unique natural capacity for sensing the fitting and decent, and, again like Cicero, Smith perceives that there is no understanding of the fitting and decent outside of the cultural situations in which they appear. With Cicero, perhaps most importantly, Smith sees decorum of speech and action to be closely interwoven concepts. And yet Smith differs from the classical tradition of propriety as well. With Shaftesbury and Hume, Smith holds that the cultivation of taste in the linguistic arts is capable of improving our sense of the moral. With Addison (*contra* Locke), Smith holds that appropriately chosen words may give hearers or readers a "more lively impression" of the things they stand for than vision. And yet, like so many of those who have written on propriety, Smith's concept depends heavily on the analogous relationship between verbal description and vision. Commonalities such as these are probably inevitable, not only because Smith had at least some acquaintance with the work of all of the authors discussed in chapters 2 and 3, but because the experience of propriety is so deeply rooted in the human condition.

These similarities notwithstanding, Smith's approach is ultimately unique, owing in part to his importation of a rhetorical understanding of propriety into his theory of moral conscience. I have argued that perhaps the most unusual aspect of *TMS* is that, by implication at least, Smith supplants moral epistemology with a theory of appropriate communication. He seems to prefer the kind of knowing about sentiments and intentions that is achieved through appropriate communication to other kinds of knowing. Unusual as this move is, however, it supplies Smith with a unique way of handling some of the philosophical problems posed by the concept of propriety when applied to the sphere of human action.

The theoretical weakness of propriety has always been understood to be its non-specifiability outside of particular contexts and incidences of practice. From Smith's point of view, this weakness is precisely the strength of a rhetorically conceived paradigm of moral thought. With some notable exceptions, moral philosophy has often seen the situatedness of action as a problem that theory needs to surmount through, say, a casuistically abstracted moral grammar, a "moral sense," a metaphysics of obligation, a final aim such as utility, or some other transcendent truth. By framing the operation of sympathy in rhetorical terms, Smith makes situatedness the very starting point and center of morality yet without wholly obviating theory, for the theory of appropriate and perspicuous communication describes the ways it is possible to perfect sympathy. The benefit to ethics, from Smith's point of view, is that this approach prevents theory from ever drifting away from the contextually bound nature of human action. The autonomy that can be achieved in moral conscience is made possible through the internalization of a kind of rhetorical activity, an activity that itself never ducks below the horizon of contingency and circumstance, and may (and often does) return to the real rhetorical venue where there is a real audience before and to whom one must act appropriately.

Seen from this point of view, Smith's impartial spectator concept is less a metaphysics of conscience or a moral epistemology than it is a description of a kind of perpetually situated practice. It is a practice with which, as Smith's remarks in *TMS, WN,* and *LJ* about the primacy of rhetorical experience in human life suggest, people are readily and intimately familiar. Smith's description of moral conscience as a rhetorical practice shares something with Addison's conception of aesthetic taste as a practice in that it asks for a special conception of "practice." Alasdair McIntyre has insightfully described such a conception of "practice" as "any coherent and complex form of socially established cooperative human activity through which goods internal to that form of activity are realized in the course of trying to achieve those standards of excellence which are appropriate to, and partially definitive of, that form of activity, with the result that human powers to achieve excellence and human conceptions of the ends and goods involved, are systematically extended" (1984, 187). In other words, practices so conceived open the possibility for the development of humanly praiseworthy qualities even while they are directed to achieving proximate ends that are conventionally determined and socially situated. Ends pursued as mere proximate goals of such practice (e.g., achieving sympathy, or persuading one to act) are capable of cultivating within the agents who pursue them ends that are not simply terminal outcomes but are teleologically inherent goods issuing from the human nature of those agents. The situated, conventional aspects of practices are not a hindrance, an obstacle consisting of mere appearances, but absolutely essential to the achievement of those goods. As Smith describes moral development, virtue is possible as an unintended consequence of rhetorical practice. This consequence is not merely random or fortuitous, but comes out of the nature of communication: humans cannot communicate intentions or sentiments directly to one another and so avail themselves of the adaptations of language to speaker, audience, subject, and context to do this. Smith thus rejects the either/or fallacy of a choice between foundational knowledge (or transcendent criteria) on the one hand or pure contingency of value on the other as a basis for morality.

This interpretation of Smith's moral thought may perhaps provide some grounds for tempering the rejection of his ethics by contemporary philosophers. For instance, McIntyre sees a salutary republicanism in Smith's ethics, but he tends to view Smith as participating in the eighteenth-century project of displacing Aristotelian and Christian conceptions of virtue with an emotivist conception based on virtue's relationship to the passions. McIntyre sees this shift as "not so much or at all the replacement of one set of criteria by another, but a movement towards and into a situation where there are no longer any criteria" (36). A rhetorically infused understanding of Smith's concept of moral conscience suggests that the very notion of moral "criteria" is the crux of the problem. By making rhetorical practice part and parcel of becoming-moral, Smith shows how virtue can evolve without appeal to overarching moral criteria, and yet without lapsing into either radical skepticism or relativism. Smith's philosophy of moral sentiment offers quite literally a "theory." Through observations of how people transact sympathy through communication, he implies a human teleology yet without committing to either a rationalist or emotivist essentialism. Intriguingly, this sentimentalism is tolerably compatible with recent developments in neuroscience, which have powerfully suggested a much closer convergence and interdependence between emotion and reason than most post-Cartesian moral philosophy has allowed, but that rhetoric has long understood.[2]

Another important weighing of Smith's ethics has come in the work of Allan Gibbard, perhaps the most prominent noncognitive ethicist writing today. In his *Wise Choices, Apt Feelings*, Gibbard tries to save emotivist ethics from its own skepticist and relativistic tendencies with an approach he calls "norm expressivism." While agreeing with the emotivist line that there are no moral facts (such facts are merely sentiments in disguise), he argues that moral judgments may yet avail themselves of a "modestly objective" criterion, namely, "the extent to which they compromise with ones interlocutors' preferences, and promote coordination and cooperation with them." Such "normative discussion," which involves both influencing and being influenced by others, can improve our individual normative judgments and lead to consensus. "Such socio-psychic mechanisms combine, at times, to make norms as impersonal as trees" (294). This is in part because normative discussion inevitably forces interlocutors to answer the meta-ethical question, "How do you know?" If moral demands are to be legitimate and coherent, they must answer this question with what Gibbard calls an "epistemic story." He considers and rejects various manners in which such a story could be "written." We could rely, for instance, on utter self-trust in our own individual feelings, but this would commit us to a radical skepticism about higher ethical norms. We could on the other hand invoke pragmatism, but this too can offer nothing beyond a fundamental moral relativism. (Norm expressivism ultimately offers a kind of hybrid of these two "stories" refracted through "normative discussion.") Another "story" Gibbard considers is Smith's "impartial spectator," but he rejects this as too idealized: we would have to know what such a detached observer is like—"informed, alert, sober and the like." This is a fair enough critique if one reads *TMS* by itself, for Smith does not add these stipulations. They are amply present, however, if we read the impartial spectator not as a wholly abstract "detached observer" (as Gibbard paraphrases) but as an internalized rhetorical audience applying the standards of discursive evaluation that are developed in Smith's rhetorical theory. Gibbard also objects that Smith's theory requires that "proper feelings" within a group be essentially the same, while our everyday experience tells us that "the ways it makes sense to feel" are situationally dependent. Again, the rhetorical core of Smith's ethical theory works to pull the impartial spectator down from any idealized heights into the parochial situatedness to which Gibbard insists any "normative discussion" must be responsive. And Smith's ethics, if read as underwritten by the theory of appropriate communication offered in *LRBL*, offers something rhetoricians would find conspicuously absent from Gibbard's notion of normative discussion: namely, stylistic criteria that would abet the effectiveness of such discussion. Gibbard takes for granted the *form* of "normative discussion," the style of epistemic narrative.

A more substantial consideration of Smith's concept of moral conscience has come from the phenomenologist Robert Sokolowski. Sokolowski has highlighted "the centrality of actual performances" to the philosophical task of clarifying what moral action is, and so it is not surprising that he would give some consideration to Smith's theory (1992, 261). As Sokolowski explains it, humans recognize the moral through a special phenomenological "identificational form": "A performance becomes a moral performance when it becomes wanted and done, or unwanted and averted precisely as good or bad for the target of the action" (265). He considers but rejects Smith's concept of sympathy and the "imaginative change of situation" enacted through the device of the impartial spectator as a version of this identificational form. He does so for two reasons. First, he sees Smith as being too concerned with sentiments, rather than with actions, as the substance of the moral. This causes Smith to underrate the way actions are made moral by the "understanding that informs them" (271). This is largely a valid critique. Smith does say that the appropriate object of praise and blame is solely the intention from which action "proceeds," treating action itself rather anemically, as no more than bodily motion: "He who shoots a bird, and he who shoots a man, both of them perform the same external movement" (2.3.intro.2).

The rhetorical view of Smith's concept of propriety, however, can temper this objection, by showing that what Smith held in theory he did not entirely hold in practice. As I have attempted to show, sentiments for Smith are not just raw affect but are passions that extend themselves as judgments; through the refraction of the impartial spectator they communicate and coidentify the good and bad between moral agents, and so, to a significant extent they partake in the realm of action. This is especially so in that sentiments are bound to be morally relevant mainly insofar as they are communicated through speech. Furthermore, when Smith notes that there is an "irregularity of sentiment" wherein humans in fact praise and blame actual outcomes, he is acknowledging, under pressure of his observation of rhetorical practice and even against his own premises, that actions themselves and not just the intentions that lead to them are the substance of what we call "moral." This "irregularity" is so pervasive in human affairs that Smith sees it as based in nature (*TMS*, 2.3.3.2). Intentions, as Smith treats them, are simply not knowable outside of the actions that follow from them, and the predominant way in which they are manifested to the mind is through appropriate speech. While appropriate speech action is not the only kind of moral action, it is an important, even essential kind, for, as Smith describes it, propriety in speech helps us to discern others as the proper object of our concern as individuals and hence discloses situations as morally relevant.

Sokolowski's second objection is more serious. He charges Smith with underrating the role of reason in making the coidentification of good and bad between moral agents (272). Indeed, Smith puts this recognition largely under the aegis of the imagination. Smith does grant, "That virtue consists in conformity to reason, is true in some respects, and [reason] may very justly be considered as, in some sense, the source and principle of approbation and disapprobation, and of all solid judgments concerning right and wrong"; yet reason's role is only to induce from experience "general rules of justice by which we ought to regulate our actions" (*TMS*, 7.3.2.6). The "first perceptions of right and wrong" can come only from "immediate sense and feeling" (*TMS*, 7.3.2.7).

Smith makes this plea for the "immediateness" of sense and feeling, however, in the context of a passage that is arguing against the idea that moral consciousness is *solely* an achievement of reason. Elsewhere throughout *TMS*, however, Smith treats first moral perceptions as if they often *are* mediated through the

appropriate speech that in many cases accompanies moral actions and sentiments and in many cases is already a form of moral action. On at least one occasion, moreover, Smith does seem to implicate reason in the moral-identifying
function of the impartial spectator device. Smith notes that it is only because of
the impartial spectator that we can "see what relates to ourselves in its proper
shape and dimensions; or that we can ever make any proper comparison between our own interests and those of other people" (3.2.1). The "proper comparison," which enables us to sacrifice our own interests for the interests of
others, is only made possible through the intervention of "reason, principle,
conscience, the inhabitant of the breast, the man within, the great judge and
arbiter of our conduct" (3.3.4). This passage seems to be anomalous, but it might
appear less so when considered alongside an argument advanced in chapter 4 of
this book, namely, that Smith's theory of appropriate style actually takes over
some of the heuristic tasks typically assigned to *logos* in classical rhetorical invention, as even the use of "comparison" in the passage quoted above indicates.

Nonetheless, it must be agreed that Smith greatly deemphasizes the role
of reason in moral thinking, that he mistakenly shrivels actions in their
being-done to motion, and that he too readily attributes all consequences of
action to fortune. This can be seen as a useful deemphasis for rhetorical theorists, however, for it led Smith to explore, in ways that had not been done
before, the relevance of the aesthetic qualities of rhetorical speech to the development of moral conscience. It led Smith to see in different terms something that Thomas Farrell has argued is a discovery belonging to Aristotle:
"The aesthetic status of rhetoric is directly related to what audiences are able
to discern about their own human condition" (103). In chapter 2 I have
shown that Aristotle emphasized the way this is made true through the rational aspects of rhetorical style. Without necessarily ruling out the rational
effects of style, Smith emphasized how quasi-rational and even nonrational
aspects of style may have a role to play in helping humans discern the nature
of their own condition, particularly the moral quality of that condition. The
deemphasis of the rational component of moral thinking is probably attributable in part to Smith's aim of offering his theory as an alternative to rationalist conceptions of moral thinking. Even Sokolowski notes, "It is true that
one should not simply rationalize human agency; desires, sentiments, and
ethical perceptions must be given their proper place, and Smith's analysis of
them rings true as far as it goes." Sokolowski concludes that Smith's description is "almost like" the form of moral identification he argues for (272). Perhaps the rhetorical infrastructure of Smith's concept of moral conscience
moves him a bit closer to Sokolowski's conception of moral thinking.

Propriety and Praxis

Because rhetoric is both a theory and an art, rhetoricians are perpetually concerned with the practical application of theoretical concepts, not just their explanatory sufficiency. Does Smith's view of rhetorical propriety offer anything useful for the formulation and conduct of rhetorical discourse in the present? Quite possibly. The rhetorical cast of Smith's conception of moral propriety may be useful in addressing a paradox that McIntyre notes about the nature of public moral debate. This paradox emerges from a central difference McIntyre observes between typical grounds of argument that suffice in interpersonal persuasion versus those required in public rhetoric. Some kinds of moral arguments, writes McIntyre, are deeply related to the contexts in which they are uttered: they are "field-dependent," in Stephen Toulmin's terms (Toulmin, 15). They depend heavily upon appropriateness, on performative "felicity conditions," to use Austin's term, for their persuasive effect. If I say to you "Do this" and you respond "Why should I?" I may reply "Because I wish it." If you have some particular reason for respecting my wishes (say, I am your father, or you stand to gain something from me) then I have given you (but *only* you) a reason. The sufficiency of the argument for you depends on "certain characteristics possessed at the time of hearing . . . by you." The rational force of the command "depends this way on the personal context of the utterance" (McIntyre, 9).

But in the moral debates that so engage our public sphere, such reasons would never be deemed sufficient and hence do not occur. Instead, rhetoricians tend to justify their judgments (when they do so at all) on grounds that are pragmatic ("Because it would work"), utilitarian ("Because it would please a number of people"), deontological ("Because it is your duty"), or simply dogmatic ("Because"). Such reasons can either implicitly or explicitly assume shared objective or at least intersubjective standards of judgment, yet even when they do so it is with the troubling consequence that "the particular link between the context of utterance and the force of the reason-giving which always holds in the case of expressions of personal preferences or desire is severed in the case of other moral and evaluative utterances" (McIntyre, 9). The difficulty deepens, writes McIntyre, when we view this condition against the incommensurability of the contrary premises that underlie the most abiding and also seemingly intractable moral and political controversies of our time—just war, capital punishment, abortion, euthanasia, the equitable distribution of goods and resources in society, and so on. In many cases, this incommensurability causes public debate to become "shrill" as McIntyre puts it; to this outcome I would add other more dangerous eventualities for life in community, such as intransigent radicalism and violence at one extreme, or, on the other, apathy and the relegation of public concern to the realm of private taste. If we nonetheless continue to discuss these issues in our public discourse, McIntyre suggests, it is an affirmation of our will "or at least an aspiration be or to become rational in this area of our lives" (10).

At the very least, we can say, with Aristotle and Smith, that propriety of speech as a probable sign of our good will and willingness to engage others is a significant, even indispensable, part of the overall rationality of public discourse. And yet, as Smith shows, it need not be wholly rationalized to have its effect. Propriety simply points to our root commonality as human and social in a way that the application of rational argument alone in moral matters, with its tendency toward philosophical abstraction, tends not to. The particular value of Smith's notion of propriety here is that it never leaves behind the particularity of moment, situation, context, and persons, even when—precisely when—it is in the nature of moral argument to abstract or attempt to transcend these things. Of course, "these things"—by which I mean our shared humanity and shared world—are often right there for us to see (literally, with our eyes), but by its very nature moral debate often turns our attention from them. Rhetorical propriety may serve as an antidote to this problem, as a significant connection between the theoretically derived and ostensibly objective standards to which all moral appeals point and the finite, particular instances in which they must be articulated and applied. Smith's rhetoric alerts us to the way propriety can serve as a *topos* for unifying the particular and individual with the universal even without being a rational sign of what that universal is. While propriety may involve the rational, for Smith it is not wholly the rational that gives propriety its effect of keeping us oriented toward what is in our interests as beings who share a world. Rhetorical propriety simply restores, or barring that, is significant as a willful, ongoing attempt to restore, the severed link between the personal context of utterance and force of moral justification in public. Ethical propriety in general is an inescapable artifact of the social imbeddedness of personal interests; rhetorical propriety in particular, as a quality of speech, is uniquely able to communicate this even when moral arguments themselves may fail to do so.

This point is itself abstract, so I will offer here three very brief examples of the way propriety can be and is applied heuristically in public debate. (1) While it might be exaggerated to suggest that there has been any real "progress" in the controversy over abortion in recent years, at least some writers on the subject have sought a way around incommensurable premises by examining the language that has been used to frame the problem, finding grounds of agreement through a recognition of the architectonic function of rhetorical appropriateness. On the pro-life side, George McKenna (no relation to me) has argued that the language typically used to describe abortion is inconsistent with abortion's status as a "right." He argues that the conflicted nature of this language points to the deeply conflicted feelings most Americans have about abortion, and he uses this as a starting point for a more tolerant, pragmatic, yet principled pro-life position.[3] On the other side, Naomi Wolf has argued that the often euphemistic, rights-based rhetoric of choice is inappropriate to the undeniable moral gravity of subject matter, functions paternalistically to protect women from their own consciences, and effectively cuts off from debate the one nearly universal point of agreement—namely, that abortions, legal or not, should be rare.[4]

(2) Following a cue from legal philosopher Mary Ann Glendon, the philosopher Richard Rorty has publicly spoken about the futility of "rights talk" for bringing about social justice for the poor. He argues that change must come, as it did in the civil rights era, from a widespread consensus about the actual cruelty of real social conditions. Thus, from the recognition of the inappropriateness of a certain kind of language for addressing this problem, Rorty advocates a fittingly robust, concrete, and vivid rhetoric—something like Smith's "indirect description"—which aims to hammer home the effects of human suffering.[5]

(3) Propriety bears most naturally on the broad set of controversies generally known by the deformed phrase "political correctness." The issue has lately been the object of more ridicule than debate, as backlash against attempts to regulate certain kinds of speech has unfortunately tended to make it seem as if the words we use to characterize one another are of little real import compared to our abstract, nearly absolute right to free speech. The architectonic concept of propriety that I have sketched here, however, could be brought to the discussion to help broker agreement between free-speech absolutists and would-be enforcers of *sprachregelungen* by reconceptualizing what the term *free* in "free speech" means. No doubt it would be a productive discussion, one that would evolve from the discovery that in attempting to speak appropriately, we always relinquish radical claims to absolute "freedom" of speech. If we didn't, there would be no productive dialogue over any controversy before long.[6] In this way, propriety would function productively as a *topos* for coming to understand the subject matter, by bridging our understanding of the right with a here-and-now confrontation with the consequences of offensive, divisive speech versus the possibilities of irenic, meliorative, and inclusive speech.

If "All problems can be stated as problems of communication"—so wrote the eminent philosopher of rhetoric Richard McKeon—then paths to solving them lie in the nature of communication itself as much as in the nature of the subjects about which we communicate (1988, 90). McKeon under stood that in a technological age—one with far greater aptitude for proliferating means than for thinking and communicating effectively about ends—we would face rhetorical crises of the kinds alluded to in these examples. It was McKeon's ambition that in confronting human social and political problems, we would recognize the architectonic function of rhetorical concepts, distinctions, and devices within thought, and turn from this insight to new and productive rhetorical solutions to such problems (1987). I have argued that Smith did precisely this in attempting to solve certain problems facing moral philosophy in his day. In these concluding provocations I have further meant to suggest that what served Smith might continue to serve rhetoricians today, particularly as they try to contribute to productive debate in a world defined by pervasive doubts about and disagreements over appropriate ends. Smith's notion of propriety, rooted in the fact of human emotions and our need to communicate them as sentiments, affirms the probability or at least the plausibility of a common human nature, a *telos*, yet without necessarily stating what that *telos* is. It provides a "provisional teleology," to borrow a phrase from Thomas Farrell, affirming the presence of common ends, even while we reason about means in ways that may lead us to disagree about ends (32). The practical implication of this is clear. If we are to continue debating publicly those subjects that are most intractable in our society with any hope of reaching reasonable and acceptable solutions, we must do so with a firm regard for norms of discursive appropriateness. And we would do well to follow Smith's example by making criticism of conventional excellences in discourse a central part of education. If rhetorical propriety is a practice, in McIntyre's special sense of the word, the outcome may be more than writing improvement.

Smith and Rhetoric: A Critical Note on Sources and Scholarship

Adam Smith is truly one of the titanic intellectual figures of the modern age, whose work cuts across several modern disciplines; unsurprisingly, the scholarship and other secondary writing on him is both vast and varied. It would be impossible to survey more than a tiny portion of that work here. This note simply aims to provide some preliminary guidance to researchers interested in pursuing further reading on Smith and his rhetorical theory and practice; it is limited to discussing mainly works that bear directly on *LRBL*. Those working in the very interdisciplinary field of rhetoric need not be told that other secondary materials beyond this limited scope, such as those addressing Smith's aesthetics and his method of inquiry, may pertain to their interests.

The bulk of Smith scholarship has been directed to Smith's economic thought; to a (mistakenly) lesser degree he has been studied as a moral philosopher, though this has begun to change in the last decade. Even within scholarship articulating a holistic vision of Smith as a systematic thinker and writer—a vision according with Smith's own understanding of his intellectual activity—comparatively little has been said about him as either a theorist or practitioner of rhetoric. From the time of their discovery until just recently, the rhetoric lectures were largely regarded as an interesting, perhaps suggestive, but largely inconsequential element of his thought. These circumstances pose both challenges and opportunities to scholars and students interested in pursuing research on Smith as a rhetorician.

Fortunately, there is Oxford University Press's *Glasgow Edition of the Works and Correspondence of Adam Smith*, an eight-volume set of critical editions of Smith's complete opera, including posthumously published essays, the student notes of *LRBL* and *LJ*, an index, and sundry other documents. (The Liberty Fund's Liberty Press/Liberty Classics has published an exact reproduction of the *Glasgow Edition* in inexpensive paperback.) The very inclusion of *LRBL* in this edition should be reason enough for scholars to take seriously the integrated place of Smith's rhetorical theory within his full corpus. In the words of the *Glasgow Edition*'s general editor, Andrew Skinner, "It is hoped that the most complete edition of Smith's works will facilitate perception of the fact that individually they form the parts of a single whole which embraces theories of knowledge and of communication together with the main components of ethics, jurisprudence, and political economy" (promotional copy). Those interested in the full publication and reception history of Smith's works should consult *A Critical Bibliography of Adam Smith*, edited by Keith Tribe.

The *Glasgow Edition* of *LRBL*, edited by J. C. Bryce, includes a detailed introduction by Bryce and concludes with Smith's "Considerations Concerning the First Formation of Languages." Bryce's work, particularly notable for his assertion that *LRBL* and *TMS* constitute "two halves of one system," supercedes the only other published edition of *LRBL*, John M. Lothian's 1963 edition (brought out five years after Lothian himself discovered the student notes), though Lothian's introduction may still be read with profit by those wishing to build an understanding of the historical and literary context within which Smith first delivered his lectures. The index to the *Glasgow Edition* is quite good, but researchers interested in analyzing connections between *LRBL* and Smith's major published works may also wish to consult the newly available digital *Glasgow Edition*, published as part of the Liberty Fund's Online Library of Liberty (http://oll.libertyfund.org).

A necessary step in studying any aspect of Smith's work is to gain an orientation to the whole of his corpus; much scholarly error has been abetted by reading parts of Smith's work in isolation. A solid foothold is to be gained with Jerry Z. Muller's carefully historicized reading of Smith in *Adam Smith in His Time and Ours: Designing the Decent Society*, a compact yet extensive and accurate overview of Smith's intellectual project. Muller's "Guide to Further Reading" offers a basic roadmap to some of the more important Smith scholarship beyond that mentioned here. *Adam Smith,* by R. H. Campbell and A. S. Skinner, is a short but useful intellectual biography, which includes a chapter summarizing *LRBL*. Ian Simpson Ross's biography is the most complete to date, but while it adds a great deal of useful context to the basic facts available in earlier biographies (such as Rae's), it is a rather drier read for it and provides relatively little that is essentially new. Skinner's *A System of Social Science: Papers Relating to Adam Smith* presents an overview of Smith's work intent on illustrating its overall coherence, beginning with an essay summarizing some key parts of *LRBL* and suggesting links to the rest of Smith's oeuvre. Among book-length critical works on Smith, the most extensive and philosophically oriented assessment is Charles L. Griswold Jr.'s *Adam Smith and the Virtues of Enlightenment*, of particular interest for its analysis of Smith's own rhetoric in *TMS* (his use of a protreptic first person plural narrative, vivid examples, and strategic arrangement). Given Griswold's aim of demonstrating the unified nature of Smith's corpus, however, it is disappointing that he has very little to say about Smith's rhetorical theory. A footnote suggests that material in the Edinburgh lectures (and then mainly material "not just about rhetoric") may have been of some formative importance (28n42).

Shortly after the publication of the Lothian edition of *LRBL*, several scholars produced articles on the lectures that made significant improvement over Lothian's introduction. Vincent Bevilacqua's 1965 article asserts the importance of Smith's treatment of propriety, traces the lectures' shift from traditional to belletristic rhetorical concerns, and weighs some broad similarities between *LRBL* and *TMS*. Three years later, Bevilaqua produced another article, which focuses on the general agreement of Smith's theory with eighteenth-century British and Continental attitudes toward rhetoric and communication. The same year, James L. Golden covered similar ground (seemingly unaware of Bevilacqua's earlier article), again summarizing main aspects of the lectures and giving them signal importance in the eighteenth-century shift to belletristic rhetoric. Golden is more sensitive, however, to classical and neoclassical influences in Smith that Bevilacqua tends to dismiss

The most important early analysis of *LRBL*, more probing than those thus far noted and which still stands as the major pilot study of Smith's rhetorical theory, is Wilbur Samuel Howell's "Adam Smith's Lectures on Rhetoric: an Historical Assessment." Howell's essay was first published in *Speech Monographs* in 1969, was reprinted as the largest part of chapter 6 in his *Eighteenth Century British Logic and Rhetoric*, and appeared yet again in *Essays on Adam Smith*, a collection edited by Andrew Skinner and Thomas Wilson. Howell's work is important in several ways. First, working closely from textual evidence and correcting some previous inaccuracies, he sets *LRBL* in a more precise historical context than had been done, finely gauging Smith's innovative positioning of rhetoric as the master art of nonpoetical communication against the traditional relationships between dialectic and rhetoric. Second, he carefully develops a judgment that the student notes provide an essentially accurate record of what Smith said. Third, Howell convincingly demonstrates that the lectures constitute a coherent system of rhetoric, one remarkably comprehensive, original, and valid in comparison to other contemporary theories.

Howell's verdict notwithstanding (or perhaps owing to the authority and insight of his analysis), very little subsequent scholarship has been devoted to Smith's rhetorical theory. Patricia Spence's 1974 article, "Sympathy and

Propriety in Adam Smith's Rhetoric," is noteworthy as the first attempt at a more sustained examination of the relationship between sympathy and propriety in *LRBL* and *TMS* and provides an expanded discussion of key points of complementarity; however, mainly on the evidence of *TMS*'s vastly greater detail, Spence assumes the conceptual priority of *TMS* as a source upon which *LRBL* is dependent (this book argues the opposite). Like many of the scholars who have assessed *LRBL*, Michael Carter treats the lectures' paradigmatically belletristic character, though in Carter's astute interpretation, the belletristic focus on arrangement and style in Smith was less a thoroughgoing dismissal of invention than a sublation of topical heuristics as means of ordering and styling discourse—a move rather too subtle, unfortunately, to have been consciously carried on in subsequent belletristic and "current-traditional" rhetorics.

The only scholar to fully recognize the import of Smith's theory of indirect description is J. Michael Hogan, whose excellent "Historiography and Ethics in Adam Smith's Lectures on Rhetoric, 1762–1763" takes Smith's theory of historical and narrative description as the most innovative element of *LRBL*. Hogan analyzes the role of indirect description in *TMS* where Smith proposed the value of historical examples as a source of ethical insight, though he fails to see that propriety provides both a rationale for the use of the indirect method and a check against mistaken perception and base emotion dominating the process. Susan Jarratt also attributes importance to Smith's theory of description, addressing Smith's treatment of ekphrasis in both Marxist and Freudian terms and diagnosing within his discussions of painting symptoms of a "disturbance in the construction of a rhetorically effective [Scottish] subject." (54). Hers is a stimulating reading, hampered, however, by an incomplete understanding of the manner in which appropriate description can and does work to identify truly "interesting" moral and political motives in rhetorical situations, as I have argued in this book.

A similar stance is taken by Thomas Miller, who, in a chapter of his *Formation of College English* entitled "Adam Smith and the Rhetoric of a Commercial Society," argues that Smith offered an atrophied discourse of polite self-restraint in place of a robust civic rhetoric. Not to completely dismiss Miller's conclusion, it is worth noting that his argument turns almost entirely on a reading of *TMS*, making relatively little reference either to the theory in *LRBL* (seeing there merely an "introspective" turn and, mistakenly, a wholesale rejection of invention) or to the example of *WN* as itself a potent piece of civic rhetoric. Miller's argument also problematically depends on essentially equating the impartiality of appropriate moral judgment with a state of radical political disinterest, whereas Smith clearly thought (naively or not) that virtuous self-interest pursued through a rhetorical-ethical educational curriculum would be a sine qua non for the development of a just civic politics under the realities of market capitalism.

Whereas Miller estimates *TMS* as Smith's most consequential (if inauspicious) contribution to the history of English as a discipline, a number of other scholars *have* counted Smith's rhetoric lectures as essential for understanding the role belletristic rhetoric played in the academic institutionalization of English. For instance, in "Rhetoric and the Novel in the Eighteenth-Century British University Curriculum," Paul G. Bator gives consideration to Smith's treatment of the romance as part of a broader analysis of how eighteenth-century rhetorics used rhetoric's epistemological reach across disciplines to help establish the novel as a literary form worthy of serious study. Less pessimistic than Miller is Franklin E. Court, whose *Institutionalizing English Literature* assigns more of the blame for belletrism's purported antirhetoric (and antipolitics) to Hugh Blair. Smith's program, on the other hand, is rightly seen as "a way to transcend class-based distinctions of refinement and to promote English citizenship" (20). Ian Duncan, who criticizes Miller's view as itself ideologically skewed, argues for seeing Smith's rhetorical approach to the study of literature as offering a "cultural technology" for the construction of a modern and metropolitan identity, one that is nonetheless conducive to the civic project of nation building (41).

Following the 1985 publication of Donald McCloskey's *Rhetoric of Economics* and ensuing interest in the rhetoric of inquiry (see Nelson, McGill, and McCloskey), a number of scholars have sought connections between *LRBL* and rhetorical aspects of *WN*. The importance of this line of research had been suggested as early as 1962, albeit in a little-noticed Italian article by Allesandro Guiliani. The only scholar to date to bring to such analysis an awareness of the centrality of propriety to Smith's rhetoric is A. M. Endres, who argues that in book four of *WN* Smith self-consciously mixes narrative, didactic, and rhetorical styles (as adduced in *LRBL*) for ultimately persuasive aims and in ways appropriate to both his own temperament and the predilections of his target audience. "Money Talks, Adam Smith's Rhetorical Project," a chapter in Charles Bazerman's *Constructing Experience,* reads *WN* as essentially constructed according to the Newtonian method of arrangement Smith discusses in lecture 24 of *LRBL*. Bazerman then argues that Smith's economic theory is presented in the form of a persuasive program designed according to and powered by the terms of a universe of essentially rhetorical discourse already imagined in *LRBL* and *TMS,* though with a crucial difference: by a natural extrapolation within the Smithian discursive universe, Bazerman argues, *WN* and indeed modern economics in general have supplanted language with money as the medium of persuasion. Bazerman sees a pernicious effect upon public discourse, as "talking money" drowns out other means of advancing weakly capitalized social interests. A similar ideological interpretation emerges in Mary Poovey's *A History of the Modern Fact: Problems of Knowledge in the Sciences of Wealth and Society*. Poovey combines an account of Smithian historical description and Newtonian arrangement in *LRBL* with an analysis of his application of such methods in *WN* en route to concluding that Smith's economic rhetoric in part "laid the groundwork for the method of theoretical-cum-descriptive analysis that rapidly became the preferred instrument for producing knowledge about wealth and society" (248). Her interpretation depends heavily, however, on an easy equation of linguistic argument and numerical data.

Two recent works on rhetoric and *WN* emphasize the place Smith gives to speech and persuasion at the root of the human propensity to trade. Thomas J. Lewis, relying primarily on Smith's references to persuasion in *LJ* (in fact making no mention of *LRBL*), reads Smith's view of markets as infused with a rhetoric of recognition having the potential to temper the human love of domination. In a strikingly similar argument, Andreas Kalyvas and Ira Katznelson survey a coherent discursive outlook across Smith's works to locate a basic human need for moral praise and social esteem as a fundamental element in Smith's understanding of markets. Drawing on Smith's views on sympathy and language in *LRBL*, *LJ*, and *TMS*, they argue that Smith helped transform rhetoric in the modern era into the "natural language of recognition." This position is abetted, however, by the authors' conflating of deliberative and epideictic rhetoric, an error that in turn licenses their liberal optimism. Rather than seeing a historic shift wherein money eclipses language as the dominating form of symbolic exchange, Kalyvas and Katznelson (*contra* Bazerman, whom they yet fail to cite) regard monetary exchange unproblematically as a "complex symbolic system of linguistic interaction" (570), then use this position to defend liberalism against communitarian critique.

As previously noted, Smith scholars have dispensed with the old "Adam Smith Problem," according to which self-interest as cast in *WN* and sympathy as cast in *TMS* were thought to be in conflict. Vivienne Brown, however, has resisted any movement toward a unified reading of Smith's oeuvre that might obscure what she takes to be important tensions in his work, and her analysis is critically dependent on a reading of *LRBL*. Brown's *Adam Smith's Discourse: Canonicity, Commerce, and Conscience* argues that stylistic differences between Smith's two main published works color each with a distinct and conflicting ethical status. Eschewing any possibility of reclaiming authorial intention, Brown uses Bakhtinian theory to locate a dialogic and fundamentally Stoic model of conscience operating in *TMS*, while diagnosing in *WN* a monologic, didactic and "amoral" discourse (218). Her reading is provocative and no doubt will be of interest to rhetoricians; it is not without problems, however. Leaving aside potential historicist or philosophical objections to her thoroughgoing renunciation of any claim to the recovery of authorial intention, it may nonetheless surprise readers to find that she frames her reading from the outset according to what she takes Smith to have meant in *LRBL*. This Brown mistakes for a purely antirhetorical doctrine of stylistic plainness based on a naïve theory of linguistic realism. While her approach helps keep in focus the rich textual variation in Smith's writing, this comes at the expense of a nuanced grasp of Smith's understanding of rhetoric—in particular the way rhetorical propriety requires discourses to be adapted to their differing rhetorical situations—a failing that at best weakens her alignment of discursive styles and ethical orientation in *TMS* and *WN*.

In addition to gleaning insight about Smith's main works from *LRBL,* scholars have paid particular attention to Smith's "Considerations concerning the First Formation of Languages," the essay first developed as part of the rhetoric lectures and later published both independently (in *The Philological Miscellany*, 1761) and as an appendix to the third (1767) and subsequent editions of *TMS*, there titled "A Dissertation on the Origin of Languages." One source of interest is that "Considerations" offers intellectual historians a particular and early model of a kind of conjectural genetic history that Smith also employs in his other works. In his reading of the essay, Stephen K. Land assesses this as part of his critique of Smith's assumptions, methods, and conclusions, which he takes to have been distorted in part by the rhetorical context attending their genesis. Other scholars have seen the essay's key ideas as logically prior to those of his rhetoric, and have sought to historicize Smith's views rather than critique them from the point of view of later developments in linguistics. Thus, Christopher Berry's treatment of "Considerations" contextualizes it among contemporary works in language theory, placing Smith within an "organic school" of eighteenth-century language speculation—that is, among theorists who treat language growth principally in terms of social development. As part of his analysis, Berry shows that Smith's views of the relative "perfection" of different languages accounts for the remedies *LRBL* supplies for the defects endemic to English. Likewise, Frans Plank examines the essay as a pioneering work of language typology,

offering a close critical exegesis, a comparison with its sources and prece-
dents, and some insightful connections to *LRBL* (e.g., the evolution of noninflected languages allows for the syntactical latitude required by Smith's
view that word order should correlate with the degree to which the objects
of language affect the speaker). In a very different kind of study, John R. R.
Christie uses de Manian analysis to discover a proto-grammatological awareness of "slippage" between grammar and rhetoric in Smith's prose, a representational tension Smith saw but ultimately could not reconcile and thus
had to repress. Christie's diagnosis stems from metadiscursive comments in
Smith's writing, but also from Smith's view in "Considerations" of the figural
origins of grammar and the consistency of this position with ambiguities in
Smith's treatment of grammar and figuration in *LRBL*. As Christie's provocative essay suggests, there is a great deal more that might be said about the
relation between Adam Smith's theory and practice of rhetoric.

Notes

Chapter 1. Smith and the Problem of Propriety

1. In his critique of the modern reliance on a radically subjectivized idea of reason, Max Horkheimer similarly saw that "[i]f tradition, so often denounced in modern and scientific and political history, is now invoked as the measure of any ethical or religious truth, thus truth has already been affected and must suffer from a lack of authenticity no less acutely than the principle that is supposed to justify it. . . . The very fact that tradition has to be invoked today shows that it has lost its hold on people"; Max Horkheimer, *Eclipse of Reason* (New York: Continuum: 1947), 33–34.
2. Lanham specifically cites Richard Harvey Brown's concept of reason as "isomorphic with the 'decorum' of classical rhetoric"; Richard Lanham, *A Handlist of Rhetorical Terms* (Berkeley: University of California Press, 1991), 46. See Richard Harvey Brown, "Reason as Rhetorical: On Relations among Epistemology, Discourse, and Practice," in John S. Nelson, Allan Megill, and Donald M. McCloskey, eds., *The Rhetoric of the Human Sciences* (Madison: University of Wisconsin Press, 1987).
3. For an important revision of the older interpretation of nineteenth-century rhetoric, see Nan Johnson, *Nineteenth Century Rhetoric in North America* (Carbondale: Southern Illinois University Press, 1991).
4. See Gregory Clark and Michael Halloran, eds., *Oratorical Culture in Nineteenth Century America: Transformations in the Theory and Practice of Rhetoric* (Carbondale: Southern Illinois University Press, 1993).
5. See Henry Hamilton, *An Economic History of Scotland in the Eighteenth Century* (Oxford: Clarendon, 1963); also R. H. Campbell, *Scotland since 1707: The Rise of an Industrial Society* (New York: Barnes and Noble, 1965).
6. These questions involve at least several key issues: the extent to which the Scottish Enlightenment had deeper origins in the seventeenth century: see David Allen, *Virtue, Learning, and the Scottish Enlightenment: Ideas of Learning in Early Modern History* (Edinburgh: Edinburgh University Press, 1990); to what extent it was a construct of late eighteenth, nineteenth and twentieth-century historiography: see Paul Wood's "Introduction: Dugald Stewart and the Invention of 'the Scottish Enlightenment,'" in Paul Wood, ed., *The Scottish Enlightenment: Essays in Reinterpretation* (Rochester, NY: University of Rochester Press, 2000); its relation to enlightened thought in England and France: see Roy Porter, *Creation of the Modern World: The Untold Story of the British Enlightenment* (New York: W. W. Norton, 2001), especially 1–23; and the

diversity of views the Scottish Enlightenment accommodated: see Dwyer, *The Age of the Passions: An Interpretation of Adam Smith and Scottish Enlightenment Culture* (East Linton: Tuckwell, 1998), especially 1–12.

7. Hume's term is from the introduction to his *Treatise of Human Nature* (1739); Kames's from his *Loose Hints upon Education, Chiefly Concerning The Culture of the Heart* (1781).

8. On Moderatism, see Richard Sher, *Church and University in the Scottish Enlightenment: The Moderate Literati of Edinburgh* (Princeton: Princeton University Press, 1985).

9. The leaders of the Scottish Enlightenment were male, but women were not without influence, especially in education; see Rosemarie Zagarri, "Morals, Manners, and the Republican Mother," *American Quarterly* 44:2 (1992): 192–215.

10. Quoted in J. F. Bell, "Adam Smith, Clubman," in John Cunningham Wood, *Adam Smith: Critical Assessments*, 4 vols. (London: Croom Helm, 1984), 1:97.

11. See Hiroshi Mizuta, *Adam Smith's Library: A Catalogue* (Oxford: Clarendon, 2000).

Chapter 2. Smith and Propriety in the Classical Tradition

1. Pohlenz, in his pioneering study of *to prepon*, argues that "Die ganze Theorie wurzelt in der Tiefe des griechischen Geistes, in seinem Gefallen an Wohlgeformtheit un Proportionalität der sinnlichen Erscheinung, aber auch an der Harmonie von Erscheinung und Wesen, von Darstellungsform und Inhalt, von Einzelgeste und Gesamthaltung"; Max Pohlenz, "*Tò Prépon*: Ein Beitrag zur Geschichte des griechischen Geistes," *Nachrichten von der Gesselschaft der Wissenschaften zu Göttingen, Philologisch-historische Klasse* 1 (1933), 53. Pohlenz sees a direct connection between the earliest and later uses of the term: *prepein*, the verb first designating the falling of the eyes on some external appearance, later came to denote the characteristic outline of one's visible features, then eventually developed its normative aspect as *to prepon*, which referred to the sense of "fitness" between a person's appearance, manner, and habits.

2. See also Wesley Trimpi, *Muses of One Mind: The Literary Analysis of Experience and its Continuity* (Princeton: Princeton University Press, 1983), 130. Through an Aristotelian analysis, Trimpi presents stylistic decorum as involving the balanced discursive relation between conveying knowledge of a subject "in itself" with expression of emotion commensurate to the experience of that object (that is, knowledge "relative to us"). Unlike the archaic phenomenology Prier describes, the poles of subject and object are clearly articulated in the Aristotelian perspective, but, perhaps as a late resonance of the archaic idea, both are mutually dependent.

3. *Prepein* and the state of wonder are directly connected at *Iliad* 18.370, where Thetis finds Hephaestus's house to be "preeminent among mortal dwellings" (*metaprepe athanatoisi*); along with other trappings, it is "a wonder to behold" (*thauma idesthai*).

4. Brian Donovan takes the latter position; see his "The Project of Protagoras," *Rhetoric Society Quarterly* 23:1 (1993): 35–47. Donovan draws support from Edward Schiappa, *Protagoras and Logos: A Study of Greek Philosophy and Rhetoric* (Columbia: University of South Carolina Press, 1991), 52, 186; and from G. B. Kerferd, *The Sophistic Movement* (Cambridge: Cambridge University Press, 1981), 105–106, 112–13. Untersteiner (110) notes that in Pythagorean philosophy, justice (*dikaion*) and "the right moment," or *kairos*

are related concepts; see Mario Untersteiner, *The Sophists*, trans. Kathleen Freeman (Oxford: Basil Blackwell, 1954), 110. He quotes an apposite remark by Rostagni (1922): "[*dikaion* and *kairos*] found their application in the relations and communications between man and man, communications which are bound to vary according to age and office and kinship and state of mind." *Kairos* was thus "a manifestation of *harmonia* which reduces the opposite qualities of the universe to a unity" (Untersteiner, 82).

5. Philostratus (*Lives of the Sophists* I,9) reports that Gorgias "improvised easily" and was known for his use of "the grand style for grand subjects," "detached phrases and transitions, by which speech becomes sweeter than it has been and more impressive" and poetic ornament; quoted in Rosamond Kent Sprague, ed., *The Older Sophists* (Columbia: University of South Carolina Press, 1972), 30–31. Some indication of the difficulty of the subject of *kairos* is supplied by Dionysius of Helicarnassus in his remark that up to his time no orator had adequately defined the art of the timely, "not even Gorgias, who first tried to write about it." He added, "nor did he say anything worth mentioning" (quoted in Sprague, 63). Plato attributes an interest in *to prepon* to Gorgias (see *Gorgias* 503e and *Phaedrus* 268d.)

6. This is not a contradiction, explains Untersteiner, if the *Helen* is viewed as dramatizing the theory of (not-) knowing expounded in *On Nature*. Helen must be exonerated, because: (a) humans cannot oppose the will of God; (b) they cannot object to violence because it is an "expression of the divine"; and (c) they are powerless against a *logos* which could be violence, intellectual power, and/or magical force (105–107). This deceptive capability (*apate*) inherent in *logos* is a result of *kairos*: it is the situatedness of speech in time and circumstance which unmoors meaning (110–11). *Logos* in this view is not merely *pseudos* (objective falsehood, mistaken or intentional) but *apate*, subjective and intentional deceptiveness—but as such it is also a creative force or process, a play of the imagination (109).

7. Pohlenz notes that Gorgias's influence led Isocrates to argue for the essentially creative nature of rhetoric and hence its status as a true art: unlike arts with "hard and fast rules," rhetoric requires "fitness for the occasion [*kairón*]" and "propriety of style [*prepontós*]" (54). For related comments, see *Against the Sophists*, 13, 16; *Panegyricus*, 9; and *Helen*, 11. Isocrates is not a theorist, however, and instead of developing the assertion, he trusts that these principles can be learned through much study, so long as the student has a "vigorous and imaginative mind" (*Against the Sophists*, 17).

8. Pohlenz notes one exception: In *Statesman* (286d) it is argued that the right measure for the length of an inquiry or discourse is determined not mathematically but qualitatively—according to "due occasion, due time, and due performance" as described at 284e, later called simply the "standard of suitability" (*to prepon*) at 286d. But suitability here is subordinated to the ultimate end of the discourse, which is always to find real forms.

9. For examples, see *Symposium*, when Agathon is said to have spoken "fittingly [*prepontos*] for himself and with regard to the god" (198) or in the *Laws* when Megillus responds to a speech by the Athenian criticizing absolute freedom and praising the authority of law: "The observation sir, is not only perfectly just, but most becoming [*prepontós*] to yourself and your countrymen" (699d). In the *Parmenides*, Zeno notes that it would be "unsuitable" (*aprepê*) for Parmenides to give a long and complex discourse before a large audience, adding that it would be

particularly so "in a man of his age" (136d). And Laches, in the dialogue named for him, remarks: "[W]hen I hear a man discoursing of virtue, or of any sort of wisdom, who is a true man and worthy of his nature, I am delighted beyond measure, and I compare the man and his words, and note the harmony and correspondence [*pre-ponta . . . kai harmottonta*] of them" (188c-d).

10. A notable exception is at *Charmides* 158c, where Socrates, having asked Charmides whether he possesses temperance (*sophrosyne*), notes that "Charmides blushed, and the blush heightened his beauty, for modesty is becoming [*eprepsen*] in youth." Given that *sophrosyne* meant more than simply "temperance" in a narrow sense but also implied "accepting the bounds which excellence lays down for human nature, restraining impulses to unrestricted freedom, to all excess, obeying the inner laws of harmony and proportion," the placement of this remark seems not to be accidental (Editors' intro-duction to *Charmides* in Plato, *The Collected Dialogues of Plato including the Letters*, ed. Edith Hamilton and Huntington Cairns (New York: Pantheon, 1961), 99). Charmides' suitable reaction is answer enough to Socrates' question, for, as Charmides explains, a flat yes or no answer to the query would be evidence of intemperance. Thus, here at least, Plato attests to the appropriateness of a disposition in relation to a given age, and he takes its immediacy as concrete evidence of an ideal virtue.

11. Interestingly here, Socrates remarks that a knowledgeable musician would not harshly rebuke the one who pretended or thought he knew harmony by knowing a few notes, but would respond to him "in the gentler language befitting his profes-sion" (268e). He then repeats the remark, saying that in the same manner, those rhetoricians with knowledge of dialectic shouldn't be "rude" or "coarse" in their language to those who think they have knowledge of rhetoric simply because they know a few oratorical techniques. The implication here is that appropriate speech (according to Socrates' view) follows not from any knowledge of appropriateness per se, but from knowledge of the subject matter.

12. See James L. Kinneavy and Catherine R. Eskin, "*Kairos* in Aristotle's *Rhetoric*," *Writ-ten Communication* 11.1 (1994): 133.

13. See Larry Arnhart, *Aristotle on Political Reasoning: A Commentary on the "Rhetoric"* (Dekalb: Northern Illinois University Press, 1981), 169. The only other single con-cept in the *Rhetoric* that integrates all three *pisteis* is the enthymeme; it is striking then that *to prepon* has not been the subject of more critical discussion.

14. Elsewhere Aristotle notes that metaphors give perspicuity, pleasure, and a "foreign" air, but only if they are appropriate (*harmottousas*). This is achieved by "observing due proportion [*analogon*]; otherwise there will be a lack of propriety [*aprepes*], because it is when it is placed in juxtaposition that contraries are most evident" (1405a9–13).

15. Thomas Farrell conceives of rhetoric as an art of practical reason, drawing heavily on just such an understanding of Aristotelian rhetorical propriety: "[E]ven in the most poetic of rhetorical forms, there is a triumphantly intractable existential reality an-chored to the discourse, which inexorably shapes its meaning. This reality also helps us mark and define what is the quintessential aesthetic quality of rhetoric as a lan-guage. The quality is *propriety*. The overriding emphasis of Aristotle's rhetorical aes-thetic is the transformation of what is available as proof into what is *proper* to the occasion, audience, speaker and subject"; Thomas B. Farrell, *Norms of Rhetorical Cul-ture* (New Haven: Yale University Press, 1993), 130 (emphases original).

16. This view of the role of emotion in cognition agrees with recent neurological research. For an overview, see Antonio Damasio, *Descartes' Error: Emotion, Reason, and the Human Brain* (New York: G. P. Putnam's Son's, 1994), particularly on knowledge as requiring "dispositional representations" (102–105); on the need for social situatedness for the development of biological neural mechanisms that generate the human capacity for "a moral point of view" (123–26); on rational decision making as requiring emotive dispositionality (127–64); on emotions functioning as "somatic markers" that enable practical reasoning through the development within individuals of "'theories' of their own minds and the minds of others" (173–75). Damasio's interpretation is framed in strong Humean terms; Dylan Evans's survey and synthesis of recent research on "emotional intelligence," however, applauds Smith as having basically gotten it right on the relation between reason and emotion. See Dylan Evans, *Emotion: The Science of Sentiment* (Oxford: Oxford University Press, 2001), xi, 64, 70.

17. Aristotle distinguishes between the non-necessary or fallible sign (*sêmeion anônumon*) and the necessary sign (*tekmêrion*) (see 1357b3ff). The latter indicates what it signifies with apodictic certainty, and allows the construction of an irrefutable logical syllogism. The former indicates what it signifies with probability, even strong probability, but not certainty. The fallible sign is further distinguished from general probabilities (*eikota*) however: whereas an *eikos* is general in nature and therefore does not specify any relation to a given instance (e.g., "Politicians are liars"), a fallible sign is specific and immediately indicates the probability of an inference (e.g., "This politician's demonstrated lie indicates immoral character"). Thus, propriety is a *sêmeion anônumon* and not an *eikos*. Both lead to probable conclusions, but the fallible sign does so more strongly. See William M. A. Grimaldi, S. J., *Aristotle, Rhetoric I: A Commentary* (New York: Fordham University Press, 1980), 64.

18. This is analogously true in poetic discourse as well for Aristotle, who includes appropriateness (*ta harmottonta*) as the second of four requisites for achieving dramatic character (1454a21).

19. Beyond those signs of *êthos* supplied by style, other indices of character may be found in explicit statements about character, good sense, and good will. Though Aristotle does not develop the idea, it is possible that the topical form(s) of argument a speaker habitually chooses indicate moral character; such a position is developed by Richard Weaver in his *The Ethics of Rhetoric* (South Bend: Regnary/Gateway, 1953), especially chapters 3 and 4.

20. Pohlenz notes that Isocrates had connected the idea of propriety with his notion of enthymeme (54). See *Against the Soph*ists, 16: one must adorn the speech with "appropriate thoughts [*enthumêmasi prepontôs*]"; and *Panegyricus*, 9: one must regard past deeds with the "right sentiments [*ta prosêkonta peri ekastês enthumêthênai*]." The sense of *enthumêma* is similar but not identical in the two authors (there is no indication that Isocrates means "rhetorical syllogism"), but there was evidently in Isocrates a connotative connection between the reasoned qualities of thought and propriety.

21. Aristotle discusses the fallacy of sign at 1401b9. Grimaldi comments that while the proof from sign is liable to being disproved as fallacious, "there can be no question that the non-necessary sign argument can be a form of valid inference, which, however, is not logically conclusive . . ."; Grimaldi, *Aristotle, Rhetoric II: A Commentary*

(New York: Fordham University Press, 1988), 344. See also *On Sophistical Refutations*, 167b1–20.

22. See Lois Self, "Rhetoric and *Phronesis*: The Aristotelian Ideal," *Philosophy and Rhetoric* 12:2 (1979): 130–45.

23. See *Nicomachean Ethics* 2.1.

24. Which means of persuasion a speaker will choose to employ is a practical matter, but as a form of political action it is also clearly a moral matter; there is no reason to think that choice of style is morally irrelevant. See 1361b1: "The virtues must also be a good thing; for those who possess them are in a sound condition and they are also productive of good things and practical."

25. See *Rhetoric* 1410a: "[Antithesis] is pleasing, because contraries are easily understood and even more so when placed side by side, and also because antithesis resembles a syllogism; for refutation is a bringing together of contraries." Arnhart notes in regard to this passage that "[s]tyle gives pleasure by making speech more 'knowable' than it would otherwise be; thus it contributes to the rational character of rhetoric" (174).

26. Grimaldi's translation used here better reflects the compatibility of Aristotle's definition of pleasure in both the *Rhetoric* and the *Nichomachean Ethics*. In the latter, Aristotle insists that pleasure is not a motion (*kinêsis*) but an activity (*energeia*). The definition in the *Rhetoric* actually indicates two senses of pleasure: (1) the vulgar one denoting bodily pleasure; (2) the proper one denoting pleasure as an *energeia* accompanying the exercise of an unimpeded faculty or habit (*hexis*). The *Rhetoric's* emphasis on the first definition here is explained by the context: The aim here is to discuss the motives of voluntary action (particularly criminal action). Thus, it is enough for the purposes of rhetorical practice to understand pleasure in its common sense. But the proper definition is relevant for rhetorical theory. The translation and a more detailed explanation of the consonance between the definitions in both works appear in Grimaldi, *Rhetoric I*, 243–46. See also Arnhart, 93–4.

27. See also 1456a14: lengths of the parts of a piece of dramatic artwork are determined by appropriateness (*prepon*) to the genre: a long section that is fine in epic poetry may fail on stage in a tragedy.

28. See also 1367b13, where Aristotle speaks of "arguments suitable [*harmottei*] to the occasion." In addition, he notes with regard to the use of maxims as a form of argument, that "it will be readily apparent on what subjects, and on what occasions [*kairoi*], and by whom it is appropriate [*harmottei*] that maxims should be employed"(1394a27). Specifically, they are suitable (*harmottei*) for use by elders, unseemly (*aprepes*) in the young (1395a2).

29. Propriety applies to arrangement as well: for Aristotle, style must be adapted to the parts of the speech. For instance, although the exordium should, like a musical overture, set the key for the speech, "even an unrelated subject, skillfully worked in, can be fitting [*harmottei*]; this is better than making the speech monotonous" (1414b29). Whereas repetition is not advised for exordia, recapitulation is said to be appropriate (*harmottei*) in the epilogue (1419b28), the appropriate (*harmottei*) style of which will be without connecting particles (1420b2).

30. George Kennedy shows that differently enumerated categories of style are present in Greek literature as early as mid-fourth century BC; see his "Theophrastus and Stylistic Distinctions," *Harvard Studies in Classical Philology* 62 (1957): 93–104.

31. Hermogenes, 108. John Monfasani argues that *deinotês* "clearly reflects the tradition of *to prepon* or *decorum*" and is thus not really a type of style like the others but "mastery of the forms and their use *eis deon kai kata kairon* [as called for and at the right time]"; John Monfasani, *George of Trebizond: A Biography and Study of His Rhetoric and Logic*. London: E. J. Brill, 1976), 253. This is directly supported by Hermogenes' mention (102) of a Homeric passage previously cited in this study, *Odyssey* 8.170. Annabel Patterson holds that *deinotês* is both control of the other styles *and* a powerful style itself; Annabel Patterson, *Hermogenes and the Renaissance: Seven Ideas of Style* (Princeton: Princeton University Press, 1970), 6.

32. For Patterson, this neo-Platonic quality in part explains the subsequent popularity of Hermogenes in the Renaissance (Patterson, 33).

33. The connection between *ornatus* and decorum is abetted by Latin. *Ornatus* literally means "equipped" or "fitted out" and it carries these connotations when applied to language. Similarly, *decorum*, "well suited," also means "decorated."

34. This fusion of virtue and style was adopted by Cicero's great admirer, Quintilian, in his *Institutio Oratoria*. He catalogues much of the lore of classical propriety in 11.1. Because for Quintilian rhetoric's aim is not simply persuasion but "speaking well," propriety is subordinate less to the situation than to the need to do what is becoming (*quid deceat*) (11.1.8). So long as one has "a clear conception in his mind as to what aims are honorable and what are not" (11.1.35), propriety will take care of itself (11.1.42).

35. Propriety remained a concern in medieval rhetoric, but seems to have undergone little development, and was of less exigency where Christian doctrine could determine the appropriate. It mainly persisted in its Ciceronian form as in St. Augustine, *De Doctrina Christiana*, 4.6.9, 4.7.17. See also Alcuin, *The Rhetoric of Alcuin and Charlemagne*, trans. and ed., W. S. Howell (Princeton: Princeton University Press, 1941), 133. Marc Fumaroli makes wide-ranging reference to this "nouveau decorum" continuing among Christian humanists in the Renaissance, who summoned decorum in defense of the sacred use of a profane art of rhetoric; Marc Fumaroli, *L'age de L'eloquence: Rhetorique et "res letteraria" au seuil de l'epoque classique* (Geneva: Librairie Dros, 1980).

Chapter 3. Rhetorical Propriety in Eighteenth Century Theories of Discourse

1. See Ralph Adolph, *The Rise of the Modern Prose Style* (Cambridge: MIT Press, 1986): "[Bacon's] rhetorical theory is permeated by what we could perhaps call today 'form following function' or what Aristotle called 'appropriateness'"(47). Adolph sees this as an entailment of Bacon's "utilitarianism," however, not as a matter of classical influence. In broad agreement are Karl Wallace, *Francis Bacon on Communication and Rhetoric* (Chapel Hill, University of North Carolina Press, 1943); Maurice B. MacNamee, *Literary Decorum in Francis Bacon* (St. Louis: St. Louis University Studies, 1950); Wilbur Samuel Howell, *Logic and Rhetoric in England, 1500–1700* (Princeton: Princeton University Press, 1956) 364–75.

2. This famous phrase was adumbrated in Boyle's *Considerations*, wherein Scriptural ornament is God's way of "hinting the usefullest and sublimest truths" in passages that

"contain more matter than words." Human writings, on the other hand, have "more words than matter"; Robert Boyle, *The Early Essays and Ethics of Robert Boyle*, ed. John T. Harwood (Carbondale: Southern Illinois University Press, 1991), 299. Scientific writing, according to the formulation in Sprat's *History*, would be precisely in between.

3. Boyle is explicit in this indictment: "I will not say . . . that our strict Ciceronian rules are crutches, that may be helps to weak or lame fancies, but are clogs or burdens to sound and active ones" (Boyle, *Early Essays*, 300).

4. John J. Richetti analyzes some of the broader implications of this point for later philosophical writers, noting, for example, that although its style is rhetorically toned down, "Augustan philosophical writing needs the voice established by style as a way of stabilizing the disorderly possibilities and implications of thought"; see his *Philosophical Writing: Locke, Berkeley, and Hume* (Cambridge: Harvard University Press, 1983), 30.

5. D. W. Jefferson puts eighteenth-century theories of taste into three categories: sensationalist (Dubos, Burke, Hume), internal sense (Shaftesbury, Hutcheson), and associationist (Alexander Gerard, Archibald Alison, Payne Knight, Dugald Stewart). All three draw upon developments in science and epistemology, though Shaftesbury and Hutcheson to a lesser extent; D. W. Jefferson, "Theories of Taste in the Eighteenth Century," *Proceedings of the Leeds Philosophical and Literary Society, Literary and Historical Section* 5 (1938–1943): 1–9.

6. In an early notebook, Shaftesbury had likewise described a practice he calls *chrêsis phantasiôn*—the "right Use of Ideas and Appearances," which involves testing mental contents through verbalization: "This is the Art & Method to be learnt: how to put these into words; so as to reason with them: force them to speak; hear their Language and return them in their answer. This is ye Rhetorick, Eloquence & Witt wch we should affect"; quoted in Lawrence E. Klein, *Shaftesbury and the Culture of Politeness, Moral Discourse, and Cultural Politics in Early Eighteenth Century England* (Cambridge: Cambridge University Press, 1994), 88–89.

7. I have retained Shaftesbury's extravagant typography, as it does much to convey the exuberant quality of his prose style.

8. Hutcheson elsewhere refers to virtue as "beauty of action" (68) and discusses "degrees of moral beauty" (114); Francis Hutcheson, *An Inquiry into the Origin of Our Ideas of Beauty and Virtue* (Westmead: Gregg, 1969). Shaftesbury discusses "moral beauty and deformity" in "An Inquiry concerning Virtue"; Shaftesbury, Anthony Ashley Cooper, Third Earl of, *Characteristics of Men, Manners, Opinions, Times*, 3 vols. (London: 1732), 2:29–30. For a treatment of Hutcheson's full debt to Shaftesbury, see Peter Kivy, *The Seventh Sense: A Study of Francis Hutcheson's Aesthetics and its Influence in Eighteenth Century Britain* (New York: Burt Franklin, 1976), 1–21.

9. Though not mentioning synecdoche, David Paxman reads the whole of Hutcheson's *Inquiry* in compatible terms: for Hutcheson, aesthetics . . . offers a mode of 'knowing' without knowledge"; see his "Aesthetics as Epistemology, or Knowledge without Certainty," *Eighteenth Century Studies* 26 (1992): 294–95.

10. See Jean-Baptiste Dubos, *Réflexions Critiques sur la Poésie et sur la Peinture* (Paris: 770): "La nature a donc pris le parti de nous construire de maniere que l'agitation de tout ce qui nous approche eut un puissant empire sur nous, afin que ceux qui ont besoin de notre indulgence ou de notre secours, pussent nous ébranler avec facilité" (17).

11. Ibid: "Le cris d'un homme que ne tient à nous que par l'humanité, nous sont voler à son secours par un mouvement machinal qui précéde toute délibération."

12. Kames makes a similar assertion in his earlier essay, "The Foundation of the Law of Nature": "[A] voluntary agent is an object which produces a peculiar modification of beauty and deformity, which may readily be distinguished from all others"; Kames, Henry Home, Lord, *Essays on the Principles of Morality and Natural Religion* (New York: Garland, 1983), 48.

Chapter 4. Propriety in Smith's Rhetoric Lectures

1. For analysis of the development between editions of *TMS*, see D. D. Raphael and A. L. McFie, eds., "Introduction," *TMS 15–20.*

2. In *Nicomachean Ethics* (1171b31), Aristotle uses the occurrence of praise and blame to set off the sphere of moral action from the sphere of involuntary behavior, even before he defines the involuntary as that done under compulsion or due to ignorance. Both Smith and Aristotle treat praiseworthiness and blameworthiness as inherent properties of action; hence, epideictic speech is the source of our awareness of the moral sphere. Smith, like Aristotle, often uses praise and blame to litmus moral distinctions, for example where he distinguishes between emotional self-control over sorrow versus that over joy (*TMS* 1.3.1.6); or more significantly, where he uses praise and blame to locate moral responsibility in intent rather than in the bodily movement or consequences of action (*TMS* 2.3.intro.3). Likewise, Aristotle calls upon praise and blame to help make the distinction between the equitable and the just (1137b1) and between false and genuine self-love (1168b27). For more on the Aristotelian qualities of Smith's ethical thought, see Lawrence Berns, "Aristotle and Adam Smith on Justice: Cooperation Between Ancients and Moderns?" *Review of Metaphysics* 48 (1994): 71–90; and Charles L. Griswold, "Rhetoric and Ethics: Adam Smith on Theorizing about the Moral Sentiments." *Philosophy and Rhetoric* 24:3 (1991): 213–37, especially 219–21.

3. This same concern arises in Smith's review of Johnson's dictionary. Though largely laudatory, the review finds fault in that "the different significations of a word . . . are seldom digested into general classes, or ranged under the meaning which the word principally expresses. And sufficient care has not been taken to distinguish the words apparently synonymous" (*EPS* 232–33).

4. Smith holds that substantives are *among* the first part of speech contrived, but in neither *LRBL* nor "Considerations" does Smith argue for an original part of speech. In a letter of 1763, however, he comments in reference to a book of grammar he has reviewed that in his estimation verbs are the "original parts of speech, first invented to express in one word a complete event" (*Corr.*, 88). On the originary contextuality of verbs see Robert Sokolowski, *Presence and Absence: A Philosophical Investigation of Language and Being* (Bloomington: Indiana University Press, 1978), 15–16.

5. Other passages in Hume's *Treatise* coidentifying sympathy and communication include 2.1.11, 2.2.5, 2.2.9, 2.2.12.

6. See Bevilacqua: "[T]he scope of mid-eighteenth-century rhetoric was limited to style and the communication of subject matter previously revealed by logic and

extra-rhetorical inquiry"; Vincent Bevilacqua, "Adam Smith and Some Philosophical Origins of Eighteenth Century Rhetorical Theory," *Modern Language Review*
63 (1968): 563. Bevilacqua sees Scottish rhetoricians as conceiving discovery, evaluation, and communication of truth as three distinct phases. For Smith however,
they clearly are not.

7. David Marshall follows Jonas Barish's assertion that Smith's impartial spectator
device is an "essentially theatrical construction"; see his "Adam Smith and the Theatricality of Moral Sentiments," *Critical Inquiry* 10 (1984): 170. See also Jonas Barish,
The Antitheatrical Prejudice (Berkeley: University of California Press, 1981), 244. Inas-
much as all communicative situations—all social interactions—are performative, this
is inarguably valid, and Marshall provides an elegant reading of *TMS* which it is not
my aim to supercede. Curiously, however, neither author adverts to Smith's rhetoric
lectures, which, as this study intends to show, are deeply concerned with the way discourse mediates sentiments and as such suggest that Smith's spectator concept is
largely inspired by the situatedness of communicative interaction, the genus to
which theater is species, and which Smith viewed under the rubric of rhetoric. The
theatrical and the rhetorical readings of *TMS* are ultimately compatible, however.

8. Michael Carter sees these two types of description as transformations of the *topoi* into
"structural modes"—that is, as ways of arranging material; Michael Carter, "The Role
of Invention in Belletristic Rhetoric: A Study of the Lectures of Adam Smith," *Rhetoric
Society Quarterly* 18 (1988): 10. Certainly they *can* have the effect of organizing material, but Smith's purpose is not so narrow. He is concerned with how appropriate
description effectively presents objects so as to make them compelling and persuasive.

9. Poussin is a particularly apt choice: his classicism espoused the ancient Greek doctrine of musical modes, which, when translated to painting, gave the artist's work
moderation and propriety: "The Modes of the ancients were a combination of several things . . . in such a proportion that it was made possible to arouse the soul of
the spectator to various passions. . . . The ancient sages attributed to each style its
own effects. Because of this they called the Dorian Mode stable, grave and severe,
and applied it to subjects which are grave and severe and full of wisdom"; quoted in
E. G. Holt, ed., *Literary Sources of Art History* (Princeton: Princeton University Press,
1947), 380. Smith knew Poussin's artistic philosophy: In lecture 21 he approves of
Poussin's avowed preference for "tranquill pieces" (2.95). Such pieces have greater
propriety in painting, because spectators can "enter into" them—that is, sympathize
with their subjects—more easily than they can pieces depicting violent emotions.

10. The date of composition of this essay, published posthumously, is uncertain: The
evidence suggests that it was complete by 1777, though versions of it may have been
presented as early as 1764, or possibly earlier. See P. D. Wightman's introduction to
the Glasgow edition, *EPS*, 172.

11. On this social aspect of perception, see Robert Sokolowski, *Pictures, Quotations, and
Distinctions: Fourteen Essays in Phenomenology* (Notre Dame: University of Notre
Dame Press, 1992): "Even if we are all alone, we experience things—trees and
rivers—as capable of being perceived by others; however, this sense in things is
established for us by the achievement of experiencing things in the actual company
of other people, who see the same objects we see but see them from different angles.
We appreciate the thing as also perceived by others who are there with us. This prox-

imate shared perception is a condition for our solitary perception of the tree and river as still capable of being perceived from another viewpoint by someone else while we perceive it from the spot that is the 'here' for us" (11).

12. Citations to Berkeley are to section number within the respective text as contained in George Berkeley, Bishop of Cloyne, *The Works of George Berkeley, Bishop of Cloyne*, 9 vols., ed. A. A. Luce and T. E. Jessop (London: Thomas Nelson and Sons, 1953).

13. In his last work, *Siris*, Berkeley writes that "[t]he phenomena of nature, which strike on the senses and are understood by the mind, form not only a magnificent spectacle, but also a most coherent, entertaining and instructive discourse . . ." (254); see also 252: "There is a certain analogy, constancy, and uniformity in the appearances of nature, which are a foundation for general rules: and these are a grammar for the understanding of nature . . ."

14. The point is made explicit in the title of Berkeley's last work on vision: *The Theory of Vision or Visual Language, Showing the Immediate Presence and Providence of a Deity, Vindicated and Explained* (1733).

Chapter 5. Propriety in *The Theory of Moral Sentiments*

1. Smith criticizes Mandeville not only for his faulty premises, but because "The ingenious sophistry of his reasoning is . . . covered by ambiguity of his language" (*TMS* 7.2.4.11).

2. Bevilacqua notes this in passing, but does not explicate the point, as is my aim; see his "Adam Smith's *Lectures on Rhetoric and Belles Lettres*," *Studies in Scottish Literature* 3 (July 1965): 53.

3. The importance of vision is evidenced even in Smith's choice of title. A capable scholar of ancient Greek, he was no doubt aware of the visual connotation of the word *theory* (*theôrein*: "to observe"), not a commonly used term in philosophical works of the day.

4. Marshall similarly recognizes that Smith "insists that neither sight nor the other senses will suffice to communicate the feelings and experience of another person" (170).

5. Smith uses no single term to refer to the individual who has a certain emotion; he usually refers to "the person principally concerned," "the person in whom we observe [emotions]," or some similar construction. For the sake of brevity and to avoid confusion between references to the person who is the dative of emotion and to the person who is a spectator of others' emotions, I will henceforth refer to the former as "the principal."

6. The point is reminiscent of Aristotle's concept of pleasure as it is discussed in the *Rhetoric* as a "settling down into one's normal state" [1369b33–70a5] and his remarks that persuasion involves learning, which itself occasions pleasure.

Chapter 6. Conclusions, Provocations

1. See for example Charles Bazerman's "Money Talks, Adam Smith's Rhetorical Project," in his *Constructing Experience* (Carbondale: Southern Illinois University Press, 1994), discussed also in my Critical Note on Sources and Scholarship.

2. See chapter 2, note 16.

3. George McKenna, "On Abortion: A Lincolnian Position," *Atlantic Monthly,* Sept. 1995, 51–68.

4. Naomi Wolf, "Our Bodies, Our Souls: Re-thinking Pro-Choice Rhetoric," *The New Republic,* Oct. 16, 1995, 26–35.

5. Richard Rorty, "The Intellectuals and the Poor," speech delivered in February 1996 at Pomona College, Pomona, California; excerpted as "What's Wrong with 'Rights,'" *Harper's,* June 1996, 15–18.

6. Stanley Fish reaches a comparable conclusion—though by a markedly different, skepticist route—in *There's No Such Thing as Free Speech and It's a Good Thing, Too* (New York: Oxford University Press, 1994), 103–104.

References

This list contains all works cited in this book; it also includes several works that were consulted but not directly cited, as well as some items that were not cited but may be of interest to those pursuing further research on Adam Smith and rhetoric.

Addison, Joseph, and Richard Steele. *The Spectator.* Cincinnati: Applegate, 1862.

Adolph, Ralph. *The Rise of Modern Prose Style.* Cambridge: MIT Press, 1986.

Aeschylus. *Aeschylus.* Trans. H. W. Smith. London: Heinemann, 1927.

Alcuin. *The Rhetoric of Alcuin and Charlemagne.* Trans. and ed. W. S. Howell. Princeton: Princeton University Press, 1941.

Allen, David. *Virtue, Learning, and the Scottish Enlightenment: Ideas of Learning in Early Modern History.* Edinburgh: Edinburgh University Press, 1990.

Arendt, Hannah. *Between Past and Future: Eight Exercises in Political Thought.* New York: Viking, 1954.

Aristotle. *Athenian Constitution, Eudemian Ethics, Virtues and Vices.* Trans. H. Rackham. Cambridge: Harvard University Press, 1961.

———. *The "Art" of Rhetoric.* Trans. J. H. Freese. Cambridge: Harvard University Press, 1982.

———. *Nichomachean Ethics.* Trans. David Ross. Oxford: Oxford University Press, 1988.

———. *The Categories. On Interpretation.* Trans. H. P. Cooke. Cambridge: Harvard University Press, 1948.

———. *On Sophistical Refutations and On Coming-to-be and Passing-away.* Trans. E. S. Forster. Cambridge: Harvard University Press, 1955.

———. [Longinus], Demetrius. *Poetics, On the Sublime, On Style.* Trans. Stephen Halliwell, W. Hamilton Fyfe, Doreen C. Innes. Cambridge: Harvard University Press, 1932.

Arnhart, Larry. *Aristotle on Political Reasoning: A Commentary on the "Rhetoric."* Dekalb: Northern Illinois University Press, 1981.

Augustini, S. Aureli. *De Doctrina Christiana.* Trans. with commentary, Therese Sullivan. Washington, DC: Catholic University of America Press, 1930.

Austin, J. L. *How to Do Things with Words.* Cambridge: Harvard University Press, 1962.

Bacon, Francis. *Works.* 14 Vols. Ed. James Spedding. Starnberg: Frommann-holzberg, 1989.

Barish, Jonas. *The Antitheatrical Prejudice.* Berkeley: University of California Press, 1981.

Barthes, Roland. *Criticism and Truth.* Trans. and ed. Katherine Pilcher Keuneman. Minneapolis: University of Minnesota Press, 1987.

Bator, Paul G. "Rhetoric and the Novel in the Eighteenth-Century British University Curriculum." *Eighteenth Century Studies* 30:2 (1997): 173–95.

Bazerman, Charles. *Constructing Experience*. Carbondale: Southern Illinois University Press, 1994.

Bell, J. F. "Adam Smith, Clubman." *Journal of Political Economy* 7 (June 1960): 108–16. Rpt. John Cunningham Wood, ed. *Adam Smith: Critical Assessments*. 4 Vols. (London: Croom Helm, 1984), 1:94–101.

Berkeley, George, Bishop of Cloyne. *The Works of George Berkeley, Bishop of Cloyne*. 9 Vols. Ed. A. A. Luce and T. E. Jessop. London: Thomas Nelson and Sons, 1953.

Berns, Laurence. "Aristotle and Adam Smith on Justice: Cooperation Between Ancients and Moderns?" *Review of Metaphysics* 48 (1994): 71–90.

Berry, Christopher. "Adam Smith's *Considerations* on Language." *Journal of the History of Ideas* 35 (1974): 130–38. Rpt. *Adam Smith*. Ed. Knud Haakonssen. Aldershot: Ashgate, 1998.

———. *Social Theory of the Scottish Enlightenment*. Edinburgh: Edinburgh University Press, 1997.

Bevilacqua, Vincent M. "Adam Smith's *Lectures on Rhetoric and Belles Lettres*." *Studies in Scottish Literature* 3 (July 1965): 41–60.

———. "Adam Smith and Some Philosophical Origins of Eighteenth Century Rhetorical Theory." *Modern Language Review* 63 (1968): 559–68.

Bineham, Jeffrey L. "The Cartesian Anxiety in Epistemic Rhetoric: An Assessment of the Literature." *Philosophy and Rhetoric* 23:1 (1990): 43–62.

Bitzer, Lloyd F. "The Rhetorical Situation." *Philosophy and Rhetoric* 1 (1968): 1–24.

Boswell, James. *Life of Johnson*. Ed. R. W. Chapman. Oxford: Oxford University Press, 1980.

Boyle, Robert. *The Early Essays and Ethics of Robert Boyle*. Ed. John T. Harwood. Carbondale: Southern Illinois University Press, 1991.

———. *The Works*. 6 Vols. Ed. Thomas Birch. Hildesheim: George Olms, 1966.

Brown, Vivienne. *Adam Smith's Discourse: Canonicity, Commerce, and Conscience*. New York: Routledge, 1994.

Burke, Edmund. *A Philosophical Enquiry into Our Ideas of the Sublime and Beautiful*. Oxford: Oxford University Press, 1990.

Campbell, R. H. *Scotland since 1707: The Rise of an Industrial Society*. New York: Barnes and Noble, 1965.

———, and A. S. Skinner. *Adam Smith*. New York: St. Martin's, 1982.

Carter, Michael. "The Role of Invention in Belletristic Rhetoric: A Study of the Lectures of Adam Smith." *Rhetoric Society Quarterly* 18 (1988): 3–13.

Christie, John R. R. "Adam Smith's Metaphysics of Language." In *The Figural and the Literal: Problems of Language in the History of Science and Philosophy, 1630–1800*, ed. Andrew E. Benjamin, Geoffrey N. Cantor, and John R. R. Christie, 202–29. Manchester: Manchester University Press, 1987.

Cicero. *De Inventione*. Trans. H. M. Hubbell. Cambridge: Harvard University Press, 1989.

———. *De Officiis*. Trans. Walter Miller. Cambridge: Harvard University Press, 1968.

———. *De Oratore*. 2 Vols. Trans. E. W. Sutton and H. Rackham. Cambridge: Harvard University Press, 1948.

———. *Brutus and Orator*. Trans. G. L. Hendrickson and H. M. Hubbell. London: Heinemann, 1939.

[Cicero]. *Rhetorica ad Herrenium.* Trans. H. Caplan. Cambridge: Harvard University Press, 1986.

Clark, Gregory, and S. Michael Halloran, eds. *Oratorical Culture in Nineteenth Century America: Transformations in the Theory and Practice of Rhetoric.* Carbondale: Southern Illinois University Press, 1993.

Conley, Thomas. *Rhetoric in the European Tradition.* Chicago: University of Chicago Press, 1990.

Consigny, Scott. "The Style of Gorgias." *Rhetoric Society Quarterly* 22:3 (1992): 50.

Coseriu, Eugenio. "Adam Smith und die Anfänge der Sprachtypologie." In *Wortbildung, Syntax und Morphologie,* ed. H. E. Brekle and L. Lipke, 45–54. The Hague: Mouton, 1968.

Crawford, Robert, ed. *The Scottish Invention of English Literature.* Cambridge: Cambridge University Press, 1998.

Court, Franklin E. *Institutionalizing English Literature: The Culture and Politics of Literary Study, 1750–1900.* Stanford: Stanford University Press, 1992.

Daiches, David, ed. *Hotbed of Genius: the Scottish Enlightenment, 1730–1790.* Edinburgh, Edinburgh University Press, 1986.

Damasio, Antonio. *Descartes' Error: Emotion, Reason, and the Human Brain.* New York: HarperCollins, 1994.

Davie, George. *The Scotch Metaphysics: A Century of Enlightenment in Scotland.* London: Routledge, 2001.

Donovan, Brian R. "The Project of Protagoras." *Rhetoric Society Quarterly* 23:1 (1993): 35–47.

Dubos, Jean-Baptiste. *Réflexions Critiques sur la Poésie et sur la Peinture.* Paris: 1770.

Duncan, Ian. "Adam Smith, Samuel Johnson, and the Institutions of English." In *The Scottish Invention of English Literature,* ed. Robert Crawford, 37–54. Cambridge: Cambridge University Press, 1998.

Dwyer, John. *Virtuous Discourse: Sensibility and Community in Late Eighteenth Century Scotland.* Edinburgh: John Donald, 1987.

———. *The Age of the Passions: An Interpretation of Adam Smith and Scottish Enlightenment Culture.* East Linton: Tuckwell, 1998.

Dykstal, Timothy. "The Politics of Taste in the *Spectator.*" *The Eighteenth Century* 35:1 (1994): 46–63.

Eagleton, Terry. *Literary Theory: An Introduction.* Minneapolis: University of Minnesota Press, 1983.

Endres, A. M. "Adam Smith's Rhetoric of Economics: An Illustration Using 'Smithian' Compositional Rules." *Scottish Journal of Political Economy* 38 (1991): 217–49.

Enos, Richard Leo. *Greek Rhetoric Before Aristotle.* Prospect Heights, IL: Waveland, 1993.

Evans, Dylan. *Emotion: The Science of Sentiment.* Oxford: Oxford University Press, 2002.

Fantham, Elaine. "*Orator* 69–74." *Central States Speech Journal* 35 (1984): 123–25.

Farrell, Thomas B. *Norms of Rhetorical Culture.* New Haven: Yale University Press, 1993.

Fénelon, François. *Fénelon's Dialogues on Eloquence.* Trans. Wilbur Samuel Howell. Princeton: Princeton University Press, 1951.

Fish, Stanley. "Rhetoric." In *Critical Terms for Literary Study,* ed. Frank Lentriccia, Thomas McLaughlin. Chicago: University of Chicago Press, 1990.

———. *There's No Such Thing as Free Speech and It's a Good Thing, Too.* New York: Oxford University Press, 1994.

Fränkel, Hermann. *Early Greek Poetry and Philosophy: a History of Greek Epic, Lyric, and Prose to the Middle of the Fifth Century.* Trans. Moses Hadas and James Willis. New York: Harcourt Brace Jovanovich, 1975.

Fumaroli, Marc. *L'age de L'éloquence: Rhétorique et "res letteraria" de la Renaissance au seuil de l'époque classique.* Geneva: Librairie Dros, 1980.

Giuliani, Alessandro. "Le *Lectures on rhetoric and belles letters* di Adamo Smith." *Rivista Critica di Storia della Filosophia* 17 (1962): 328–36.

Golden, James L. "The Rhetorical Theory of Adam Smith." *Southern Speech Journal* 33:3 (1968) 200–15.

Gray, Hanna. "Renaissance Humanism: The Pursuit of Eloquence." *Journal of the History of Ideas* 24 (1963): 497–514

Grean, Stanley. *Shaftesbury's Philosophy of Religion and Ethics: A Study in Enthusiasm.* Athens, OH: Ohio University Press, 1967.

Grimaldi, William M. A., S. J. *Aristotle, Rhetoric I: A Commentary.* New York: Fordham University Press, 1980.

———. *Aristotle, Rhetoric II: A Commentary.* New York: Fordham University Press, 1988.

Griswold, Charles L., Jr. *Adam Smith and the Virtues of Enlightenment.* Cambridge: Cambridge University Press, 1999.

———. "Rhetoric and Ethics: Adam Smith on Theorizing about the Moral Sentiments." *Philosophy and Rhetoric* 24:3 (1991): 213–37.

Hamilton, Henry. *An Economic History of Scotland in the Eighteenth Century.* Oxford: Clarendon, 1963.

Hermogenes, 2nd cent. *Hermogenes' On Types of Style.* Trans. Cecil W. Wooten. Chapel Hill: University of North Carolina Press, 1987.

Hobbes, Thomas, and Bernard Lamy. *The Rhetorics of Thomas Hobbes and Bernard Lamy.* Ed. John T. Harwood. Carbondale: Southern Illinois University Press, 1986.

Hogan, J. Michael. "Historiography and Ethics in Adam Smith's Lectures on Rhetoric, 1762–1763." *Rhetorica* 2 (1984): 75–91

Holt, E. G., ed. *Literary Sources of Art History.* Princeton: Princeton University Press, 1947.

Homer. *The Odyssey.* Trans. W. H. D. Rouse. New York: New American Library, 1937.

———. *Odyssey.* Trans. A. T. Murray. Cambridge: Harvard University Press, 1966.

———. *Iliad.* Trans. A. T. Murray. Cambridge: Harvard University Press, 1966.

Hooker, Edward Niles. "The Discussion of Taste, from 1750 to 1770." *PMLA* 49 (1934): 577–92.

Hope, V. M. *Virtue by Consensus: The Moral Philosophy of Hutcheson, Hume, and Adam Smith.* Oxford: Clarendon, 1989.

Horkheimer, Max. *Eclipse of Reason.* New York: Continuum: 1947.

Howell, William Samuel. "Adam Smith's Lectures on Rhetoric: An Historical Assessment." *Speech Monographs* 36 (November 1969): 393–418. Rpt. Andrew S. Skinner and Thomas Wilson, eds., *Essays on Adam Smith,* 11–43. Oxford: Clarendon, 1975.

———. *Eighteenth Century British Logic and Rhetoric.* Princeton: Princeton University Press, 1971.

———. *Logic and Rhetoric in England, 1500–1700.* Princeton: Princeton University Press, 1956.

Hume, David. *Of the Standard of Taste and Other Essays.* Indianapolis: Bobbs, 1965.

———. *The Letters of David Hume.* 2 Vols. Ed. J. Y. T. Greig. Oxford: Clarendon, 1932.

————. *A Treatise of Human Nature.* 2d. ed. Ed. L. A. Selby-Bigge, with text revised and variant readings, P. H. Nidditch. Oxford: Clarendon, 1978.

Hutcheson, Francis. *An Inquiry into the Origin of our Ideas of Beauty and Virtue, in two treatises: I. Concerning Beauty, Order, Harmony, Design; II. Concerning Moral Good and Evil.* Westmead: Gregg, 1969.

Isocrates. *Isocrates.* 3 Vols. Trans. George Norlin. Cambridge: Harvard University Press, 1980.

Jarratt, Susan. "Ekphrastic Rhetoric and National Identity in Adam Smith's Rhetoric Lectures." In *Scottish Rhetoric and its Influences,* ed. Lynee Lewis Gaillet, 43–55. Mahwah, NJ: Erlebaum, 1998.

Jefferson, D. W. "Theories of Taste in the Eighteenth Century." *Proceedings of the Leeds Philosophical and Literary Society, Literary and Historical Section* 5 (1938–43): 1–9.

Johnson, Nan. *Nineteenth Century Rhetoric in North America.* Carbondale: Southern Illinois University Press, 1991.

Johnson, Samuel, and James Boswell. *A Journey to the Western Islands of Scotland and The Journal of a Tour to the Hebrides.* New York: Penguin, 1984.

Kahn, Victoria. *Rhetoric, Prudence, and Skepticism in the Renaissance.* Ithaca: Cornell University Press, 1985.

Kalyvas, Andreas, and Ira Katznelson. "The Rhetoric of the Market: Adam Smith on Speech, Recognition, and Exchange." *Review of Politics* 63 (2001): 549–79.

Kames, Henry Home, Lord. *Elements of Criticism.* New York: Huntington and Savage, 1847.

————. *Essays on the Principles of Morality and Natural Religion.* New York: Garland, 1983.

Kant, Immanuel. *Critique of Judgment, Including the First Introduction.* Trans. Werner S. Pluhar. Indianapolis: Hackett, 1987.

Kennedy, George A. *The Art of Persuasion in Greece.* Princeton: Princeton University Press, 1968.

————. *Classical Rhetoric and Its Christian and Secular Tradition from Ancient to Modern Times.* Chapel Hill: University of North Carolina Press, 1980.

————. "Theophrastus and Stylistic Distinctions." *Harvard Studies in Classical Philology* 62 (1957): 93–104.

Kerferd, G. B. *The Sophistic Movement.* Cambridge: Cambridge University Press, 1981.

Kinneavy, James L. *A Theory of Discourse: The Aims of Discourse.* New York: W.W. Norton, 1971.

————, and Catherine R. Eskin. "*Kairos* in Aristotle's *Rhetoric.*" *Written Communication* 11:1 (1994).

Kivy, Peter. *The Seventh Sense: A Study of Francis Hutcheson's Aesthetics and its Influence in Eighteenth Century Britain.* New York: Burt Franklin, 1976.

Klein, Lawrence E. *Shaftesbury and the Culture of Politeness: Moral Discourse and Cultural Politics in Early Eighteenth-Century England.* Cambridge: Cambridge University Press 1994.

Land, Stephen K. "Adam Smith's 'Considerations Concerning the First Formation of Languages.'" *Journal of the History of Ideas* 38:4 (1977): 677–90.

Lanham, Richard. *A Handlist of Rhetorical Terms.* Berkeley: University of California Press, 1991.

Leff, Michael. "Decorum and Rhetorical Interpretation: The Latin Humanistic Tradition and Contemporary Critical Theory." *Vichiana* 1 (3rd series, 1990): 107–26.

Lentricchia, Frank, and Thomas McLaughlin, eds. *Critical Terms for Literary Study.* Chicago: Chicago University Press, 1990.

Lewis, Thomas J. "Persuasion, Domination, and Exchange: Adam Smith on the Political Consequences of Markets." *Canadian Journal of Political Science* 33:2 (2000): 273–89.

Lidell, Henry George, and Robert Scott. *A Greek-English Lexicon*. Oxford: Clarendon, 1986.

Lightwood, Martha Bolar. *A Selected Bibliography of Significant Works About Adam Smith*. Philadelphia: University of Pennsylvania Press, 1984.

Locke, John. *An Essay Concerning Human Understanding*. Ed. Peter H. Nidditch. Oxford: Clarendon, 1975.

[Longinus]. *Longinus on the Sublime*. Ed. W. Rhys Roberts. Cambridge: Cambridge University Press, 1899.

MacIntyre, Alasdair. *After Virtue*. 2d ed. Notre Dame: Notre Dame University Press, 1984.

———. *Whose Justice? Which Rationality?* Notre Dame: Notre Dame University Press, 1988.

MacNamee, Maurice B. *Literary Decorum in Francis Bacon*. St. Louis: St. Louis University Press, 1950.

Marshall, David. "Adam Smith and the Theatricality of Moral Sentiments." *Critical Inquiry* 10 (1984): 592–613.

———. *The Figure of Theater: Shaftesbury, Dafoe, Adam Smith, and George Eliot*. New York: Columbia University Press, 1986.

McCloskey, Deirdre N. "Bourgeois Virtue and the History of P and S." *The Journal of Economic History* 58:2 (1998): 297–317.

McCloskey, Donald. *The Rhetoric of Economics*. Madison: University of Wisconsin Press, 1985.

McKenna, George. "On Abortion: A Lincolnian Position." *Atlantic Monthly*, Sept. 1995, 51–68.

McKeon, Richard. "Communication, Truth and Society." In *Freedom and History and Other Essays: An Introduction to the Thought of Richard McKeon*, ed. Mark Backman. Chicago: University of Chicago Press, 1988.

———. "The Uses of Rhetoric in a Technological Age: Architectonic Productive Arts." In *Rhetoric: Essays in Invention and Discovery*, ed. Mark Backman. Woodbridge, CT: Oxbow, 1987.

Miller, Carolyn. "The *Polis* as Rhetorical Community." *Rhetorica* 11:3 (1993) 211–40.

Miller, Thomas P. *The Formation of College English: Rhetoric and Belles Lettres in the British Cultural Provinces*. Pittsburgh: University of Pittsburgh Press, 1997.

Mizuta, Hiroshi. *Adam Smith's Library: A Catalogue*. Oxford: Clarendon, 2000.

Monfasani, John. *George of Trebizond: A Biography and Study of His Rhetoric and Logic*. London: E. J. Brill, 1976.

Morrow, Glenn R. "The Significance of the Doctrine of Sympathy in Hume and Adam Smith." *The Philosophical Review* 33:1 (1923): 60–78.

Muller, Jerry Z. *Adam Smith in His Time and Ours: Designing the Decent Society*. New York: Free Press, 1993.

Nelson, John S., Allan Megill, and Donald M. McCloskey, eds. *The Rhetoric of the Human Sciences*. Madison: University of Wisconsin Press, 1987.

Noordegraaf, Jan. "A Few Remarks on Adam Smith's Dissertation (1761)." *Historiographia Linguistica* 4:1 (1977): 59–67.

Patterson, Annabel M. *Hermogenes and the Renaissance: Seven Ideas of Style*. Princeton: Princeton University Press, 1970.

Paxman, David. "Aesthetics as Epistemology, or Knowledge without Certainty." *Eighteenth Century Studies* 26 (1992): 285–306.

Pindar. *Odes of Pindar*. Trans. John Sandys. Cambridge: Harvard University Press, 1978.

Plank, Frans. "Adam Smith: Grammatical Economist." In *Adam Smith Reviewed*, ed. Peter Jones and Andrew S. Skinner, 21–55. Edinburgh: Edinburgh University Press.

Plato. *Collected Dialogues of Plato including the Letters*. Ed. Edith Hamilton and Huntington Cairns. New York: Bollingen, 1961.

Polenz, Max. "*Tò Prépon*: Ein Beitrag zur Geschichte des griechischen Geistes." *Nachrichten von der Gesselschaft der Wissenschaften zu Göttingen, Philologisch-historische Klasse*, Heft 1 (1933): 53–92. Rpt. in Heinrich Dorrie, ed., *Kleine Schriften*. Vol. 2. Hildescheim: G. Olms, 1965.

Poovey, Mary. *A History of the Modern Fact: Problems of Knowledge in the Sciences of Wealth and Society*. Chicago: University of Chicago Press, 1998.

Porter, Roy . *Creation of the Modern World: The Untold Story of the British Enlightenment*. New York: W. W. Norton, 2001.

Prier, Raymond Adolph. *Thauma Idesthai: The Phenomenology of Sight and Appearance in Archaic Greek*. Tallahassee: Florida State University Press, 1989.

Puttenham, George. *Arte of English Poesie*. Ed. G. D. Willcock and A. Walker. Cambridge: Cambridge University Press, 1936.

Quintilian. *Institutio Oratoria*. 4 Vols. Trans. H. E. Butler. Cambridge: Harvard University Press, 1989.

Rae, John, and Jacob Viner. *The Life of Adam Smith (1895) with an Introduction "Guide to John Rae's Life of Adam Smith" by Jacob Viner*. New York: August M. Kelley, 1965.

Richetti, John J. *Philosophical Writing: Locke, Berkeley, and Hume*. Cambridge: Harvard University Press, 1983.

Rorty, Richard. *Philosophy and the Mirror of Nature*. Princeton: Princeton University Press, 1979.

———. "What's Wrong with 'Rights.'" *Harper's*, June 1996, 15–18.

Ross, Ian Simpson. *The Life of Adam Smith*. Oxford: Clarendon, 1995.

Saussure, Ferdinand de. *Course in General Linguistics*. Eds. Charles Bally, Albert Sechehaye, and Albert Riedlinger. Trans. Wade Baskin. New York: McGraw-Hill, 1959.

Schiappa, Edward S. *Protagoras and Logos: A Study of Greek Philosophy and Rhetoric*. Columbia: University of South Carolina Press, 1991.

Scott, Robert L. "On Viewing Rhetoric as Epistemic." *Central States Speech Journal* 18 (1967): 9–17.

Seigal, Jerrold. *Rhetoric and Philosophy in Renaissance Humanism: The Union of Eloquence and Wisdom, Petrarch to Valla*. Princeton: Princeton University Press, 1968.

Self, Lois. "Rhetoric and *Phronesis*: The Aristotelian Ideal." *Philosophy and Rhetoric* 12:2 (1979): 130–45.

Shaftesbury, Anthony Ashley Cooper, Third Earl of. *Characteristics of Men, Manners, Opinions, Times*. 3 Vols. London: 1732.

Sher, Richard. *Church and University in the Scottish Enlightenment: The Moderate Literati of Edinburgh*. Princeton: Princeton University Press, 1985.

———, and Jeffrey R Smitten, eds. *Scotland and America in the Age of the Enlightenment*. Princeton: Princeton University Press, 1990.

Shipley, Joseph T., ed. *Dictionary of World Literature*. New York: The Philosophical Library, 1943.

Sipiora, Phillip, and James S. Baumlin, eds. *Rhetoric and Kairos: Essays in History, Theory, and Praxis*. New York: State University of New York Press, 2000.

Skinner, A. S. *A System of Social Science: Papers Relating to Adam Smith*. Oxford: Clarendon: 1996.

Smith, Adam. *The Correspondence of Adam Smith*. Ed. E. C. Mossner and I. S. Ross. Indianapolis: Liberty Classics, 1987.

———. *Essays on Philosophical Subjects (and Miscellaneous Pieces)*. Ed. W. P. D. Wightman. Indianapolis: Liberty Classics, 1982.

———. *An Inquiry into the Nature and Causes of the Wealth of Nations*. Ed. R. H. Campbell and A. S. Skinner. Indianapolis: Liberty Classics, 1981.

———. *Lectures on Jurisprudence*. Ed. R. L. Meek, D. D. Raphael, and P. G. Stein. Indianapolis: Liberty Classics, 1982.

———. *Lectures on Rhetoric and Belles Lettres*. Ed. J. C. Bryce. Indianapolis: Liberty Classics, 1985.

———. *Lectures on Rhetoric and Belles Lettres, delivered in the University of Glasgow by Adam Smith, reported by a student in 1762–63*. Ed. John M. Lothian. Carbondale: Southern Illinois University Press, 1971.

———. *The Theory of Moral Sentiments*. Ed. D. D. Raphael and A. L. MacFie. Indianapolis: Liberty Classics, 1982.

Sokolowski, Robert. *Pictures, Quotations, and Distinctions: Fourteen Essays in Phenomenology*. Notre Dame: University of Notre Dame Press, 1992.

———. *Presence and Absence: A Philosophical Investigation of Language and Being*. Bloomington: Indiana University Press, 1978.

Spense, Patricia. "Sympathy and Propriety in Adam Smith's Rhetoric." *Quarterly Journal of Speech* 60 (1974): 92–99.

Sprague, Rosamond Kent, ed. *The Older Sophists*. Columbia: University of South Carolina Press, 1972.

Sprat, Thomas. *The History of the Royal-Society of London*. Eds. John I. Cope and Harold Whitmore Jones. St. Louis: Washington University Studies, 1958.

Struever, Nancy. "Lorenzo Valla: Humanist Rhetoric and the Critique of the Classical Languages of Morality." In *Rhetoric Eloquence: Studies in the Theory and Practice of Renaissance Rhetoric*, ed. James J. Murphy, 191–206. Berkeley: University of California Press, 1983.

———. "The Conversable World: Eighteenth Century Transformations of Rhetoric and Truth." In Nancy Struever and Brian Vickers, *Rhetoric and the Pursuit of Truth: Language Change in the Seventeenth and Eighteenth Centuries*. Pasadena: Castle Press, 1985.

Teichgraeber, Richard F, III. *"Free Trade" and Moral Philosophy: Rethinking the Sources of Adam Smith's Wealth of Nations*. Durham: Duke University Press, 1986.

Toulmin, Stephen. *The Uses of Argument*. Cambridge: Cambridge University Press, 1958.

Townsend, Dabney. "From Shaftesbury to Kant: The Development of the Concept of Aesthetic Experience." *Journal of the History of Ideas* 48:2 (1987): 287–305.

Tribe, Keith, ed. *A Critical Bibliography of Adam Smith*. London: Pickering and Chatto, 2002.

Trimpi, Wesley. *Muses of One Mind: The Literary Analysis of Experience and its Continuity*. Princeton: Princeton University Press, 1983.

Tuve, Rosamond. *Elizabethan and Metaphysical Imagery: Renaissance Poetic and Twentieth Century Critics*. Chicago: University of Chicago Press, 1947.

Untersteiner, Mario. *The Sophists*. Trans. Kathleen Freeman. Oxford: Basil Blackwell, 1954.

Wallace, Karl. *Francis Bacon on Communication and Rhetoric*. Chapel Hill: University of North Carolina Press, 1943.

Warnick, Barbara. *The Sixth Canon: Belletristic Rhetorical Theory and its French Antecedents*. Columbia: University of South Carolina Press, 1993.

Weaver, Richard. *The Ethics of Rhetoric*. South Bend: Regnary/Gateway, 1953.

Williamson, George. *The Senecan Amble: A Study in Prose Form from Bacon to Collier*. Chicago: University of Chicago Press, 1951.

Wilson, Thomas. *The Art of Rhetoryke*. Gainesville: Scholars' Facsimiles and Reprints, 1961.

Wolf, Naomi. "Our Bodies, Our Souls: Re-thinking Pro-Choice Rhetoric." *The New Republic*, 16 Oct. 1995, 26–35.

Wood, John Cunningham. *Adam Smith: Critical Assessments*. 4 Vols. London: Croom Helm, 1984.

Wood, Paul, ed. *The Scottish Enlightenment: Essays in Reinterpretation*. Rochester, NY: University of Rochester Press, 2000.

Zagarri, Rosemarie. "Morals, Manners, and the Republican Mother." *American Quarterly* 44:2 (June 1992): 192–215.

Index